Being Texan

Being Texan

ESSAYS, RECIPES, AND ADVICE FOR
THE LONE STAR WAY OF LIFE

BY THE EDITORS OF

TexasMonthly

HARPER WAVE

An Imprint of HarperCollins*Publishers*
www.harpercollins.com

HarperCollins books may be purchased for educational, business, or sales promotional use. For information, please email the Special Markets Department at SPsales@ harpercollins.com.

Portions of the material contained herein were previously published in whole or in part in *Texas Monthly*, between the years of 1994 to 2020.

FIRST EDITION

Designed by Bonni Leon-Berman

Illustrations by Christopher DeLorenzo

Library of Congress Cataloging-in-Publication Data has been applied for.

ISBN 978-0-06-306854-4

21 22 23 24 25 LSC 10 9 8 7 6 5 4 3 2 1

The rosebuds here

Endure heat and frost

And sprout new hearts in every spring's leaf

Whether planted by concrete or field

Today or yesterday

Deep purple to fall's beckoning gold

Drawing in all the wandering bees

To the feast of a Texas shade

This ever-promising bloom

This sanctuary of disparate bodies

Worshipped in breath and lone starred skies

Welcomes us into its arms

In the swell of cicada cry

—*Deborah D.E.E.P. Mouton*

Contents

Contents

III: Arts & Entertainment

Contents

IV: Food & Drink

Being Texan

What Does It Mean to Be Texan?

By Dan Goodgame

TWO CENTURIES AGO, HOMES and businesses across the American South could be seen freshly abandoned, with a sign on the door that read "Gone to Texas." Their former occupants often fled misfortune—or the law—and sought a fresh start in a place that promised great opportunity and adventure (at least if you were white). Texas fired the imagination of Americans like no place other than perhaps California, its only real peer in size and self-regard—but one that now, in a typical week, is losing to Texas some 1,600 migrants, many of them well educated, along with the headquarters of marquee companies such as Charles Schwab, Hewlett Packard Enterprise, and Oracle.

Today, more than a third of Texans were born elsewhere, up from a record low of about 25 percent in 1940. That proportion is rising rapidly as thousands more arrive each week, from locations as far-flung as Los Angeles and Lagos, Lucknow and León. I am among those migrants: a proud Mississippian by birth and upbringing, but also happily a Texan for the past dozen years. I work in Austin and enjoy its energy, but live with my wife in San Antonio, a beautiful, friendly, historic, Tejano-majority city that we love. When friends visit, we have a strict requirement that they cycle with us down the river to visit the Spanish missions, ride horses in the nearby Hill Country, and shoot clay pigeons at the skeet range within earshot of our house.

I've been fascinated by Texas from age eight, when my family took a leisurely drive across it, en route to visit relatives in California. We toured the Alamo and Big Bend National Park, and scarfed down what for us were exotic delights such as *tacos de lengua* and smoked brisket. I knew I'd be back. Some two decades later, writing for *Time* magazine, I covered the campaign, and then the presidency, of George H. W. Bush. I became friendly with many of his Texas allies and rivals. I got to know the Lone Star State, visiting its wildly varied regions, from the subtropical Rio Grande Valley to the piney woods along the Louisiana border to rugged parts of the Panhandle that get as much snow as Philadelphia.

I also came to admire a magazine called *Texas Monthly*. Founded in 1973, *TM* has vividly chronicled the current events and culture of Texas, including the ways that newcomers have constantly changed what it means to be Texan, in every sphere from politics to music. Today, I'm proud to serve as the magazine's editor in chief, and to present this book on the state's many pleasures, and its evolution.

In today's Texas, cowboys still tend cattle—and sometimes perish while saving their herds from range fires. Wildcatters still strike it rich, and go broke, in the Permian Basin. And the state's pitmasters and *taqueros* are still the most passionate and creative in the country. Theirs are iconic lifestyles here. But being Texan can also mean moving here from New Orleans and launching a food truck that specializes in gumbo tacos. It can mean being twelve years old and Black with a Stetson pulled low over your dreadlocks as you learn to ride rodeo bulls. It can mean walking into a Starbucks and hearing conversations in Arabic and

Introduction

Farsi and Nigerian-accented English. It can mean packing into a football stadium to hear the prime minister of India court your support and that of some 50,000 others among the 450,000 Texans who hail from that country.

What brings all these migrants here? The answer is very different for the Salvadoran fleeing gang violence than it is for the Silicon Valley software developer with stock options who compares his state's top income-tax rate of 13 percent with the rate in Texas: zero. But both often come to appreciate much of what stirs the hearts of the native-born. Most newcomers learn to love the state's diverse landscapes and people and cultures. They take pride in its triumphs, in everything from space exploration to sports championships. They develop a fierce attachment to homegrown brands, from Whataburger and Dr Pepper to Southwest Airlines and the ginormous gas-station-cum-country-store that is Buc-ee's.

Texans are divided, even more than the rest of the country, on the role of government. Even as they recognize big shortcomings in racial justice, education, and health care, many are reluctant to raise taxes or add civil-rights protections. But they're glad to help a neighbor and join with him for a practical cause. I recall breaking away from the Bush campaign in 1988 to see Democratic presidential nominee Michael Dukakis bungle what should have been a moving address on this topic. Speaking from a stack of hay bales in Idalou, Dukakis harked back to the Great Depression, when at night, much of Texas was lit only by fire. Texans Sam Rayburn and Lyndon Johnson worked with President Roosevelt to pass and implement the Rural Electrification Act, against opponents who described it as socialism. "But your grandparents and your parents didn't believe the naysayers," I remember Dukakis saying, "and they dug the holes and sunk the poles and strung the lines—and the lights came on, all over Texas." Dukakis was trying to link that tradition to his pitch for a much bigger federal role in health insurance. But he missed a key ingredient in Texas's support for the REA: neighbors tangibly helping one another.

If you get a flat tire in Texas, odds are someone will pull over pretty quickly to assist with the jack. But as my friend Paul Hobby, former publisher of *Texas Monthly*, adds with a smile: "We don't want the gub'mint telling us we have to do so."

Being Texan means taking risks and building things. My Texan friend of longest standing, Bo Baskin, grew up in Midland in West Texas and founded a boutique private-equity firm in Austin. Bo studied and worked for a time on the East Coast, and he observes that when someone from there meets someone new, what he or she first wants to know is "Where'd you go to college?" Someone from the Deep South wants to know "Who ah yo' people?" Someone from Texas asks, "How can you

and me partner up and make us some money?" To be sure, commercial and social hierarchies shape the lives of Texas cities, but I've found them more open to newcomers than in any of the dozen cities where I've lived in the United States and abroad.

NOT LONG AGO, I was waiting at London's Heathrow Airport for a flight back to Austin and grabbed some breakfast at a café near the gate. In the booth behind me, a woman with a distinct Brooklyn accent was chatting with friends, one of whom asked how she was enjoying her recent move to the Texas capital. "I love Austin," she replied, praising its cuisine and the music and tech scenes, but then added, "I'm trying to get used to it being in Texas."

I chuckled, but the exchange also made me sad. My mama taught me better than to interrupt a conversation among strangers. But I badly wanted to encourage that new Austinite to give the rest of Texas a chance. Drive ninety minutes west of the capital and tour a winery in Fredericksburg. Stop along the way at the Garrison Brothers distillery for a sip of my favorite bourbon. Drive (or cycle!) fifty miles south of the capital for a float trip down the Guadalupe, and then some live music at Gruene Hall. Hike Big Bend. Kayak on moss-draped Caddo Lake. Check out the hip-hop scene in Houston, and the exceptional Cameroonian and Vietnamese restaurants. Spend a weekend touring the fine museums in Fort Worth and grab some *birria* wontons at the King Kups truck in McKinney.

As we planned this book, I and its editor, Tom Foster, agreed that no single volume can hope to capture all there is to appreciate about Texas. It's too vast and shifting. It contains multitudes. Our modest goal was to craft a well-informed, thoughtful sampling of the best the state has to offer. Throughout this work, I've thought of Ms. Brooklyn Accent, and also of a certain native-Texan friend who takes a dim view of most writing about the state. My hope is that both of them, and you, read *Being Texan* and find it entertaining and inspiring.

I

Identity & Culture

The Birth of Texas Pride

By Stephen Harrigan

"WE WERE HUNTED DOWN as the felon wolf," Sam Houston declared in his inaugural address as the first elected president of the Republic of Texas, "our little band driven from fastness to fastness, exasperated to the last extreme; while the blood of our kindred and our friends was invoking the vengeance of an offended God, was smoking to high heaven, we met the enemy and vanquished them."

This was in October 1836, six months after Houston's rebel army defeated the forces of Santa Anna at the battle of San Jacinto and seized Texas from the rest of Mexico. The bones in Houston's ankle that had been shattered by a musket ball during the fighting were still unhealed. The adrenaline rush that had followed his unlikely victory was still unquelled, the blood of the dead kindred of the Alamo and other battlefields still smoking. At least that's the feeling you get from reading Houston's words of righteous amazement, and no doubt he delivered the speech in person with all the theatrical force of his personality.

Texas—"A spot of earth almost unknown to the geography of the age"—was no longer a restive frontier state in the Mexican federation. It was, all of a sudden, its own nation. And as anyone who has ever met a bombastic Texan can attest, the state can't stop thinking of itself that way. All of the clichéd signifiers of Texas identity—boldness, defiance, self-reliance, self-infatuation—echo through Houston's inaugural speech, and were incubated in Texas's hard-won national consciousness.

The Republic of Texas claimed the vastly sweeping Rio Grande as its southern and western borders, making it a far larger entity at the time than when its borders as a state in the United States were ultimately fixed in 1850. At 389,166 square miles, the country was almost twice as large as France. But there was no European palace to house its president or to serve as its seat of government. The national capitol was a clapboard shack. The new senators and congressmen slept, as often as not, on the ground under a live oak tree. The secretary of state, the official entrusted with representing Texas to the world, was Stephen F. Austin, the man who had first brought Anglo colonists to Mexican Texas. His governmental appurtenances were no grander. He lived in a shed and soon died of pneumonia after the cold winds of a norther gusted through the cracks. From the beginning, Texas was a republic of bigness, of rawness, of pugnacity.

Other states had been or would be independent countries before they joined the union. Vermont declared itself a republic in 1777 before entering the United States in 1791. The Bear Flag Republic of California existed for twenty-five days in 1846. And after the 1894 overthrow of Queen Lili'uokalani, the ruler of the Hawaiian Kingdom, the new Republic of Hawaii spent four hovering years as it waited to be annexed to the United States.

Most Texans expected to be annexed as well, but the Republic of Texas turned out to be not just a transitional entity but something like a real country. It lasted just shy of ten years, from 1836 to 1845. It was eventually recognized by other nations, by the United States, France, England, and the Netherlands. It had a flag, an official state seal, a navy, a Supreme Court, and a postal system—though the country was so immense and so broke it paid its mail carriers in land instead of money.

What kept Texas from immediately becoming part of the United States was its status as, and insistence on remaining, a haven for slavery. Its economic well-being was dependent upon a plantation cotton economy, which in turn was dependent upon enslaved workers. Cotton made up ninety percent of its exports. Without slavery, Austin had written a decade before the Texas revolution broke out, "we will have nothing but poverty for a long time, perhaps the rest of our lives."

But Texas's insistence on remaining a slave republic collided with the seething and unsettled argument in the United States over the expansion of slavery. In the words of the Quaker activist Benjamin Lundy, who had been keeping a wary eye on Texas for years, the real purpose of the revolution had always been to bring into the union a "a vast and profitable slave-market."

Being spurned by the country they wanted to join only perpetuated the sense of grievance and isolation Anglo Texas had already felt in being an ignored part of Mexico. Texas was accustomed to being regarded as a chronic problem for unseen decision makers in faraway capitals. And it had plenty of its own problems to solve.

One way to understand how Texans developed such a proud and embattled self-consciousness is to realize that for the ten years of its existence the Republic of Texas found itself, and kept itself, at war.

Santa Anna's army may have been beaten at San Jacinto, but the Mexican government never quite bought into the idea that Texas now belonged to the American outlanders that Santa Anna had regarded as land pirates. Mexico, affirmed a Veracruz newspaper, was "not aware of the existence of a nation called the republic of Texas, but only a horde of adventurers in rebellion against the laws of the government of the republic."

There was an overall atmosphere of combativeness that had barely paused after the battle of San Jacinto. New arrivals from the United States kept pouring in, eager to reanimate the fight they had missed out on. Mirabeau Lamar, an ambitious politician and ardent poet, made it to Texas in time to fight Santa Anna as a common soldier and six months later was the vice president of the new republic. He became president after the end of Houston's first two-year term, declared annexation "as the grave of all [Texas's] hopes and happiness," and decided that Texas might as well be a national powerhouse in its own right. His policies were brutal and bankrupting. He made war on the Cherokees and rekindled long-running hostilities with the Comanches. He sent a disastrous expedition to Santa Fe to try to coerce the recalcitrant inhabitants there into believing they were now Texans and not the Mexicans they thought they were. "Everywhere a Texan sets foot," Lamar told them, in one of the first and grandest empty boasts of Texas history, "he transforms barrenness into fertility."

After Lamar's disastrous term was over and Houston was returned to office, Mexico invaded Texas not once but twice. The armies were beaten back, and then Texas was beaten back when it in turn tried to invade Mexico. By the time Texas was finally annexed to the United States in 1945, it was exhausted and broke. But the creation story it told of itself during the decade of the Republic's existence—its battle for freedom from Mexico, its holy sacrifice at the Alamo and glorious victory at San Jacinto—had been so carefully nourished that it ended up being not just remembered but enshrined.

The annexation of Texas led to war between the United States and Mexico, which led to the acquisition by the States of vast new territories, which superheated the bitter debate over the expansion of slavery. The result was the Civil War, in which Texas seceded from the union that had grudgingly welcomed it, just as it had once seceded from the Mexican nation. In a sense, it also seceded from the defeated South. Texas worked hard to think of itself as its own thing. It had no use for the reveries of the Lost Cause when it still had a western frontier to be exploited and Indian resistance to be crushed.

The Texas state song was adopted in 1929, sixty-four years after the end of the Civil War. Unlike the wistful and nostalgic official songs from other states of the defeated South—with their references to sweetly warbling birds and "proud armorial trees"—"Texas, Our Texas" is a vibrant imperial anthem. The phrase "Largest and grandest" had to be changed to "Boldest and grandest" after Alaska joined the Union in 1959, but "boldest" is probably more to the point anyway. Otherwise the song remains intact, as does the nationalistic pride it celebrates. Texas was for a time, and still not-so-secretly wants to remain, an "empire wide and glorious."

Strong Texas Women

By Mimi Swartz

I RECENTLY CAME ACROSS a roast of Ann Richards on C-SPAN that took place in Port Arthur in 1992. It seemed like something out of another era—that year George H. W. Bush was president and Richards was governor. It had been four years since she wowed the Democratic convention with her claim that the forty-first president had been "born with a silver foot in his mouth," and she was well on her way to icon status, if she hadn't already settled into it. But this East Texas event was clearly one held among friends, mostly among the good-ole boys whom Richards had tolerated and cajoled and maybe even bullied to get her way in the statehouse. Once powerful Democratic state senator Carl Parker was there, as was the crazy rich East Texas plaintiff's lawyer and Democratic donor Walter Umphrey. Bum Phillips, former coach of the former Houston Oilers, gave a testimonial; then-congressman Jack Brooks, the longtime lead of the Texas delegation, got a hot-mic dressing-down about a crime bill from Richards just before the proceedings began. Of course, Richards's bff, Molly Ivins, was there, claiming her rightful place on the dais.

This was not a group who could ever be mistaken for, say, denizens of a posh Connecticut suburb. A lot of the men were kind of tubby, pasty white, and poorly tailored. Unless you had an assertive Texas accent, you might have been denied admission. Many of the jokes were the kind you couldn't tell today without attracting a lawsuit. But Ann and Molly—that's what everyone called them, whether they knew them personally or not—fit right in, giving every bit as good as they got. Ivins, slathering on her thickest Texas patois, began by saying, "I've known Ann Richards since both Ann and Exxon were still Humble." After the applause died down, she added that Richards was "one of the finest public officials Texas ever sent to California for Treatment."

Richards began her portion of the evening by stepping to the podium, picking up the yardstick used as a pointer by a previous speaker, and casually putting it aside. "There's nuthin' big enough [here] to measure with that," she muttered, breaking up the place before she'd even started her speech, one she proceeded to deliver with expert comic timing.

It was easy to see from even a musty old performance why the two women had become Texas icons: they were very funny and very smart, of course, but more important, they had a way of bridging all the gaps that can separate us. They were of Texas but also outside it, in a way that could win friends and disarm potential enemies. Whatever difficulties these women had in their lives—and they had them—they were successes by any measure, and in a male-dominated world that, as Richards's most famous metaphor put it, required them to follow like Ginger Rogers, dancing backwards in high heels. I was well into middle age before I understood that their histories are my history, and that of so many Texas women before me.

GROWING UP IN San Antonio in the 1960s, I didn't have that many female role models to choose from, or it seemed that way to me at the time. I was sure, in fact, that the Richards/Ivins option was the sole alternative to the obvious if impossible path many of my girlfriends had selected: the Farrah Fawcett route. If you are younger than, oh, seventy-something, you remember Farrah at her height: the breathless, stunning blond star of the first iteration of *Charlie's Angels* and the poster that fueled the fantasies of countless teenaged boys. She was the personification of Texas beauty, the gorgeous, fresh-faced sorority sister type, the one who inspired severe self-image problems for any female who wasn't blond, blue-eyed, long-legged, and expertly flirtatious. (Mine were the paleolithic days; pre-Selena, pre-Beyoncé, much less Lizzo and Megan Thee Stallion.)

My high school, like most Texas high schools of its time, was dominated by mini-Farrahs, often but not always cheerleaders who seemed to possess some secret knowledge of makeup application, hair color, and whatever feminine wiles it took to get the attention of the cutest guys in school. I didn't so much envy them as I just didn't see the point. I was pursuing other interests; I wasn't going to wear lipstick or color my hair. I was reading *Siddhartha* and protesting the construction of a freeway through town. My high-school game plan was to get the hell out of Texas and never come back. As it turned out, I did come back, and over the years I came to realize that the only person who thought I had to choose between role models was me.

Maybe surveying the list of Most Popular Texas Women would cause anyone to go a little binary, to set up an either/or equation. Either Richards and Ivins and the stentorian-voiced Barbara Jordan were representative, or victory went to the Farrah type. To my mind, Group A was smart, flinty, and funny, while Group B was beautiful, sexy, and well groomed. Of course, anyone who bothered to carefully examine the lives of both groups would quickly see that some of their qualities overlapped, and that both flourished because they'd found ways to exercise power in a world still controlled by men.

Certain qualities that have made Texas women so noteworthy are also ones they share with Texas men: resilience, shrewdness, a boundless if sometimes ill-advised optimism, along with the ability to hold the floor just by virtue of being great company. I would submit, too, that Texas women have had to pick up the pieces of so many dunderheaded men that they have honed these qualities to a fine art.

These women weren't reserved like New Englanders and eschewed (with some contempt) the fragility of southern belles. People were drawn to Ann Richards because there was no one else like her—the snowy white hair, the merciless humor, the quickness, the fearlessness. Whatever demons and insecurities she battled privately couldn't deter her from being anyone but herself. I love to imagine the Houston-born super-hostess and philanthropist Lynn Wyatt in her mansion in the South of France, more cleverly dressed than all those other jet-setters, her voice and accent unmodulated ("Well, haaaaaaaaa!!!!!! How *RRR* yew?"), surely knowledgeable of but incapable of kowtowing to all the unwritten rules of European society.

One other thing: most of these women we now call icons came of age when Texas was making that epochal transition from a rural to an urban state. In them you can see (and hear) vestiges of a past that did not include video games or shopping malls or quickie weekends in Cozumel or Aspen. Molly Ivins went to Smith College in Massachusetts when few of her River Oaks contemporaries even considered venturing out of state. Houston still had Black and white water fountains when she was a kid, a factor that, along with that overbearing daddy of hers, no doubt shaped her politics. When there were still places on the west side of San Antonio where bad drainage caused houses and streets to flood after every rain, Rosie Castro was taking her twin sons, Julián and Joaquin, to the polls and teaching them to pass out leaflets for Raza Unida candidates.

In short, most of these women came of age at a time (before, say, the oil boom of the late 1970s and early '80s) when jokes about backward Texans contained more than a grain of truth. Anti-intellectualism flourished, because it comforted the vast number of folks who were uneducated. Rich people were celebrated (and celebrated themselves) because there weren't very many of them; most people knew exactly how hard life could be. Texas was a place where people had to learn to entertain themselves, to find beauty and joy amid harshness. This job fell to the women, of course. Not for nothing were Richards and Wyatt famous for their parties. Richards's entertaining tips included (a) never washing her floor beforehand and (b) never feeding her guests until it got really late. She served homemade bread and vegetables from her organic garden; egg dishes came courtesy of her yard chickens. She kept a box of costumes at the ready, and she wasn't above dressing as Santa Claus, Dolly Parton, or, famously, a Tampax. Wyatt gave seated dinners for up to sixty guests with themes like "Denim and Diamonds," "Think Pink," and the "Gypsy Party."

"Your life sounds like so much fun," I once said to Wyatt, whom I was interviewing for one story or another, who had probably just finished telling me about visiting with Prince Charles or Elton John. "Oh," she said, her voice softening, "if you only knew." Her tone suggested that her life hadn't been all fun and games—she was, after all, married to a man many

considered the Darth Vader of the Oil Patch. But maybe that was the secret of so many Texas women I admired: focus on the good times. The hard times will come again soon enough.

MOST OF US don't recognize the veins of ore running through our own pasts—I for one was too busy rebelling against my hometown to see that anything there could possibly have any lasting value. But now I understand that I was always surrounded by unconventional women—that the iconography of Texas females came not from those at the top but evolved from the ground up, from women who learned to create, by whatever means necessary, not just a room of one's own but a world more suited to one's dreams and desires. It's no accident that my childhood neighbor Robert Hammond would go on to develop the High Line in New York; his mother, Pat, turned their house into a world of wonders that could stir even the most stunted imagination. She collected everything—kites, brooches, cicada shells stored in jars. There were strings of lollipops as window treatments, old magic tricks she bought from a closing shop on Broadway.

My best friend's mom offered ballet and tap lessons on her patio, which doubled as a recital stage. (There's a picture of me in a tutu with a very Texas-like sequined bodice. I do not look happy.) Someone else's mom taught us to batik in her garage with dyes she'd ordered from India; another friend's mom made hand-carved melons for elaborate Chinese dinners. My mother used to take me to the junk shops on McCullough Avenue, where we'd pick through piles and piles of stuff, until I learned to spot genuine treasures amid all the Asian souvenirs San Antonio's soldiers brought back from overseas. She taught me to restore neglected furniture and to tell the difference between loquat and kumquat trees, mesquite and hackberry. She put me on a horse when I was six or so—without a helmet, of course—and I learned that falling off

and getting back on was the most essential life lesson of all.

If I surprised myself by hightailing it back to Texas after college on the East Coast—to then-booming Houston—it was equally surprising that the women I was drawn to were not East Coast exiles but those, like myself, who had grown up here. They had a gift for self-preserving—as opposed to self-deluding—optimism. We didn't have to always be storming the barricades; it was okay to enjoy ourselves. A friend of mine once broke up a tedious dinner party by showing everyone how to wipe their spoons clean and then stick them so they hung from their noses. "I was brought up to be decorative and amusing," another friend mused the other day. Which may have been true but didn't stop her from becoming an attorney.

I am still ashamed when I think of how I initially discounted my friend Sally, whom I met when we were coworkers at a law firm more than forty years ago. She seemed to me a dark-haired, taller version of Farrah—

a Group B type—who even in her twenties was stylish beyond her years; she had a whiskey-and-cigarettes laugh that carried down hallways. I imagined Sally had been given every sort of advantage as a child of old Houston; it was only later that I learned that her upbringing had been as full of trials as anyone's. She just wore them with grace and humor, the same way she wore a cape embroidered with the Virgin of Guadalupe to stodgy River Oaks soirees. When my mother died eleven years ago, Sally brought me a gigantic rosemary plant, with branches twirling every which way, that exuded an intoxicating woodsy aroma. The message was clear: sometimes all we can do in the face of loss is breathe in as much beauty as we can.

I wonder if young women growing up have anyone to tell them such things. I don't think we will ever see the likes of Ann or Molly again, or their surrogates in small towns and suburbs. Texas has become so much more connected to the rest of the country and the world, and women are, maybe, not quite so thwarted that they have to obscure their dreams and ambitions behind costumes and pointed humor. They can work in oil fields and big law firms; they have the diction of Ivy League professors. And now, they have so many homegrown role models to choose from: Beyoncé and Lizzo, Simone Biles and Eva Longoria, Cecile Richards and Harris County judge Lina Hidalgo, just to name a few—women who haven't been bound by all the rules and biases of previous generations. But maybe there's a little of Wyatt's tasteful flamboyance in Queen Bey, Ivins's nose-thumbing in Lizzo's posturing. Lina's resolve may be polite, but she's as relentless as Rosie Castro. And no one could ever doubt that Cecile Richards is her mother's daughter; thanks to the likes of Ann, Cecile now dances ever so gracefully, not backwards in high heels, but forward. In whatever shoes she likes.

Something in the Water

By Christopher Hooks

IN THE EARLY MORNING hours of July 31, 1981, state representative Mike Martin arrived at the trailer park in east Austin where he stayed during sessions of the Texas Legislature. He stepped out of his car and felt the blast of a 12-gauge shotgun. Sometime later, an associate found him bleeding: Martin told him to call his publicist.

The police came up empty-handed, but in time, Martin solved the case himself. The perpetrators, he said, were members of a Satanic cult, the Guardian Angels of the Underworld. This seemed unlikely, and a growing number of observers began connecting the shooting to the fact that Martin was angling to run for an open state senate seat. Police went looking for him, with a growing list of questions in hand, and found him hiding in a stereo cabinet at his mother's house in Longview. Soon after, his cousin confessed: he had been the triggerman, and the whole thing had been staged to help elevate Martin to higher office.

In an inferior state, one of those corners of the union that God loves less, the story of the legislator who faked his own shooting and blamed satanists would be taught to schoolchildren in history classes. His face would hang on the wall in every newsroom. A plaque would commemorate the shooting, maybe even a statue of him in his hometown. The fact that hardly anyone in Texas remembers Martin's name—that his story has been washed out by a thousand other stories of eccentricity, derangement, ambition, and chronic inability—indicates a political culture of uncommon excellence.

Texas politicians are not like politicians elsewhere, and alongside wind and sun they are one of the state's most important renewable resources. Politicians in Sacramento, Albany, and Baton Rouge are no less crazy or corrupt, of course, but the way those attributes manifest themselves differs from place to place, and the men who have ruled or misruled Texas—mostly men—have a distinctive spiciness. The reasons for this are much debated. I have always had a sneaking suspicion there is something in the water.

But it's not hard to come up with exacerbating factors. There is the Texan's general appreciation for loudmouths, braggarts, hucksters, and schemers. The state's voters reward men and women who can perform, and who have strong personalities, and the state capital has hosted a seemingly endless list of crackpots and crooks. About the worst thing you can say about politicians here is that they are boring.

There is also the fact that Texas has had a proper two-party system for about fifteen of the last hundred and fifty years, and that most everything is decided within political parties, which rewards ideological intransigence. There are also no real ethics laws of note—some for show, of course, but hardly worth the paper they're written on. It used to be possible to hand out checks on the floor of the Texas senate; brothels and hotels where lobbyists could be found to pick up the tab lined several blocks just off Austin's Congress Avenue.

Our rickety nineteenth-century constitution practically orders lawmakers to get rich in office, and they frequently do. This combines neatly with the fact that there is a tremendous amount of money in the state for the taking, much of it held by millionaires and billionaires who are just as eccentric as the politicians they buy off.

A few great leaders, and many not-so-great leaders, have spilled out of that cauldron. The first half of the twentieth century saw extraordinary figures like "Ma" and "Pa" Ferguson, a husband-and-wife team of governors who combined extraordinary corruption with populist economics, and

"Pappy" O'Daniel, a businessman who became governor thanks to his noontime radio program and Western swing band, the Hillbilly Boys. Up through those ranks slipped Lyndon Baines Johnson, one of the strangest men who has ever walked the earth, who remade the United States in his image after a journey begun unpromisingly at Southwest Texas State Teachers College.

But while the upper cadre of Texas politicians have produced three presidents in the last sixty years—and quite a few others who would like to be president—the lower ranks, as found in the legislature, are populated by a sort that inspires a different kind of awe. Throughout the decades, the Texas state capitol was as much a place for heavy drinking, drug use, and sexual exploits as it was for politicking. The Texas house has played host to so many fistfights and scuffles in the last century they could hardly be counted. In 1961, a fight rolled on so long that four lawmakers formed an ad hoc barbershop quartet at the front

mic to provide revelers with some musical accompaniment. In 1969, land commissioner Jerry Sadler choked a state representative in the presence of a radio journalist who caught it all on tape.

Bob Bullock, a top statewide official for a quarter century, would threaten to shoot a reporter one weekend and be off on a private plane for a seventy-two-hour bender in New Orleans the next. In 2007, state representative Borris Miles was accused of drunkenly storming a holiday party at the St. Regis Hotel, brandishing a pistol, and forcibly kissing a woman. He is now a state senator.

With excellent politics comes excellent political writing. That's a thin silver lining, to be sure, but it's there. The best fictional work about politics in America is Billy Lee Brammer's *The Gay Place*; the best nonfiction work Robert Caro's *The Years of Lyndon Johnson*. The state has produced more than its fair share of great columnists, essayists, and reporters—Molly Ivins, Lawrence Wright, and Willie Morris a few among them—and the endlessly ridiculous and entertaining nature of the state's politics is probably one reason, albeit a small one, that the state's media is so much healthier and stronger than it is in many less fortunate states.

A few years ago, after a long and sloppy budget debate on the floor of the Texas house, in which members appeared to have imbibed something stronger than civic spirit and in which one member asked another for details regarding his premarital commitment to virginity, I got in touch with a friend who had recently started covering Idaho's state legislature. That must be fun, I said, imagining what Idaho's Bob Bullock would sound like.

Hardly, she said, it was impossibly boring. On one recent Friday, staffers cut out early to play Putt-Putt golf, and there had hardly been anything to put in the newspaper. I recoiled in horror, and then I understood. In Texas our forefathers and foremothers worked hard over many generations to ensure there is always something to put in the newspaper. As much as bluebonnets and tamales and pecan pie, this is our birthright. Never take it for granted.

From Amarila
to Wad-a-loop

By John Nova Lomax

THE TEXAS MAP DRAWS inspiration from as many cultures as any state in America. There's Czech: Praha, Moravia, Dubina. And German: Breslau, New Baden, New Ulm, and New Braunfels, to name just a few. Scattered across the landscape are small towns with names coming from the Polish (Panna Maria), Swiss (New Bern), Norwegian (Oslo), Danish (Danevang), and Russian (Marfa, Odessa) pioneers who got there first. Plus, to visit most of the great European cities, you never have to leave the Lone Star State: We've got Paris, Athens, New London, Berlin, and Dublin (plus Edinburg, if you'll forgive the un-Scotsman-like spelling. And Rhome, for that matter).

But aside from family names and others deriving from English and Native American sources (Comanche, Quanah, and anything with Caddo attached), Spanish is the most common wellspring of inspiration for our place names. Often as not, we Texans butcher it, whether we are referring to a town or a street or a river. (Although maybe not so often as those Californians do.)

Yes, we get a few right. We pretty much nail Laredo, Del Rio, Seguin, Comal (as in the county), and aside from some emphasis and flattened vowels, mostly do okay with El Paso, San Antonio, Bandera, and Concho (again, as in the county). Bosque County is sort of a typically Texan hybrid: locals pronounce it "boskie," which is close to the Spanish "boas-kay," but not all the way there, yet nevertheless much closer than "bosk" or "boss-cue," to rhyme with barbecue.

But others we render unrecognizable. It should be "ah-ma-ree-yo," not "amarila," or "mo'-rila," as I've heard in bars. "Sahn ha-seen-toe," not "san jacinna." Refugio should be "ray-few-hyo," not "r'-feery-o," and the nearby shrimp port of Palacios should be "pah-lass-ee-os," not "p'lashus." Don't get me started on how Austinites render Menchaca "man-shack" and Guadalupe "wad-a-loop" or "gwadda-loop." Like that extra "s" that all-too-often slides into New Braunfels, how did that extra "r" creep into the Pedernales River, rendering it the purda-nalleez?

But my favorite is the northeast Texas town of Bogata. It's named after Bogotá, Colombia, but the locals pronounce it, roughly, as "B'goda," and that is what you must call it unless you want to be mocked as an outsider.

Hell, the entire state is a mispro-nunciation: If we want to get right down to it, it should be "tay-hoss" instead of Texas, though the Span-ish landed on that name by adapt-ing a word from Caddo Indians. But should we care? Should we cede our traditional Texan mispronunciations because there are now more Anglo Texans with knowledge of Spanish and more native Spanish speakers im-migrating from south of the border? Should we be ashamed of our butch-ery of the Spanish (or Caddo, or other) tongue?

Probably not, says Gustavo Arel-lano, the former editor of *Orange County Weekly* and former author of a weekly syndicated column called Ask a Mex-ican. "To me it just shows we have a shared heritage," he says. "Whether we are fifth- or sixth-generation or not, we are going to call it whatever locals were calling it when they got here."

Of course there are exceptions. Arellano, a Southern California na-tive of Mexican heritage, cites the relatively recent migration to South-ern California from the Midwest. He blames those middle America accents for turning Los Angeles into that soft g sound we hear universally today ("an-juh-les" instead of "ahn-heles"), and areas like Los Feliz from "fae-leez" to "fee-lez."

To Arellano, the linguistic change is inevitable. "It's gonna happen," he adds. "Americans are going to butcher Spanish names, but I have to say it goes both ways. There is a town [in California] called Cudahy, and growing up I always heard it [from native Spanish speakers] was 'Carra-hie.' The white locals called it 'Cudda-hay.'" The same phenomenon is on view in Houston, where Tellepsen Street, named after a Norwegian immigrant, has been rendered into "tailspin" by those living in the barrio nearby.

For some longtime Texans, a sense of guilt is creeping in. Pronounce street names as you've always heard them and you risk being shamed by those with a better understanding of correct Spanish. But consider this: Nashvillians don't pronounce Demonbreun correctly, nor do denizens of "Glasgie" (Glasgow, Scotland). In "Noo Yawk," locals have so long and so routinely slaughtered the Dutch place names that littered the landscape, we no longer even know that places like Yonkers, the Bronx, and Flushing ever had any connection to the land of tulips and dikes.

Given that, why should residents of Refugio, Bogata, San Jacinto County, or San Felipe Street feel ashamed when they say their place names the way they were taught to?

Whatever will be, will be—*que será, será*. Or, as we might say, kay sirrah sirrah.

More Colorful Texas Sayings Than You Can Shake a Stick At

By Anne Dingus

COMMON AS CORN BREAD. Old as dirt. Funny as all get-out. Homespun expressions still color how modern Texans talk. Using them can be an affectation, but it can also be a genuine link to the plainspoken humor of Texas pioneers. Plenty of these sayings are good for provoking reactions. If you find yourself offended—well, that may be the point.

Bad Idea. That dog won't hunt.

Bad, Mean. Would steal the flowers off his grandma's grave.

Busy. Busy as a one-legged man at an ass-kicking contest.

Caution. Don't dig up more snakes than you can kill.

Cheap. Has short arms and deep pockets.

Cold. Cold as a cast-iron commode.

Difficult. Like putting socks on a rooster.

Dry. So dry the trees are bribing the dogs.

General Advice. Just because a chicken has wings don't mean it can fly.

Immoral, Wild. They ate supper before they said grace.

Inept, Worthless. Couldn't organize a pissing contest in a brewery.

Noisy. Learned to whisper in a sawmill.

Phony. All hat and no cattle.

Putdown. Anytime you happen to pass my house, I'd sure appreciate it.

Sad. Looks like the cheese fell off your cracker.

Sick. Got a hitch in his gitalong.

Timid. Yellow as mustard but without the bite.

Unsophisticated. So country he thinks a seven-course meal is a possum and a six-pack.

Vain. Broke his arm patting himself on the back.

YOUR DRAWL, YOUR SELF

By David Courtney

A GOOD DRAWL (mild, medium, or Lufkin) is a useful part of every Texan's ensemble. Think of it like the tail plumage of the male peafowl, which when fanned leaves no doubt in the minds of nearby birds as to who is the peacock in the room. There are occasions, usually up north, when Texans find it advantageous to parade around with their feathers flared, so to speak (see Ann Richards, Ross Perot, George W. Bush). As the former president can attest, though, extended stays in localities where the dialect is different from one's own can often have a distorting effect on the native tongue. And the internal turmoil caused by the diminishing of such a defining characteristic can be painful. You have lost your plumage and must appear to all as a pigeon or grackle and not the splendid peacock you are. The only way to guarantee its safe return is for you yourself to return home. And it will when you do.

The Wildcatters

By Bryan Burrough

OF ALL THE IMAGERY that defines Texas, one of the most vital and enduring archetypes, perhaps second only to the cowboy, is the headstrong, hard-
living oilman, the lone wildcatter silhouetted against a lone derrick on a lonely
prairie, mopping his brow day after day as his pipe disappears into the earth,
sleepless, suffering, one step ahead of the banks, until that glorious dawn when
the ground begins to shake, the derrick shudders, and out of nowhere a geyser
of black crude erupts from below, bathing him, finally, in a shower of inky gold.

It's how Texas fortunes, and modern Texas, were made.

And while it's been decades since the last real gusher arced across the Texas skies, you can still glimpse that wildcatter ethos, that sense of a single bullheaded iconoclast doing battle against a world of doubters, in the careers of Texas business figures as diverse as Robert F. Smith, Mark Cuban, and Thai Lee. A lot of Texans believe this is no accident, that there's something inherent in the Texas character, something self-propulsive and entrepreneurial, that helps explain the stream of rags-to-riches Texans who have risen to national prominence over the last hundred fifty years.

Many Texans—certainly the Anglo ones—had that mindset almost from the beginning. As citizens of the only future state to single-handedly defeat a foreign nation in war, they rarely lacked for self-confidence. As they saw it, they had settled a rugged wilderness by themselves, bested Mexico by themselves, and formed a unique state police force, the Texas Rangers, that grew into arguably the most effective fighting force in mid-1800s North America. Swaggering? Yeah, pretty much. They were arrogant victors. The "Texas brag" was already a thing in the first years after the revolution in 1836.

But outsiders noticed something different about Texans as well. "These people are rough and wild, but their constancy and courage are admirable," a British diplomat wrote in the 1840s. "These strange people *jolt* and *jar* terrifically in their progress, but *on* they do get, and prosper too, under circumstances when our people would starve or die." The legacy of violence had produced combative loners who relied on themselves and their families and had little use for bureaucrats or technocrats of any kind.

Some of the first notable Texas businessmen, the wildcatter's precursors, were the brawny cattlemen who monetized the stringy, obstreperous longhorn cow in the years after the Civil War. Millions of longhorns—unable to get to market during the fighting—milled about South Texas afterward. Cattle barons such as Richard King, Charles Goodnight, and John Chisum gathered them into vast herds and drove them to the nearest railheads, in Kansas, and also to California, New Mexico, Colorado, and as far north as Montana. Within fifteen years Texas cattle, and Texas cattlemen, pretty much dominated a new open-range ranching empire that spread across fifteen western states and territories.

Theirs was a world of self-made men and self-made laws. On and off the trail, Native American tribes and cattle rustlers were a constant menace, and frontier Texas cattlemen had no second thoughts about administering swift justice to just about anyone who eyed their stock crossways, either with a bullet or a noose. There was no legal authority or bank or credit union to help a cattleman in his daily life out on the plains. Ranchers created a business entirely their own, with their own rules, their own laws, their own ways to survive. Those who failed fell,

forgotten, beside the corpses of the rustlers and Comanches they left behind. Those who thrived became millionaires. Their worldview—you're on your own; swim or drown; it's every Texan for himself—came to define the Texas ethos, or at least the popular conception of it.

Which made Texas an ideal venue for the business that suddenly burst from a scraggly little hill south of Beaumont in 1901: oil. Spindletop changed everything, of course, about Texas, about the world. Those first gushers were able to produce more oil than the rest of the planet; they made practical everything from the combustion engine to the automobile to modern factories. The man who found Spindletop was a one-armed thug named Pattillo "Bud" Higgins, and his struggles are a metaphor for the infant Texas oil industry. Higgins lost control of the well even before it was drilled, much as Texans swiftly lost control of an industry by rights they should have been supervising. The Big Boys from back east rolled in, making Texans serfs on their corporate manors. Those early Texas oil workers didn't get rich working for the big oil companies, but the smart ones got a valuable education.

That feudal system lasted almost twenty years, until World War I ended in 1918 and the economy exploded, the Roaring Twenties arrived and everyone and their mother bought a car. Suddenly oil companies wanted to drill anywhere and everywhere, but Texas was simply too big to drill all the land they had leased themselves. So they began shoveling intel to an army of sharp young Texas boys who agreed to split the profits on any oil they found. The wildcatter was born.

During the '20s you could see them in the courthouses in Mexia and Luling and Burkburnett, men in muddy Witch-Elk boots poring over maps and land records, ducking their heads and whispering to each other. In every corner of the state—on the scrubby flats east of Austin, in the deserts along the New Mexico line—you could glimpse their rickety wooden

derricks slowly going up. Most came up dry. A few of the men found oil, and a handful actually got what you might call rich. But not seriously rich. Not yet.

Thank God for the Depression. The economic collapse that began in 1929 was, simply put, the best thing that ever happened to the Texas wildcatter. The major oil companies scaled back their exploration budgets and quit leasing almost any new land. Into the vacuum charged a legion of lone Texas wildcatters whose discoveries during a brief six-year window, from 1930 to 1935, would change the state forever.

It wasn't easy. Like the ranchers who rounded up longhorns roaming the Nueces Strip sixty years before, they did it almost entirely on their own—their own hunches, their own sweat, their own money, sometimes with a partner or two and a little bank money here and there. But the bankers weren't there to drill the wells, which was always a challenge. Down in Conroe, north of Houston, George

Strake begged and borrowed the equipment he needed to drill a promising tract. Out in far West Texas, Sid Richardson paid his tool pushers in groceries. Back in Fort Worth, he glanced both ways before leaving his makeshift office—actually a seat at a pal's pharmacy counter—always worried one of his creditors would serve him with papers.

And lo and behold, they found oil. Oceans of oil. And because the majors had pulled in their claws, almost all the profits went straight into their own pockets. Dozens of men literally became millionaires overnight. The oilfields Strake, Richardson, and their peers discovered during the Depression enshrined the Texas wildcatter as an American icon. Strake found the Conroe field, the state's third largest, and ended up one of the country's wealthiest men. Richardson struck the Keystone field in 1935, and was soon hobnobbing in the White House. His buddy Clint Murchison made money in pipelines and seemingly every corner of the industry; his son founded the Dallas Cowboys. Houston's richest wildcatter, a stern scold named Hugh Roy Cullen, found the Tom O'Connor field and ended up bickering with a string of US presidents, bankrolling the University of Houston, and underwriting much of the city's medical infrastructure.

But the greatest wildcatter of all was Dallas's H. L. Hunt, a gambler and card shark who blundered upon the biggest oilfield in American history to that point: East Texas. A deeply strange man whose pastimes including serial bigamy—he would hide not one but two secret families—Hunt hornswoggled a character named Dad Joiner into handing over leases Joiner had romanced out of a string of widows and, after a fateful gusher, woke up one morning as arguably the wealthiest man in America. By the '50s, the great heyday of Texas wildcatter wealth, Hunt and Cullen and Richardson and Murchison would take turns trading the title. Texas would never be the same.

Ever since, the wildcatter has been

the state's defining symbol of what's possible, of what it takes, of the notion that a lone individual with the right character, the right business plan, or simply the right kind of luck can make it very, very big. "One riot, one Ranger" goes the saying, and it's a principle you can just as easily apply to the wildcatter, or to many of the state's up-and-coming modern businessmen, whether they're fracking in South Texas, erecting windmills in the Panhandle, or scrambling for start-up money in Austin. Whether it's a real thing or just an oft-told tale probably doesn't matter. It's what a lot of Texans believe.

The Lure of a Good Truck

By Wes Ferguson

WHEN I WAS FIFTEEN, my mom bought a pickup truck so I could drive myself to work. I had a hardship driver's license issued by the state of Texas and a summer job in the East Texas oil patch, where I put in fifty or sixty hours a week of sweaty, dirty labor, usually on top of rigs that swabbed out clogged oil wells.

Behind the wheel of my family's new-to-us Chevy, I didn't realize in the mid-nineties that our truck was such a classic. I just thought it was old: an

'83 model complete with bench seat, two-tone brown paint, and a bed so ridiculously long, I could haul around both of my little brothers, our friends, our four-wheeler, a dirt bike, and perhaps a few sacks of fireworks, all of us bouncing down the rutted backroads of the Piney Woods anytime I was off the clock or not at school. It was a solid truck. My brother Dan took to calling it Brownie, and the name stuck.

The previous owner had maintained Brownie in meticulous condition. A World War II veteran named Red, he lived down the gravel road from my grandparents' farm. My uncle had talked him into selling the truck to us, arguing that Red was long overdue for an upgrade. I ended up driving Brownie for three years, and the way I remember things, I kept the truck in decent-enough shape. Dan was a maniac, though. When the pickup was handed down to him, he ran poor Brownie ragged. We off-loaded our truck to a classmate who thought he could get it running again.

The last time I saw Brownie, about a decade later, my first pickup truck had broken down for good in the old classmate's backyard, abandoned to rust and dry rot. I left East Texas not long after that and developed into a city slicker. My wife, Laura, and I rented a small apartment in Central Austin. A couple of bus passes, a shared car, and our own two feet were sufficient modes of transportation. I never made a secret of my desire for another truck, a far-off longing that seemed to intensify as I entered middle age. My dad and uncles had always owned pickups. So did my Papa Corky, who let me drive his farm truck ever since I could see above the steering wheel, so long as I was hauling hay for him. I was even beginning to miss the cloud of smoke from unfiltered Camels that used to fill the cab of my other Grandpa Bill's truck when I rode shotgun to open farm gates and gauge oil wells for him.

Nostalgia alone couldn't justify the cost of a gas-guzzling pickup truck on city streets. That is, until Laura and

I lost our apartment in Austin and washed up in suburbs unserved by public transportation. My uncle told me that Red, the first owner of Brownie, had died at the age of ninety-five. His last truck, a 2005 GMC Sierra with a tan finish and diamond-plated toolbox, was just sitting in front of his old house, collecting dust and tree sap. Did I need that truck? Probably not. And yet, I had to have it. With a new battery, it cranked on the first try. The AC went out right off the bat, and a check-engine light came on. Red's old truck made the drive just fine, though, from the red-dirt farm fields where he and my grandparents had lived and died, on freeways through downtown Dallas and Austin, to its new home, parked on a curb in the Texas 'burbs, where it comes in handy from time to time.

The Evolution of Juneteenth

By Kayla Stewart

I REMEMBER SITTING IN the passenger seat of our green, two-door Ford pickup as my mom drove me to the Museum of Fine Arts on a scorching summer day in Houston and taught me about the origins of Juneteenth. Though technically the Emancipation Proclamation freed slaves in the Confederate states on January 1, 1863, she explained, that news didn't make it to Texas until two and a half years later—on June 19, 1865. "That's our true day of freedom," she said. I stared out the window, imagining what the world must've been like for my ancestors who were enslaved in the South.

I'm grateful that my mom took the time, because I didn't learn much about Juneteenth in school. Black history lessons rarely reflected the full breadth of our past. We learned about slavery, Rosa Parks, Martin Luther King Jr., and not a whole lot else. But my mom, a third-grade teacher, made sure I knew how important Juneteenth was. The fact that the holiday remained relatively obscure, she said, was a lesson in how white people manipulated history to serve themselves.

Mom outlined a straightforward narrative that filled me with Texas pride: standing in Galveston on June 19, Union Army major general Gordon Granger read General Order Number Three, effectively emancipating the last enslaved people in the United States, who should've been freed two years prior. Within a few years, African Americans in Houston and Austin celebrated that fateful June day, beginning an annual tradition.

In my family, we marked Juneteenth by gathering in Houston's Third Ward and Miller Outdoor Theatre. Some years there were small parades and performances; other years, street festivals. Afterward, at outdoor picnics and sometimes at our church in the Hiram Clarke neighborhood, we indulged ourselves with beloved Black American foods: southern fried chicken, collard greens, peach cobbler.

Then came 2020 and the death of Houstonian George Floyd at the hands of police. Black Texas culture—perhaps most vividly seen in the horseback protest ride into Houston's Discovery Green that summer—became more nationally prominent than ever, and so did Juneteenth. Black Americans who'd never before celebrated Juneteenth began making it a tradition in their homes. Artists commemorated Juneteenth. Major corporations made June 19 a paid day off. A year later it became the twelfth federal holiday.

Why does Juneteenth resonate so powerfully? It captures the essence of so much of the Black American experience. Many of our greatest moments of exhilaration are connected to overcoming decades of tribulation. That adjacency of joy and suffering is perhaps most visible on the summer holiday. There's a texture to so much Black joy—a combination of jubilance, sorrow, and pride in our resilience—that Juneteenth perfectly captures.

Black people in Texas figured it out a long time ago. It's good to see the rest of the country finally catching on.

RETURN TO A MEXICAN REFUGE

By Wes Ferguson

EVERY YEAR ON June 19, friends and relatives from both sides of the border hold a little-known festival and reunion in Nacimiento de los Negros, a Mexican ranching village about three hours south of Eagle Pass whose name translates literally to "Birth of the Blacks." Their purpose: to celebrate

Being Texan

Juneteenth, or as it is known in Nacimiento, el Día de los Negros, the Day of the Blacks.

Although few Black people remain in northern Mexico, the region was once home to thousands who escaped slavery in the United States. Mexico outlawed slavery in 1829, an underlying factor in Texas's declaration of independence seven years later. In 1836, there were an estimated 5,000 slaves in Texas, a number that ballooned by 1860 to 182,500—more than 30 percent of the state's population.

Freedom lay just across the Rio Grande. One estimate holds that as many as 5,000 enslaved people followed a clandestine Southern Underground Railroad to Mexico. A band of people called the Negros Mascogos, or Black Seminoles, settled in Nacimiento. The group grew from runaway slaves who were given asylum in Spanish Florida and lived among the Seminoles until they were forcibly removed to Oklahoma. With few prospects in Oklahoma and the ever-present risk of being kidnapped by slave hunters and sold into bondage, this group of Black Seminoles turned to Mexico. Following the Civil War, several of Nacimiento's Mascogos came back to the United States with their families in 1870 to serve as Indian scouts in the army, first at Fort Duncan in Eagle Pass and eventually at Fort Clark in Brackettville.

On Juneteenth, Nacimiento's festivities involve a trail ride, songs passed down from Mascogo ancestors, a swim in the cool and clear Rio Sabinas, and a village-wide "Dance of the Blacks." Afterward, a few hundred Mascogos continue to wake up each morning in the village of Nacimiento. Most of the others return again to Texas.

A Tale of Two High Schools

By Dan Q. Dao

AFTER THE FIRST DAY of first grade, I asked my parents if I could go blond. I was for the first time aware of my black Vietnamese hair, which stood out at Houston's preeminent Southern Baptist institution. In 1998, I was one of the only visibly nonwhite students in my grade. This was in a city that is now, by many metrics, considered the most diverse in America.

Founded in 1946, Second Baptist is a K–12 school that, along with a megachurch, occupies a sprawling forty-acre complex of steeples, stained glass, and decorative fountains, with five satellite locations. The campus had two gyms, a restaurant, a gift shop, a small chapel, a larger sanctuary, and an even larger 1,500-person Worship Center, dubbed by fellow alum and writer Jia Tolentino as "the Repentagon." Second Baptist was, in our pastor's words, "a town within a city."

For a decade, I lived inside this white, Christian bubble. Perhaps out of a sense of self-preservation, I became enamored with the gilded mythology of Texas, from the folklore of the Alamo to the twang of country music. I wore cowboy boots, showed up for Friday night football games, and rarely missed a rodeo. Part of me believed that if I proclaimed my Texanness loudly enough, I would be spared the label of outsider. Through elementary and middle school, I lived as a Vietnamese person at home and as a Texas cliché at school.

I remember the blur of overpasses and strip malls along Highway 59 on my daily commute to school, from the suburbs of Missouri City and later

Sugar Land into the immaculate, tree-lined Memorial area of Houston proper. Even in the early 2000s, the forty-five-minute route hinted at the diversity Space City would become known for. On the way in, we'd stop for breakfast tacos at a nondescript Mexican counter on Hillcroft; after school, we'd grab wraps from Shawarma King. On weekends, we'd visit my grandma in Alief, an immigrant enclave lined with Vietnamese street signs and noodle houses.

Second Baptist was a world of its own. On one occasion in elementary school, when asked to lead class prayer, I found out the hard way that my classmates did not pray to Allah, as I'd learned to at home. My parents got a concerned call from the school that day. On another occasion, I went home hungry, ashamed of the Vietnamese dish my parents had packed in my lunch. Once I asked my mom if I could be baptized. She vetoed the idea.

My parents had no interest in joining the Second Baptist Church con- gregation, but my identity struggle didn't discourage them from keeping me at the school. For them, physical safety, a strong education, and a beautiful campus outweighed such frivolous cultural concerns. As refugees from Vietnam who had fared well in Texas, they were adamant that their sons have the best that money could buy. Like many first-generation immigrants who'd realized the American Dream, they subscribed to the notion that private school would somehow keep me out of trouble and significantly improve my chances of enrolling in a good university. "I sit in boardrooms with white men all day—it takes resilience," my mom would say. "You stand out because you're unique, so use that to your advantage."

But things deteriorated for me. I was in high school when Barack Obama was elected to his first term as president, and that was also when I began to witness and experience— and excuse—conspicuous acts of racism by my adolescent classmates.

Obama signs ripped from yards and burned in our school parking lot. Jokes about genocide made on our school intercom. Racial slurs directed squarely at me. It hardly mattered that our class had in fact become more diverse, and that I had formed a small group of friends—all nonwhite—who ate lunch together far from the student cafeteria. Or that I had become a National Merit Scholar and qualified for state in swimming. By spring 2009, I had seen enough. After being disciplined for a marijuana violation on campus, I marched out of school with all my belongings.

I was a junior by then, and I enrolled at my local public school, Kempner High, where for the first time I was able to fully appreciate the other Houston that had always existed in parallel. In 2013, the *New York Times* nodded to Kempner's diversity in a story touting the near-equal breakdown of white, Black, Asian American, and Latino populations of Fort Bend County. There were no manicured flower gardens at Kempner.

Here we had catfish tanks and pastures for cattle and sheep tended by the students. And here I embraced a new kind of Texan identity—one that had room for a Vietnamese American kid trapped between two worlds. I befriended classmates from Nigeria, El Salvador, Iraq, and rural Texas. I met some *real* country people who were nothing like the kids from ranch-owning families in River Oaks.

Public school came with its own issues, of course: with 700 students per grade rather than seventy, testing rooms would get so packed that some of us had to sit on the floor. With a critical mass of each ethnic group, students self-segregated: every hallway and lunch table belonged to a different group. But I was profoundly happier in my life.

For most of my life, my plan had involved going to my parents' alma mater, the University of Texas, studying law, and settling down in Houston. But it was my time at Kempner that convinced me to leave Texas—not because I hated the school but because it opened my eyes to broader America. I went to college in New York City and stayed there for ten years. But recently, perhaps inevitably, I moved back. For years, I would bristle when I heard East and West Coasters drag out social and political stereotypes about Texans. I'd ask them if they knew Houston was the first major American city ever to elect an openly gay mayor. I'd tell them that in 2019, Houston's non-Hispanic white population shrank to just 24.4 percent, less than half the national figure.

Texan culture, to me, today, isn't just boots and barbecue. It's speaking both English and Spanish no matter your ethnicity. It's Viet-Cajun crawfish boils, sticky hot summers, Cadillacs on swangas. It's the 11,500-square-foot limestone and marble Hindu temple in Fort Bend County. It's Megan Thee Stallion, whose aesthetic has helped many rediscover the lost history of Black cowboys.

In 2020, after the killing of Houston-native George Floyd led to a 60,000-person demonstration in his hometown, I received an invitation to sign an open letter created by current Second Baptist students and alumni imploring the administration to recognize decades of structural failings and integrate anti-racism into the curriculum. We are the city of immigrants and their children and their children's children, I thought as I signed— a place where Texanness is offered to anyone regardless of their skin or hair color.

CAN LIBERALS BE TRUE TEXANS?

By David Courtney

WAS LBJ NOT a Texan? What about the great folklorist and foe of McCarthyism J. Frank Dobie, or his antagonist-turned-friend Américo Paredes? Statesperson nonpareil Barbara Jordan? Ann Richards? Willie Nelson? The fact is, when you've got 29,360,759 notoriously individualistic and wildly disparate people living amid more than 250,000 square miles of megacities, charming small towns, and anodyne suburbs, it is pretty much guaranteed that you're going to find a few disagreements among them. Conservative Texans, liberal Texans, moderate Texans, libertarian Texans, pacifist Texans, Texans who are and are not God-fearing, vegetarian Texans, old Texans, young Texans, girl Texans, boy Texans, straight Texans, LGBTQ Texans: whatever their political, religious, sexual, musical, culinary, automotive, or cowboy-boot-toe-shape inclinations, they are all Texans. And one reason we all manage to exist in relative comity is a philosophy that has held Texans in good stead for many, many years now: live and let live.

Way Beyond Hats

By Kathy Blackwell

"I WOULD LOVE TO go to Marfa, but I don't have the right hat."

I was partly joking. While catching up over cocktails in Austin, a friend had just asked if I was attending a popular music festival in West Texas. "I totally know what you mean," she responded, and we laughed over our frozen margaritas.

I was also partly serious. I had never been to the Trans-Pecos Festival of Music + Love, held each fall in the hip artist enclave of Marfa, about a seven-hour drive away, mainly because the timing was never right. But I had experienced it vicariously through my friends' social media posts, which resembled album-cover outtakes in all of their coolness. There were sundresses paired with vintage boots, utility suits zipped over concert tees, handstitched denim jackets, and lots of badass felt hats worn by the types who could pull them off (I have never been one of those people, alas).

Would you call this aesthetic effortless Texas chic? Maybe. But those festival looks were also based on function and necessity: That unforgiving desert sun gives way to a strong night chill, requiring protection and layers. They just made it all look very, very good.

Long before I lived in Texas, my idea of Texas style was based on pop culture: Sue Ellen's silk and sequins on *Dallas*. The dueling high-end/low-end cowgirl looks of rivals Pam and Sissy in *Urban Cowboy*. The electrifying purple jumpsuit worn by the singer Selena. So I was surprised by the casual vibe that greeted me when I moved to Austin twenty-one years ago. There was a DIY sensibility to even the most stylish outfits that seemed to emanate from the city's fierce loyalty to small, local businesses ("Keep Austin Weird" was more than a tourist slogan back then). I learned how to shop vintage and how to dress up jeans for any occasion, and I saved my money to buy clothing and jewelry from hometown designers along South Congress Avenue.

As I began to visit other cities around the state, I discovered that each had its own dress code. I remember going to an arthouse cinema on a Saturday afternoon in Dallas with a friend who lived there. As we stood in the ticket line, I noted that we were in a sea of pearls and blowouts and men in khakis. "Don't they know we're here to see *Sexy Beast?*" I whispered, feeling suddenly out of place in my weekend uniform of sandals, jeans, and a vintage tee. A couple years later, a longtime Houstonian invited me to attend a Saturday night performance by the Houston Grand Opera, featuring guest star Renée Fleming. Black tie, she insisted, and boy did she mean it. That's the night I learned that Houstonians do not mess

around when it comes to black tie—I had never seen so many eye-dropping designer dresses in one place. I myself reveled in my Cher-in-*Moonstruck* moment, with a long red gown and a silky black wrap. (When I attended the Austin opera the next season, I wore a less formal but still long dress while the man seated next to me enjoyed Puccini in his shorts.)

Over the past two decades, though, I've witnessed more of a blending and a blurring of trends across the state. Austin became a little less casual as more out-of-staters poured in and high-end chains and boutiques came to town; Dallas and Houston seemed to loosen up a bit and embrace edgier fashion. This sartorial sea change was influenced in large part, I think, by the wide reach of social media and the rise of online shopping. Back in 2007, fifteen-year-old Jane Aldridge, who lived in a planned suburban community near Dallas, started a blog called *Sea of Shoes* that documented not only her love of footwear but her appreciation for vintage designer pieces in a way that was fresh and charming (a seventies orange-plaid Bill Blass coat over a basic thrift store shift and lace-up Prada boots was just as beguiling as it sounds). Adoration by the national press soon brought her fame and followers, but she never left Texas. She's married now and is also into cooking and home decor, but still maintains *Sea of Shoes*. A few years after Aldridge became one of the original social media influencers, another Dallasite, Amber Venz Box, figured out how to help make fashion bloggers money by launching RewardStyle in 2011 and later, in 2017, LiketoKnowIt, which gives users a commission on sales based on their outfits. An industry was born.

With some of pop culture's biggest names hailing from the Lone Star State, Texas style became a marketable concept, with Beyoncé and Solange Knowles leading the way in clothes and ten-gallon hats that celebrated the roots of Black cowboy culture. Country crossover star Kacey Musgraves hit the award-show circuit

in Western wear from Italian designers such as Valentino and Versace. The vivid rhinestone-encrusted suits favored by Post Malone, the white rapper from Grapevine, and Midland, the country band from Dripping Springs, helped usher in a new appreciation for the classic "Nudie Suits" worn by country stars in the last century.

Perhaps there's no better ambassador for the state's style right now than Brandon Maxwell, who, like Matthew McConaughey, hails from the East Texas town of Longview, where he spent many childhood days by his grandmother's side as she worked in a women's dress shop. He went on to gain fame as Lady Gaga's stylist before launching his own fashion label, but he's been vocal about the influence that Texas women have had on everything he designs. In 2018, he presented his new collection (part of which came together during a retreat in Marfa) in a show modeled after a Texas tailgate—Selena's "Dreaming of You" playing over the loudspeakers at the end. It was the highlight of New York Fashion Week, and a year later he won the coveted Womenswear Designer of the Year award from the Council of Fashion Designers of America.

One of Maxwell's constant muses is Houston philanthropist Lynn Wyatt, whose grandfather and great-uncle founded the Sakowitz department store chain in Galveston in 1902. Now in her eighties, Wyatt is the grand dame of Texas style. Asked in a 2009 interview to define that *je ne sais whuuut* that she pulled off so well, she responded, "Style is a sign of creativity, of knowing who you are."

The combination of artful living and confidence certainly seems to be the common denominator that I see in fashion expressions all around the state, whether in a young teenager wearing her frothy lilac quinceañera confection on the steps of the Capitol, the seventy-something couple two-stepping in their favorite worn boots on the floor of the Old Coupland Inn & Dance Hall, or in the thousands of shoppers wearing Junk Gypsy–inspired clothing and accessories at the Round Top antiques shows every spring and fall.

Can we overdo it at times? Yes. But while trends change, that Texas swagger stays the same—I just need a little bit more of it before I can finally get my own custom hat. Give me five more years in Texas.

Stanley Marcus and the Art of Shopping

By Jason Heid

NEWCOMERS TO DALLAS OFTEN wonder how the nation's ninth-largest city came to occupy a hot, flat, undistinguished stretch of prairie. Why would settlers have chosen to live so far from the beauty of the mountains or the abundance of the oceans? The truth is that Dallas, from the beginning, was a retail enterprise. Founder John Neely Bryan set up a trading post next to a convenient crossing, the only natural ford of the Trinity River for miles in either direction.

Still, it was some sixty-six years later that a trio of twentysomethings opened a store that cemented the city's status as a shopping mecca. In early September 1907, a full-page advertisement in the *Dallas Morning News* announced "the opening of the New and Exclusive Shopping Place for Fashionable Women, devoted to the selling of Ready-to-Wear Apparel." Herbert Marcus, his sister, Carrie, and her husband, Al Neiman, named their downtown Dallas shop Neiman-Marcus (they later dropped the hyphen).

Though "Neiman's" became the usual shorthand, it was the Marcuses who ran the place for decades following Al and Carrie's divorce in 1928. By then, Herbert's eldest son, Stanley, had joined the family business. In his 1974 memoir, *Minding the Store*, Stanley described the Neiman's formula for success, which he learned from his father. "There was a right customer for every piece of merchandise, and that part of a merchant's job was not only to bring the two together, but also to prevent the customer from making the wrong choice," he wrote. "I consider it a doctrine of idealistic pragmatism."

Neiman's got a big assist from the discovery of oil in Texas, which spawned "a new breed of customer. They were people who had made their money in a hurry, and they were in an equal hurry to spend it on some of the luxuries they had heard about all their lives," Stanley wrote. At a time when Texas was far more isolated than it is today, he established Dallas as a market that the couture houses of New York, Paris, and Milan could ill afford to ignore. He hosted weekly in-store fashion shows and created the Neiman Marcus Award for Distinguished Service in the Field of Fashion, which came to be known as the Oscar of the industry and lured fashion luminaries like Coco Chanel and Yves Saint Laurent to visit Texas.

"I have the simplest taste; I am always satisfied with the best," Stanley was known to say (borrowing from Oscar Wilde), and so his customers came to trust in Neiman Marcus to provide them with the best of everything. The introduction of outrageous fantasy gifts to the company's annual holiday catalog, known as the Christmas Book, further whetted their aspirational appetites. Over the decades the catalog's "his and her" gifts have included a two-seater submarine, mummy cases in the style of ancient Egypt, matching pink-striped hot-air balloons, and live camels. One year, when a set of complementary Beechcraft aircraft were on offer, a West Texas rancher reportedly wrote to Neiman's, "I already have a plane, but if you will break the pair, I'd like one for the little woman, who has been hankering for a plane of her own."

In the early fifties, when Neiman Marcus expanded its downtown Dallas store, Stanley installed a restaurant on the new sixth floor. It wasn't long before the elegant space became the de rigueur dining spot for the city's ladies who lunch and made Neiman Marcus nearly as well known for its popovers paired with strawberry butter as for its merchandise. Today that flagship store has a small espresso bar and a salon as well. The chain's second-oldest Dallas store boasts two restaurants, each with full bars, plus a salon and spa. As Neiman's expanded to Houston and later went national, most of its new shops duplicated this model of offering food, spa, and beauty services to make for a full day of luxury. Generations of well-to-do Texans would travel hours across the state for the Neiman's experience.

Shopping thus became a pastime for which Dallas was widely known, so much so that the city became home to what was then the world's largest climate-controlled retail center, which opened in 1965 with a Neiman Marcus store as its prime anchor tenant. That upscale mall, NorthPark Center, still boasts of attracting more than 26 million visitors annually, enough to qualify it as the top attraction in Dallas. Its clean lines and modern design give it the feel of a museum as much as a shopping center, and indeed, paintings and prints and sculptures by celebrated artists like Andy Warhol and Frank Stella adorn its hallways. Even as indoor shopping malls have gone endangered, NorthPark remains a gathering spot for a cross section of the city, perhaps the closest thing Dallas has to Central Park.

To a city without obvious natural resources to bolster its growth, a place built largely by the vision of its settlers, Stanley Marcus brought tastes of the outside world. In turn, Texans learned much of what they might aspire to and were further inspired to claim their place on the world's fashion runway. It's a legacy visible throughout Dallas, which has since grown into one of the world's most indulgent luxury capitals, from the couture houses of Highland Park Village and the downtown boutiques colonizing Main Street to the designer showrooms and art galleries of the Design District. It's not hard to draw a line from Neiman Marcus's influence to Dallas leaders hiring international architects like I.M. Pei to design City Hall and Santiago Calatrava a pair of bridges over the Trinity. The effect has even rippled through the city's suburban sprawl to upscale retail playgrounds such as Plano's Shops at Legacy or Southlake's Town Square. Texans of means, in Dallas and beyond, learned to expect the best. To demand the best. Mr. Stanley, as he affectionately came to be known by so many, sold them a dream. And oh did they buy it.

THE BIGGEST LITTLE
SHOPPING TOWN IN TEXAS

By Jordan Breal

WHEN THE BLUEBONNETS start popping up, another harbinger of spring is not far behind: the two-week antiques shopping bonanza in and around tiny Round Top (population: ninety) that twice a year draws thousands of amateur and professional collectors of all budgets from around the world. As the dozens of shows begin to open, it's natural for a mild panic to set in that you won't have enough time to see (or buy) it all. Unless, that is, you go armed with these tips.

Go early. If you want first dibs, join the professional merchandisers and collectors (for stores like Anthropologie and Ralph Lauren) who are known to buy merch as it's being unloaded from the trucks.

Or go late. If it's bargains you're looking for, consider going the last couple of days a show is open.

Head to "the fields" for the best bargains. You're going to have to sort through a lot of junk, but the thrill of the hunt can't be beat in the tent-strewn pastures known as "the fields," which have the mishmash vibe of a garage sale (albeit, a very large one).

Head to the admission-required shows for the best high-ticket items. If you aren't too keen on junking or picking, instead preferring a well-curated, beautifully merchandised shopping experience, the Marburger Farm Antique Show and the Original Round Top Antiques Fair will be worth the few dollars spent at the gate.

Book a hotel room well in advance. If you can't make a day trip and want to stay in one of the area's stylish B&Bs, book at least half a year in advance.

Always bargain. Don't hesitate to ask a friendly, "What's the best you can do on this?" The worst someone can do is not budge.

Bring cash. The green stuff may help you get a better deal.

Come prepared. You'll want a hat, sunscreen, rain boots, a poncho, tote bags, a wagon, a tape measure, and a list of key measurements from around your house.

If you see something you really want, buy it right then. It'll almost certainly be gone if you come back for it.

The State of the Boot

By David Courtney

WHEN THE NEPALESE AMERICAN fashion designer Prabal Gurung wanted to make a statement about American identity and inclusiveness at his 2018 New York Fashion Week show, he partnered with Dallas-based bootmaker Miron Crosby to create a line of cowboy boots in such materials as mirrored rose-gold leather and paraded them down the runway on an ethnically diverse cast of models. This came about three weeks after "Old Town Road," by the cowboy boot–wearing hip-hop artist Lil Nas X, finished its record-setting nineteen weeks atop the Billboard singles chart and became the unofficial anthem of the so-called yeehaw agenda, a pop culture movement highlighting the history and aesthetics of the black cowboy.

Cowboy boots, that is, stay relevant even as the world around them evolves. Today there are venture-capital-backed boot start-ups, like Austin-based Tecovas, whose Dallas-raised founder moved back to Texas from the Northeast to bring e-commerce to the staid old boot trade. Meanwhile, the overall Western boot market entered the 2020s expecting 50 percent growth in five years.

Texans, of course, need no reminder of the powerful appeal of the cowboy boot. It is as much a part of the state's heritage as cattle and oil. The emergence of the boot in hip new places, however, is a reminder that boots are the province of more than just Marlboro Man types. While the cowboy boot as we know it today likely wouldn't exist without the influence of Texans, the style has no single creator or birthplace that can legitimately lay claim to its "invention." The cowboy boot has always been a cultural amalgam.

For utilitarian reasons, horsemen from time immemorial have favored sturdy, high-shafted foot coverings. Genghis Khan and his marauding Mongol army wore leather boots, and so did medieval Moors, Hungarian hussars, and the vaqueros of old and new Spain. Eighteenth-century German soldiers wore smart-looking calfskin Hessian boots with tassels and a V-cut scallop at the front top of the shaft. Arthur Wellesley, the First Duke of Wellington, did away with the foppish decoration and popularized his namesake Wellington boot. Wellies, in the feedlot and grocery lot, endure still.

What we know today as the cowboy boot is a distinctive offshoot of all those styles and cultures. It arose at the zenith of the great cattle drives—between 1866 and 1890—when cowboys started asking cobblers for boots with a slimmer design, higher heels, more rounded toes, and a sturdier instep than were available at the time. Higher heels, often slightly underslung, stayed in the stirrup better. Rounded toes were roomier. And sturdier insteps made for an altogether sturdier boot. A bootmaker in Coffeyville, Kansas, near the terminus of the Chisholm Trail, began supplying Texas cowboys with such boots in the 1870s. Interestingly, as many as a quarter of working cowboys during this period were black, most of them former slaves. And Richard King had his *kineños*, families of vaqueros he'd recruited from Mexico, working the herds of his sprawling South Texas ranching empire.

Meanwhile, H.J. "Big Daddy Joe" Justin, who hung his shingle in 1879 in Spanish Fort, in Montague County, right on the Chisholm, and Sam Lucchese, who founded Lucchese in San Antonio, in 1883, were shoeing Texas cowboys too. Over the ensuing decades, notable bootmaking outfits emerged all across the state: Tony Lama Boots, founded in El Paso, in 1911; Little's Boot Company, founded in San Antonio, in 1915; M. L. Leddy's, founded in Brady, in 1922; the Nocona Boot Company, established in Nocona by Big Daddy Joe's daughter Enid Justin in 1925.

And though the cattle trailing game

faded away with the advent of barbed-wire fencing, the expansion of railroad routes, and changing economics in the beef trade, the romantic—and whitewashed—image of the Wild West cowpoke took hold in countless books, movies, and radio shows. Between the late thirties and late sixties, Hollywood's most popular genre was the Western. The likes of Gene Autry and Roy Rogers became the faces of the tradition.

Riding that wave of popularity, cowboy boots became fashionable among non-cowboys. And fancier than they had ever been before, with elaborate stitching, brighter colors, and ever more intricate inlays and overlays. Where a lone star had once sufficed to decorate the shaft of a boot, there were now multiple stars, as well as images of cacti, six-guns, lightning bolts, and so on. The first big moment of cowboy boots on fashion runways came during the Texas chic movement of the eighties, when *Dallas* ruled the TV screen and *Urban Cowboy* ruled the box office.

Texas has changed profoundly, in almost every imaginable way, since the days of the great cattle drives. The state's population has grown to more than forty times its size back then, and nearly 90 percent of Texans live in giant and diverse cities, not on the range. But one thing that hasn't changed all that much over this span is the overall essence of the cowboy boot, even as successive generations of bootmakers have continued to refine its form and turn it into a canvas for their art. The footwear that played an integral part in the creation of Texas—the actual one as well as the mythical one—remains, all these years later, a part of the colorful tapestry of Texas. If cowboy boots are the state's official footwear (as the Texas Lege itself officially named them, in 2007), then they belong to all Texans. Despite the name, they know no specific gender and belong to no specific trade or class or ethnicity. Cowboy boots are ours.

A FEW RULES OF WESTERN WEAR

By David Courtney

FASHION TRENDS—FRINGE JACKETS, kiltie boots, bolo ties—come and go like drought. But just like springtime flowers, some elements of the Texas wardrobe return year after year and never wear out their welcome—provided they're donned authentically.

What should a new Texan buy first in order to fit in: cowboy boots, a belt buckle, or a hat? Take your pick. Any one of these items can be worn by anyone right away. But in tandem they are best reserved for the homegrown, or for costume parties. Newcomers to the Midwest do not appear at their local diners in Big Smith overalls and John Deere gimme caps with wheat stalks dangling from their lips; nor do transplants to the Pacific Northwest rush out to buy bright-yellow hip waders and matching slickers. Clothes may make the man, but they may also make the man look foolish.

Should you tuck your pants into your boots? Are you a nineteenth-century Texas Ranger? Is your closet full of Western-style bib shirts? Do you have a drawer full of large kerchiefs? Do you spend most of your time atop a horse, or are you currently clearing brush? No? Then there's only one question to ask yourself: "Do I really give a damn what anybody thinks when I tuck my jeans into my boots?"

How does one break in boots? The union of foot and boot is not unlike the union of matrimony, and, as in the best marriages, the strongest bonds are forged by time—time spent traveling together, molding to each other, collecting a patina of character-building nicks and scratches in strange and foreign lands together. There is no shortcut.

What does "Western chic" dress code mean on a party invitation? Sartorial solutions for a dude are easy: boots, jeans, and a shirt, with or without a jacket or hat. It's trickier for the gals. Understatement is not a quality for which Texas women are known, especially when it comes to expressing their regional identity. A flouncy calico prairie skirt, an embroidered Mexican smock, brightly embellished boots, a buckskin kerchief with a silver and turquoise concho cinch ring, a vintage belt with a rodeo buckle, and a bolero hat wouldn't raise a single eyebrow. (One of the great things about the Texan proclivity for loud fashion is a wide margin of error.) That said, a little black dress, if paired with some nice black cowboy boots, would work out just fine. Use your best judgment and express whatever level of Western flair you'll be comfortable with.

Souls of the Departed

By Oscar Cásares

OTHER THAN A FEW framed photos of family and friends who had passed away over the years, there wasn't much in the way of decorations when my family set up our first Día de los Muertos altar. Later came the banner of *papel picado*, and the year after that tiny sugar skulls, and, most recently, the flameless candles that stay on all night after the real ones are blown out. But no matter how our family altar has changed, it always begins with the same centerpiece— a grapefruit—that takes us back to a faraway memory of how it all began.

It's 1938 and my father is a young man. He lives in Donna, just a few miles north of the Rio Grande, where he works at a packing shed. One afternoon, he's loading crates of grapefruit onto the back of a truck when he spots a group of high-school girls walking by. He tries to make eye contact with one of them and has no luck. Then he sees a little boy playing near the packing shed and has an idea. He tosses the boy a grapefruit and tells him to run over and give it to the girl in the gray gingham skirt. "Tell her there's someone who wants to meet her," he says. "Ándale." The little boy delivers the gift, and this is how my parents become my parents.

We didn't celebrate Día de los Muertos as a family when I was growing up. All I knew when I set up my first altar seven years ago was that it honored the memories of the dead. But I didn't know that the holiday dates back to Aztec times or that what I sometimes call an altar is actually known as an *ofrenda*, and that offering food and drinks, along with photos and mementos, is part of a ritual meant to welcome back the souls of the departed every year in early November.

The truth is, I didn't start celebrating it for cultural reasons; I began the tradition so my two kids would remember the people they had little to no memory of. My son, Adrian, was born three months before my father died, and my daughter, Elena, was entering kindergarten when my mother passed away. I wanted them to know who my parents were and where they were born. I wanted them to understand what mattered to my parents: whom they loved and how they died.

Of course, I set up our original *ofrenda* years before a pandemic would change life on the border and everywhere else in the world. Before I had any idea what sorrow awaited us, and what our *ofrenda* would come to include.

I WAS BORN a couple of months after my parents celebrated their twenty-fifth wedding anniversary. By that point, they weren't going out so often, but when they did, it was either to a dance or to a funeral. In Brownsville, in the seventies, Saturday nights meant dances at the Civic Center or the Friendship Garden. If they went to a funeral or rosary during the week, it was at the Treviño, Garza, Delta, or Darling-Mouser Funeral Home. Not that they had that many relatives and good friends who were dying off. It might be a lady from church they knew only from saying hello to her after Mass every Sunday. It might be the husband of the woman my mom bought her tamales from at Christmas, or the sister of a man my parents used to have coffee with at the Whataburger on Boca Chica Boulevard, or the man at the end of our street who had repaired my father's lawn mower a few summers back.

After a while, I gave up asking them why they had to go to another rosary, why they couldn't just skip this one. I'd always get the same answer: "*para cumplir*," which essentially meant "to do our part." That, or "*para acompañar*," to be with the family. It didn't matter if the grieving wife or husband or in-law even knew who my parents

were or how they knew the deceased. They weren't going there to be seen or recognized. They showed up because that's just what they did.

But if it was one of their friends I'd never met and shaken hands with— something my father put a lot of stock in—then it was okay for me to stay home. Once, though, when I was ten, my dad took me to a rosary for the father of a friend of mine from the Boys Club. The man had been killed in a bus wreck coming back from Ciudad Victoria, something that I still remember any time I'm traveling in Mexico and pass another roadside shrine.

Family was different. Losing someone close to us also meant being with those we hadn't seen and held in years. While these funerals were sad occasions, a part of me looked forward to having my uncles and aunts and cousins pour in from Chicago and Fresno and Grand Rapids. Then, after the burial, we would gather in someone's kitchen or backyard to hear the stories we hadn't heard since the last time we were together. My *tío* Nico would tell one about the afternoon he was in his backyard, in Houston, working under his car—a buttercup-yellow 1969 Chevrolet Bel Air—trying to loosen a bolt. Then, just as he turned onto his side, the car suddenly wobbled off its blocks and fell on him. It sounds awful, but not when he reenacted the whole scene, including the way he yelled for help—BELIA, *AYÚDAME . . . AYÚDAME!!!*—and then told us how he was saved, miraculously—no other way to put it—when my *tía* Belia and my cousins Hilda and Rosy grabbed hold of the bumper and raised the car just enough for him to scoot out. Then there was the one about the blowout my *tío* Héctor had in the middle of the King Ranch—a good twenty miles from the nearest service station— only to discover his spare tire was flat. He and my *tía* Nena and my *tía* Lilia hitched a ride with an eighteen-wheeler, but there was room only for him in the passenger seat, so my *tías* had to climb behind the seats and lie down in the sleeper cab, staring up at themselves in the trucker's mirrored ceiling. Or the story about my father driving a taxi one night in downtown Brownsville, around Market Square, circa 1944, when a guy backed out of one of the cantinas swinging a barstool at two other men. When my dad got closer, he realized the guy with the barstool was my mother's younger brother, Óscar (my *tocayo!*), so he slowed down enough to reach over and push open the passenger door so his *cuñado* could hop in. Those kind of stories.

After seeing my parents attend so many rosaries and funerals, I guess it shouldn't have surprised me years later when my father, already in his eighties and a full decade after retiring, took a part-time job at a funeral home. He had spent most of his life laboring under the South Texas sun as a farmworker, a deliveryman, a fireman, and then a cop, and a tick inspector for the USDA, which he did for thirty-three years, much of that time riding horseback across long stretches of the Rio Grande to make sure livestock weren't crossing over from Mexico and spreading cattle fever in this country (this explains why his belt buckle of a quarter horse also has a spot on our *ofrenda*).

As an attendant at Treviño Funeral Home, he was expected to answer the phone, greet and direct people to one of the two chapels, encourage them to sign the guest book, and give directions to guests coming in from out of town. If someone called in sick, he might need to assist one of the funeral directors at the church and burial. He loved getting dressed up for work in one of his dark suits, then slipping on a tie from the half dozen he kept hanging on a belt rack. He loved wearing real lace-up shoes, not the ones with the Velcro straps my mother had bought him when he retired and stopped wearing his work boots. He loved being the first one to arrive at work and the last one to leave, and he especially loved helping people whose families he had known for ages.

MY FATHER DIED in 2007, but I wonder how he would have reacted to seeing all the parents and grandparents, *tías* and *tíos*, and *primas* and *primos* who in 2020 became COVID-19 victims in the Rio Grande Valley—especially Hidalgo County, which is more than 90 percent Latino and became the epicenter of the crisis that summer. The county represents only 3 percent of Texas's population but accounted for 12 percent of its coronavirus deaths then. It was here in late July that we lost my father's favorite nephew—my cousin, A. C. "Beto" Jaime. A couple of days later, his wife of sixty-three years, Dora, also passed away from the coronavirus.

After a lifetime of civic involvement, including his time as the first Mexican American mayor of Pharr, from 1972 to 1978, Beto was well known in the area. But due to social-distancing mandates, his and Dora's combined funeral service was limited to immediate family, all of them wearing masks and discouraged from hugging and crying on one another's shoulders. I can't imagine how my father would have made sense of the restrictions that prevented family members from being with Beto inside the ICU, holding his hand as he took his last breath. What would my father say if I told him that we could only watch the livestream of the funeral, on my laptop? If he had watched a pair of attendants wheel the two caskets up the aisle and place them near the altar, side by side, would he have felt a terrible sob catch in his throat, as it did in mine?

Of the pandemic's many blows, perhaps the cruelest deprived us of the ritual of grieving our losses together. Growing up along the border, we were all reminded of how precarious life could be, but also of how we would always be there for one another. We understood that, no matter what, those of us left behind wouldn't carry this loss by ourselves.

Like so many others in the Valley, we're a family of touchy-feely people. We hug, we kiss, we cry, we hug some more. No one cries as long and passionately as my *tía* Minerva, who,

six years ago at my mother's burial, had to be held back from clinging to the casket as it was lowered into the ground. I still remember the *abrazo* Beto gave me at my father's rosary, patting me on the back as he squeezed me a little tighter, reminding me over and over that I wasn't going through this alone.

So, alongside my father's belt buckle and the grapefruit on the *ofrenda*, I'll need to add a photo of Beto and Dora dancing, something they loved to do at every wedding and family reunion. I can see that irrepressible smile on Beto's face as he spins Dora one way and then right back into his arms, like the song might never end.

Since Beto and Dora's burial itself wasn't livestreamed, I heard about it from their eldest son, Bert, who works as a chaplain at a nearby hospital and served as an acolyte during the Mass. Bert had planned to deliver the final prayers at his parents' burial, and when the moment came, he walked toward the gravesite, past his five sib-

lings and their families and the musician they had hired to serenade their
parents.

They were all waiting for Bert to
speak, but as soon as he opened his
mouth, he choked up, unable to get
the words out. He thought of how his
father had died, and then his mother,
within forty-eight hours of each other.
He thought of the two weeks that had
passed before the memorial service
could take place—the funeral home's
schedule had been overwhelmed. He
thought of how accepting his parents'
death felt like a test of his faith in God's
will, and he wondered if he would
even be able to make it through the
final prayer. And then he felt someone
lay a hand on his left shoulder, and
then another hand rest on his right
shoulder. He turned to see his young-
est brother, Kevin, and his own son,
Andres, standing behind him, steady-
ing him. It was all he really needed to
make it the rest of the way.

II

Town & Country

For Love of the Land

By Sterry Butcher

THE MARE PASTURE AT the Seven L Ranch is horse heaven. Just half an hour from the Gulf of Mexico and close to the little burg of Devers, this field looks level from a short distance, though really the ground undulates with tiny hummocks of thick-growing Bahia grass, salt grass, and Bermuda grass. Lines of bramble and short scrub trees grow along culverts and a live creek, delineating the pasture's wide boundaries. The sky is very blue. At the approach of a truck, the horses turn and raise their heads in unison, and when the truck stops and its occupants climb out, the horses amble toward them with the deliberate, unhurried speed of old friends greeting one another. The mare band consists of mothers, daughters, sisters, aunts, and cousins. They are slick-sided, big-barreled, and gleaming, the spires of their ears perked and their expressions soft and curious as they semicircle around their visitors.

Texans have always yearned for land and fine creatures, and here, at the Seven L, it is easy to fall in love with this grassy abundance and these robust, personable mares arching their pretty necks. It is easy to want this beauty and bounty. Virtually nothing in ranching is genuinely easy, though, and whatever success and quality the Seven L can boast come from long decades of careful planning and management. "The ranch is one hundred ten years old," says Paxton Ramsey. It's 2015. Ramsey owns the ranch along with his mother, Susan Ramsey, and his sister, Romney Velazquez. "It means everything to me. It's what

gets me up before my alarm clock, a responsibility that is one hundred ten years old."

A Texan's reverence for land ownership comes somewhat naturally. Ranching, while it has changed over time, remains one of the state's great identifiers, and while folks in other places undoubtedly forge profound connections to their properties, Texas is different. The state was born from land grabs. The Spanish claimed it, despite the presence of Native Americans who had been here for millennia, then the French, then the Spanish again, until Mexico took it from Spain and the Texicans wrenched it from Mexico. Land was everything, worth fighting and dying for.

A brief, whirlwind history lesson: In the 1700s, Spain began handing out land grants to those willing to endure the hardship of staking out lives on a sparsely populated and dangerous frontier. While the Spanish didn't settle Texas in large numbers, they were responsible for the invaluable addition of horses, cattle, and sheep to these parts. By 1821, Mexico had taken over, and to populate this vast territory, the new government courted foreign settlers with land allotments of 4,428 acres for grazing, plus another 177 acres for farming. The land wasn't free—certain fees were charged—but the grants were darned cheap even for then, about 3 cents an acre, which was less expensive than land in the United States.

As any Texas seventh-grade-history student knows, empresarios like Stephen F. Austin brought lots of single men and families to Texas. By doing so, the empresarios earned themselves premium tracts. Soldiers of the Texas Revolution were rewarded with the promise of acreage, and during the decade of the Texas Republic, the General Land Office distributed more than 40 million acres. (African Americans and Native Americans, it should be noted, were deemed ineligible for those land grants.) In 1844, when Congress was considering the annexation of Texas, land was again a primary concern: in the proposed treaty for statehood, the United States would take on the Republic's $10 million of debt, along with 175 million acres of its public territory.

Except this didn't happen. The republic's public domain wasn't worth $10 million, according to Congress, and the treaty was rejected. Texas therefore came into the Union with both its debt and its unappropriated lands. This turned out to be important. While federal lands now checker the expanse of other Western states—like Nevada, which is 80 percent federally owned, or Utah, whose land is 63 percent federal—less than 2 percent of Texas is made up of federal land. The rest is privately owned or controlled by the state. Texas, in other words, is held by Texans. Texas is ours.

There's an obvious timelessness with land—the ever-present rocks and sky—that is at odds with the very human wish to put a stamp on a property, to forge a history and attach it to a place. Paxton Ramsey, whose mother inherited the ranch from her mother, acknowledges that his tenancy is temporary, though the effort to shape, cull, and improve the Seven L, or any other ranch, is worth it. "My grandmother told me, 'This land will never be yours; you're just borrowing it from your children,'" he says. "Ranchers are focused on successors, and a key part of that is realizing that you're part of something bigger than yourself—and that you're leaving something better than you found it."

RANCHING IS FULL of promise. There is always the potential to do well. Even in poor, undernourished, or flinty country, there are things that can be produced. Use the rocks to make a fence or the pine trees to build a barn. Dig the dirt to make an adobe home. Raise a calf to eat and trade another to your neighbor for hay. Harness the wind and pull water from the ground. Grow grass. It's your country to protect or exploit, conserve or improve. What freedom there is in that notion—to do what you want on your land. Of course, the risks involved are real. You could fall off a windmill or get stomped by a mule. You could go broke if it doesn't rain. The trick is to balance the needs of the land and the animals on that land with the weather, the rhythm of the seasons, and the financial constraints of the rancher. That's some trick. Good thing that time is sometimes, usually, hopefully, on the side of the rancher.

Ranching is inherently unfettered by the sort of time that constricts us in office towers or classrooms or suburban homes. A wristwatch or an alarm ping on your phone won't change the minds of the cows who must be penned but are hiding on tiptoe in the cedar brakes. Often, you can't have exactly what you want when you want it on a ranch. It takes a long time to stack that rock wall, build that barn, raise that calf, grow that grass. It will take a lifetime to get to all that work, and then when you are gone, it will take the next person a lifetime as well. There's something soothing in that idea, an optimistic glimmer that this world will keep spinning despite far-off wars, troubles at home, shaky economies, and human frailties. As long as people manage to stay alive and sane, the need to care for the land and livestock will go on.

Much of ranching work is done alone. It takes only one person in a vehicle, for instance, to tour the ranch's windmills to check that water continues to flow from each of them. No one is around to see your antics goading two dopey steers back into the right pasture after the escapees apparently wormed through an unknown gap in the fence. No one hears the cussing when you discover the carcass of a good ewe, curled up dead at the bottom of some skinny arroyo. ("Aw, sheep," a long-ago acquaintance of mine once scoffed. "Sheep just want to die.") You're likely to be alone when you slam your hand in the tailgate, and alone when you take note that the turkey vultures have returned from migration and that the limestone seep,

gone dry from drought, has begun trickling water again.

It also means that no one is typically aware when you've done something particularly well. No one sees that extra-mile effort or your ingenuity at problem-solving. Well, accolades aren't all that important. Self-worth, however, that's a different matter. "How do you measure your satisfaction with who you are when you go to bed at night?" Paxton asks. "Other people, they may not see you riding these good colts and pulling a calf out of quicksand. I could ride away from her, and no one would know I spent four hours to pull her out. And even then, I still have a chance of losing her—but I have a clear conscience about that."

The work's aloneness may account for the reason that a chance encounter with a ranching friend at the feedstore or, in the small-town way, in two trucks pulled cab to cab in the middle of the street can induce an eagerly shared, one-sided font of information. The speaker's torrent may include family news, opinions on cattle prices, details about home improvements, or a suddenly recalled tale about a tool spied in tall grass during a ride on a broncky colt in a far-distant pasture, this tool's being a neat old thing (ancient sheep shears, a long-handled wrench, or a Model T jack) hardly ever seen or used anymore but alluring despite its mantle of rust and dirt. At times there is nowhere else I'd rather be than sitting snug in a truck with the heat blasting and the windows down, listening to a friend, red-nosed with the cold, talk about the hijinks of cornering an ornery cow and muscling her into the trailer.

It sounds fun, doesn't it, all that roaming around and wrestling with nature? I suspect it is fun, at least sometimes, in the way that hard and productive work can be deeply satisfying. This is some of the allure of ranching and of holding land—that there's an honesty and clarity to the overarching duties. Though I can't claim to be a rancher, I do admire

them. And while the little twenty-acre empire where my husband, son, and I live is captivating, I'll admit—only a bit shamefully—that we lust for more land, a bigger place, pastures and canyons and creek beds beyond the reach of earshot and eyesight. This is nuts, I know.

The yen for more property isn't a reflection of dissatisfaction or ingratitude with our present place, which, truthfully, pleases us a great deal and suits our present situation. Rather, that want for more country is simply greed, the desire for more aloneness and more majesty, for different varmints and plants and rocks. It's to have the chance to know a place, to start the long romance of finding out what birds nest in which trees, of how the water courses in a heavy rain, of stumbling across a midden of flint from some long-ago knapper or figuring out how to best cover the bare spots of land still raw and sore from when cattle and goats grazed there ages ago.

A piece of country is a living being. It's a chance to do many things. It's the potential for nearly endless work and discovery. If there is enough time, what knowledge unfolds from the stewardship of these acres? Amid the droughts and the downpours, what things do you discover? The answers are probably too numerous to grasp, though the appetite to find out is there. That, in the end, is the pull of the land.

The Seven Territories of Texas

By Wes Ferguson

DEFYING CATEGORIZATION WITH THE Southwest, the South, and the
Heartland, Texas is simply its own vast swath of country—and a diverse one at
that. Starting in the center of the state and heading in any direction, different
worlds appear before any state lines do. From desert mountains to lush forests,
briny bays to wide-open prairies, Texas is a meeting point of seven distinct
ecological regions. Each has its own identity, and yet each is deeply, essentially
Texan.

BIG BEND

Sweeping westward from the badlands surrounding the Pecos River, past the "big bend" of the Rio Grande, and toward the city of El Paso, this vast and arid region of West Texas lies within the sun-baked Chihuahuan Desert, which is home to jackrabbits and Mojave rattlesnakes and a host of spiky plants, all clinging to life in the state's most inhospitable landscape.

There are grace notes in the desert if you look for them, as in the startling oasis that is San Solomon Springs, which the Civilian Conservation Corps in the 1930s dammed into a bracing, rock-walled swimming pool that Texans know as the main attraction at Balmorhea State Park. Even more remarkable are the Guadalupe, Davis, and Chisos Mountain Ranges, which tower above the desert floors that surround them. By the sheer drama of their nosebleed-tall elevations, these so-called sky islands transform the local weather and ecology by creating a natural barrier for westerly winds.

Guadalupe Peak, at a whopping 8,751 feet, and other West Texas mountains force the winds to suddenly rise, cooling and condensing the moisture in the air and encouraging rain. The surprisingly damp conditions nurture plants and animals that otherwise couldn't survive in the region, like the slender-limbed Texas madrone, a tree otherwise known as Naked Indian and Lady's Leg, whose red berries feed the ringtail cats that forage in the canyons at night. Black bear, panther, and elk also make their home here, as do firs and maples more commonly found in the Rocky Mountains.

GULF COAST

The Texas stretch of shore that bends along the Gulf of Mexico is often described as a "working coast" trawled by shrimping boats and dotted by offshore oil rigs. Ports, refineries, and enormous terminals that export natural gas around the clock line many of the bays, estuaries, and wide mouths of rivers that feed into the sea. And yet, the Texas coast is also a mecca for those seeking more natural repose, including saltwater anglers and beachgoers flocking to wonders such as Padre Island, the world's longest barrier island, which is home to the world's smallest and most endangered sea turtle, the Kemp's ridley.

Nature and industry hang in uneasy balance throughout Texas, but nowhere is that more evident than along the coast, from the petrochemical jungles of Port Arthur and Freeport to the hundreds of thousands of acres of coastal wetlands that have been set aside as state and federal reserves for fish and other species. Of the millions of migratory birds that take advantage, the most magnificent may be the endangered whooping cranes, the tallest bird in North America, which spend each winter at a marshy wildlife refuge near the charming bayside town of Rockport.

HILL COUNTRY

The Texans who live and vacation in this region at the geographic center of the state may prefer to fix their gaze on the pretty live oaks and majes-

tic bald cypresses that line the many spring-fed streams. Truly, though, this part of Texas is cedar country. The ashe juniper, more commonly called mountain cedar, is so universally despised for its allergy-inducing releases of pollen each winter that *Texas Monthly* once described the tree as an "arboreal parasite" and "objectively the ugliest of trees."

This shrubby evergreen—a native species that is widely, though incorrectly, said to be invasive—blankets much of the Hill Country, crowding out other plants and blocking views. It wasn't always like this. When the first waves of settlers from Europe and the American South ventured northwestward in the 1840s and '50s from the coastal plains of Texas, they ascended a series of limestone ridges called the Balcones Escarpment and arrived at the Hill Country, then a seemingly endless sea of prairie grass carpeting every hill and valley within sight. Amazingly, the native grass had grown so tall, its stems reached the stirrups of the pioneers' saddles. The cedar trees, meanwhile, were largely confined to so-called cedar brakes along the tight canyon walls and other slopes that were too rocky and steep for the otherwise ubiquitous grass to root. In just a few decades, however, most of the prairie grass was gone, a casualty of intensive tilling, plowing, and grazing. As the region's thin topsoils blew away, the cedars, whose strong taproots don't need much soil, crept out of the canyons and took control.

Today Texas's most picturesque landscape is being overtaken by yet another conquering force as developers stud the hills around Austin and San Antonio—and destination towns such as Fredericksburg and Wimberley—with new homes. On mild summer evenings, the region's many charms, from limestone ledges overlooking gin-clear swimming holes to breezes that rattle the oak leaves, can make the inevitable return of cedar season feel very far away.

THE PANHANDLE

Way up in the High Plains of Texas, an old saying goes, the farmland is so flat, you can stand on your back porch near Lubbock or Amarillo—or Plainview or Levelland or the town of Plains, for that matter—and watch your dog run away for three days.

Head east, though, and all that flat land suddenly falls off a cliff. The High Plains sits on one of the largest mesas in North America, called the Llano Estacado, whose eastern edge is a weathered wall of red dirt and white caliche known as the Caprock Escarpment. The Caprock stretches north and south for some 200 miles and towers as high as a thousand feet above the wide-open ranchland that rolls back toward the east, down below.

In a landscape otherwise known for its sameness, the Caprock counts as spectacular. It's the most obvious and dramatic dividing line between any two geographic regions in Texas. On magnificent display among the cliffs and peaks of Caprock Canyons State Park near Quitaque (pronounced Kitty-Kway), the Caprock also encompasses Palo Duro Canyon southeast of Amarillo. With its colorful mesas, buttes, and chimney-shaped hoodoos standing above one of the main channels of the Red River, Palo Duro is the second-largest canyon system in the nation.

PINEY WOODS

Blessed with more abundant rain than the rest of the state—and looking nothing like popular depictions of Texas; no desert vistas or tumble-weeds in sight—this lush and pine-shrouded region of slow rivers, lakes, and gently rolling landscapes sits at the western edge of the Old South. It's just one part of an enormous forest—known, naturally, as the Piney Woods region—that also comprises parts of Louisiana, Arkansas, and Oklahoma.

Before sawmill towns sprung up in the mid-1800s to clear the stands of loblolly, longleaf, and shortleaf pine interspersed with hickory and white oak, the old-growth forests were said to be so tall, and their canopies so dense, that very little undergrowth could take hold; a person could ride horseback for hours through the heaviest forests and never need to duck a tree limb. After the trees were gone, Piney Woods landowners tried their hand at cotton and cattle. Now, the pines have returned in much of the region, often planted in monolithic tracts that supply lumber for construction in the state's more populous areas.

PRAIRIES AND LAKES

Running through much of North and Central Texas, this strip of land forms a transitional zone between the great forests of the southern United States and the wide-open prairies of the West—and borrows a little from both neighbors. In one sense, there's not much about this liminal area to distinguish it from Texas's other geographic regions. On the other hand, the Prairies and Lakes could be the most quintessentially Texan part of the state. Gentle grasslands intersperse with patches of oak woodlands, man-made lakes as blue as the sky, and expansive estates.

Sweeping south from Sherman and Paris near the Oklahoma state line, down through the Dallas–Fort Worth Metroplex, to Waco and Brenham, and ending where South Texas and the Gulf Coast begin, the Prairies and Lakes region is also home to the Blackland Prairie, a belt of dark, fertile soil once part of a vast system of native tallgrass but now mostly plowed over for crops and sprawl.

SOUTH TEXAS

Humid near the coast and arid toward the west, where it's bounded by the Rio Grande, the subtropical plains of South Texas make up a mostly flat expanse of ranchland and thorny scrub, primarily masses of prickly pear and pervasive mesquite, which to folklorist and Brush Country native J. Frank Dobie were "as native as rattlesnakes and mockingbirds, as distinctive as northers, and as blended into life of the land as cornbread and tortillas."

Often reviled by ranchers for infesting otherwise perfectly good grazelands for cattle—traditionally longhorns—the mesquite is a shrubby tree whose hot-burning wood imparts a strong, smoky flavor on grilled meats. Mesquite bean pods were also an essential food source for thousands of years and can be dried and ground into a sweet, nutty flour that is especially delicious when baked into cookies.

The brush only grows thicker as you travel southward and enter the Tamaulipan Thorn Scrub, the ideal habitat for elusive ocelots and chachalacas, whose earsplitting calls are most commonly heard in the early morning hours. In and around Brownsville, at the southern tip of the United States, the brush gives way to a number of resacas—attractive, eyelash-shaped lakes—which are remnants of long-ago Rio Grande floods, now stranded among swaying palm trees.

HOW BIG IS TEXAS, REALLY?

By Dan Solomon

ANYBODY WHO'S DRIVEN the twelve hours between Beaumont and El Paso can confirm that Texas is big. Still, "big" is a relative term. Next to Delaware, the state is huge, but compared to the infinitely expanding universe, it is but a speck. It is perhaps to stave off the feeling of cosmic insignificance that so many Texans loudly embrace sheer size as central to Texan identity. Compare the state to the United Kingdom, and it's advantage: Texas. Israel? Smaller than the Dallas–Fort Worth metro area. Spain? Ha. Texas could fit the whole Iberian Peninsula, including Portugal, with enough room left to squeeze in Bulgaria. Japan and Madagascar are both longer than Texas, but with less girth. France? Vive le Texas! Of course, Texas cannot win every landmass matchup. It would take up just 9 percent of Australia. If Texas were an African nation, it would rank as the eighteenth largest. You could fit a whopping twelve and a quarter in Brazil. Fine. But Texas is still bigger than California.

The Beauty of Small Things

By Courtney Bond

MY NEIGHBORHOOD IN NORTHEAST Austin is a fifties-era collection of ranch-style homes joined by a couple of schools, quite a few churches, and very many auto-repair shops, hair salons, and fast-food joints. Bisecting the area is a wide graffiti-decorated drainage ditch, usually choked with rampant vegetation intertwined with, at last observation, plastic debris of all sorts, someone's unopened mail, and random items of clothing—that is, until a heavy rain turns the canal into a veritable river wild, flattening the reeds and weeds and moving the detritus on down to its next stop. A walk along the tree-lined streets means navigating fast-moving cars, a chicken or two, the occasional wandering but not lost dog, and more carelessly tossed trash, of which Swisher Sweets wrappers predominate. Meticulously xeriscaped lawns alternate with greenery run amok. And every spring, one of these rowdy patches erupts into a sea of bluebonnets, what must be thousands of them, reminding me once again that the beauty of Texas is often found in diminutive forms and unexpected places.

It's not that Texas doesn't have sweeping vistas and grand landscapes. I don't know anyone who isn't awed by the austere splendor of Big Bend or the Guadalupe Mountains. But, well, we don't have a Yellowstone. Or a Denali. No Grand Canyon. We are blessed with two national parks (California has nine). When I lived in the Golden State, I never tired of the gentle hills of the wine country or the craggy coastlines. Every time I visit Colorado, as I hike alongside an icy river that's making its way down a snow-dusted mountain, I wonder if there's any terrain more beautiful. I have studied waves in varying shades of blue barreling over black volcanic rock in Hawaii. I have marveled at the towering sandstone arches of Utah, the misty waterfalls of the Smoky Mountains, the turquoise water of a Florida beach.

What Texas does have, though, is sheer variety. I picture the state, in all its gigantic and oddly shaped glory, squatting resolutely at the base of the country and quietly embracing some of its best parts, like a hen with her brood. Those who have not traveled here have trouble grasping its multitudes, distracted as they are by stereotypical images of dusty ranches on one hand and suburban sprawl on the other.

As someone who spends a lot of time exploring the parks and natural areas of Texas, I've covered many miles seeking out must-see views and can't-miss lookouts. And it's never not worth it, whether it's descending the Devil's Backbone into a jigsaw puzzle of green and yellow pasture or walking a Port Aransas beach at dawn to watch the sun rise out of the Gulf of Mexico. But sometimes I find myself lulled into complacency, almost desensitized by a postcard-pretty vision, a soft-focus tableau not too far removed from an estate-sale oil painting of, say, bluebonnets and weathered barns.

What I tend to pause and ponder over are the components of those panoramas, the brushstrokes in the canvas, like a stretch of the Frio River running clear over mossy rocks rolled smooth and round on their travels. Or the sunset-colored grapefruits bending the branches of tree after tree in Mission. Or an early morning mist floating over the glassy surface of the Angelina River. You don't know Texas beauty till you've peered into the turquoise-fading-to-black depths of Jacob's Well or seen a flame-tipped ocotillo silhouetted against a flint-colored sky in Big Bend. You don't totally get it till you've kicked over a dusty rock to find its backside encrusted in milky quartz or spotted an unbroken sand dollar or lightning whelk in the wet sand.

Back in my humble patch of Lone

Star State, I look for the yellow-crowned night heron who pokes among the shallow depths of the drainage ditch for something to take back to its nest in a tall post oak just down the street. I pocket pecans that languish on the sidewalks and pilfer *chile pequins* from wild bushes straining through the gaps in wooden fences. I marvel at the giant "asparagus spear" that shoots from a dying agave and smile whenever I pass a neighbor's mysterious handwritten sign wedged into an Oriental arborvitae that boldly declares, "I am a flower and beautiful here!" And I look forward to the day when I round the corner to discover that the bluebonnets have once again made their faithful return.

Endless Summer

By Mimi Swartz

I AM DEEPLY ENVIOUS of all those wistful photos that turn up on my Instagram feed around the end of summer: that last sail on the blue waters off the Cape, or the final sunset in the Hamptons, or that last hike in the Tetons or the Rockies, the one requiring long pants and a fleece jacket. Photos of last cookouts around the charcoal grill—and no one is sweating. I understand why the arrival of Labor Day is a bittersweet time in other parts of the country, signaling as it does the end of so many carefree days and open-windowed/AC-free nights. But before the bleakness of winter comes fall! The season when vegetable stands transition into pumpkin patches and store windows are stocked with cozy, comforting cashmere.

Unless, of course, you live in Texas. Yes, we have the same post–Labor Day pumpkin spreads and sweater specials, but without the concurrent change in temperature. Instead, there is cognitive climate dissonance. I am still traumatized by the Septembers of my school days, when bulletin boards were decorated with artificial autumn leaves while we sat cooped up in stifling rooms with nothing but rotating floor fans for relief. I was in high school before I attended my first air-conditioned class. It's a wonder I ever learned to read.

Most real Texans—or anyone who has lived here for more than twelve months—know that September feels like the hottest month of the year, meteorologically and psychologically, because we have already traipsed through June, July, and August like the Dementors in the Harry Potter series. Every year I have the same argument with my husband about whether it cools off noticeably in October (him) or November (me), and every year there we are, handing out candy on our porch steps while we slap at mosquitoes and fight for breath in the Kolkata-like humidity of Halloween. The most ambitiously costumed kids look like tiny broiled beasts, their grease-painted faces melting in rivulets before our eyes.

For relief, I stroll through the frigid climes of the Galleria Mall and study this year's winter fashions—fur-lined boots! Cable-knit sweaters! Puffer coats in royal blue!—and wonder if ever more Houstonians are traveling to places like Greenland or Mongolia, because the chance of wearing any of that stuff around here is as likely as, well, a snowstorm in hell.

Yes, I notice a change in the light around mid-September—it's yellower and dies closer to eight p.m. instead of nine—but that's about it. In the meantime, I count the weeks until November, when the air will finally crisp and a real blue norther will roll in and send us all scurrying to switch our thermostat settings from AC to heat. Maybe after that—in December or January, when the temperature ranges from a high of sixty-five or seventy during the day to a low of forty-five at night—I will start posting photos of my husband and me barbecuing in jeans and T-shirts in the backyard and walking dogs who have stopped hiding whenever we suggest a walk.

"Winters here are beautiful!" I will write. Yes, and all too brief.

We'll Always Have Austin

By Stephen Harrigan

THERE ARE PLENTY OF places more exciting and excitable than Austin, places that rouse you to wonder or stir you to accomplishment. When I arrived here as a bewildered college freshman in 1966, it wasn't much more than a self-infatuated college hamlet. There was no traffic. The water in Barton Springs had not yet been debased by nutrient-rich runoff and had an arctic purity, so startlingly clear you could not believe what you were seeing. The city itself was more or less self-contained, still largely held in check by hills and creeks and other natural barriers. There was a Chinese restaurant, Lim Ting, way out near Ben White Boulevard; otherwise, it seemed the only thing to eat was chicken-fried steak.

But the joint was jumping. Austin had an offbeat pulse of energy that was intoxicating. Planted cross-legged in my cutoffs on the floor of the Armadillo World Headquarters, feeling the sticky spilled beer against my bare legs, I would stare at Jim Franklin's painting to the left of the stage. It depicted blues artist Freddie King, his face contorted in creative rapture as he nailed a decisive note on the neck of his guitar and an armadillo burst from the bloody center of his chest. This explosive coronary embodied everything to me that was great about Austin. The armadillo was Austin's shy and absurd totemic animal, and even its timid spirit could not resist the harmonic magic that caused it to rocket out of its hiding place.

Austin's growth spurts have been something to behold over the last few decades: convention hotels, sushi restaurants, high-rise downtown condominiums, movie studios, crushing traffic, artfully rustic wineries, thousands upon thousands of networking hipsters with badges around their necks swarming into town for South by Southwest or video-gaming conventions or screenwriting conferences or social-networking seminars. The city's famous alternating current of energy and lethargy has been transformed into a steady buzz.

The surprising thing is, I like it even more now. One of the reasons I don't bother to join in the carping about how much better Austin was in the old days is because in looking back I know I'll reencounter my old sluggish, formless self, the boy who caught the Austin vibe only to learn that it was a live virus, a strain of excitement that could mutate over time into terminal inertia. Old Austin was inspiring, but if you didn't watch yourself, it could be suffocating too. The place had a native smugness, an insistence on its own laid-back wonder. It was an incubator for itself; it kept a jealous hold on your dreams. But in the new Austin the excitement feels genuine, even a little dangerous. Its latest growth spurt, typified by big new personalities like Elon Musk and a real estate market that has turned buying a house into a frenetic exercise in commodity trading, can strike us old-timers as a mad lunge toward absurdity. Its beloved civic posturing ("Keep Austin Weird," "Live Music Capital of the World") more and more seems to belong to a distant century. All of which is to say there's no turning back from the fact that it's a real city now—edgier, less complacent, far more demanding. The place that in the past could seduce you into a life-long slacker's sleep is slowly gaining the power to jolt you into definition.

City of Ghosts

By Cat Cardenas

I USED TO COLLECT ghost stories. My hometown of San Antonio overflows with them. It began with El Cucuy, the monster who lurked in the shadows behind racks of dresses in my grandmother's laundry room. Next came La Llorona, the weeping woman who had drowned her children and sent my heart racing if I went near water at night. Later the ghosts in my nightmares drove me to my mother's godmother—a *curandera*, a healer. As I lay on the floor of her home with a blanket draped over me, her prayers delivered me from the spirits' grasp.

One by one, I squirreled stories away in spiral notebooks or on typed pages stapled together and tucked into a green folder. My *tías* and *tíos* spoke of the dancing devil—a handsome man who appeared at El Camaroncito nightclub on Halloween night in 1975. Capable of romancing any woman, he impressed the crowd until his dance partner noticed that his dress shoes had become chicken feet. With his facade crumbling, the devil rushed out of the club, leaving behind a cloud of sulfurous smoke.

On the city's southside, the ghosts of children who died in a bus accident in the 1940s were rumored to haunt the train tracks. Some drivers who parked near the tracks at night reported feeling their cars move, ever so gently, as if being pushed out of harm's way. Others discovered small handprints on their vehicles. The marks were sometimes so clear they could make out the ridges and wrinkles of palms.

Perhaps it's San Antonio's own fraught history that summons the sense that spirits walk the streets, commanding attention by shooting shivers down the spines of the living. The many indigenous groups known as Coahuiltecans hunted and foraged in the region's river valley long before Spanish friars broke ground on the city's first missions in 1718. Centuries later, tourists visit these sites of the forced conversion of native tribes, unaware they're passing through cultural cemeteries where centuries of history were erased.

These fractured origins suffuse my hometown with a sort of enchantment, one that beckons folkloric figures to wander into dance halls or appear along moonlit highways or hide in my grandmother's house. Supernatural events feel possible only in a place so suffused with reminders of its past that every corner, from its missions to its markets, echoes with the stories of those who once walked there.

Survivor City

By Mimi Swartz

YOU KNOW YOU'RE A real Houstonian when you can't recall the names of all the floods, hurricanes, and tropical storms you've endured. The big ones were Alicia, Allison, Rita, Ike, Tax Day, Memorial Day, and Harvey, but I've lost count of how many others have come and gone. During one typical monsoon, my husband totaled his car when he drove into an underpass; in his trunk was a box of ancient family photos that did not survive, which seemed like a metaphor for life in Houston. Cling to the past at your peril.

It's easy for Houstonians to self-identify as survivors. Along with the atrocious weather, there are the roaches and mosquitoes, the billboards, the highways, the concrete, the pollution, the chemical plant explosions—the usual litany of obvious drawbacks weaponized by outsiders and those who pack up and slink away.

It's true that on many mornings, especially those that involve newspaper reports on state politicians or bad weather, my husband, who is from Virginia, asks, "Should we be getting out of here?" Then we run through the ritual of listing other places we might want to live, and they are always too expensive, too cold, or too far from good medical care. Once, a very rich, very worldly Houstonian explained to me why he sticks around. "It's cheap," he said, and he was just one plane ride away from just about anywhere.

I stay because in Houston, as nowhere else, it is possible to have those kinds of conversations without having to be very rich or very worldly. It's a place for the helplessly, unrelentingly curious. Even though the city has changed enormously since I moved here in the late seventies—mostly for the good—Houston remains a port city, with all the ebb and flow of humanity that suggests.

If you are out and about in Houston—and you can do that from, say, November through May—sooner or later you will encounter someone who knew George Floyd or who sends their kids to school with Ted Cruz's. It is still possible to spy an oil company CEO chowing down on a plate of ribs; to shop for Korean, Middle Eastern, and Colombian delicacies within the space of a few hours and several traffic jams; to hear a writer lay out the plot of his latest novel; to send your kid to a diverse public high school; and to hear the Tower of Babel–like chatter at the Galleria. I would never say that Houstonians are free of prejudice or intolerance, but it's not a place for people who want to live in a bubble.

Put simply, if you believe you can enjoy the richness of life without being rich, this is the place for you. As my friend Alison likes to say, paraphrasing Samuel Johnson, "He who is tired of Houston is tired of life." But it doesn't hurt to buy a generator.

Bright Lights, Big Branding

By Michael J. Mooney

OUTSIDE OF THE REGION it refers to, the word means almost nothing. "Metroplex." It sounds like the name of a city where a comic-book superhero might live, where a regular cast of colorful villains contrive simple-but-dastardly schemes that are inevitably foiled before the citizenry suffers. Even the phonetics of the word seem strange and discordant.

In the area between and around Dallas and Fort Worth, you're likely to encounter Metroplex several times a day. It's on the news. It's on billboards along the highways. It appears in ads for cars and clothing and furniture and food. It's in the name of auto shops, gyms, real estate firms. It's a string of letters and sounds signifying—well, what exactly it means is complicated.

As the story goes, the term was devised in the early 1970s by an adman named Harve Chapman, who worked at the TracyLocke agency. He'd been tasked with formulating a term, a label, a brand that could represent the region around the newly constructed DFW airport. An alliance of business interests called the North Texas Commission was reportedly hoping to promote that part of the state, which was struggling with the fresh legacy of a presidential assassination.

The other cities and towns in the area wouldn't like calling the entire metro area "Dallas"—at least partially because Dallas was still known nationally at the time as the "City of Hate." The phrase "North Texas" didn't really work either, because a lot of Texas is north of the Dallas–Fort Worth area and someone could easily

think it might mean the Panhandle. Even "Northeast Texas" would have been tricky, because Texarkana—the northeastern-est part of the state—is nearly 200 miles away.

So they portmanteau-ed the Greek word "Metropolis" and the French-by-way-of-Latin word "complex"— and never looked back. As soon as the airport was finished, this "Metroplex" started growing in every direction and hasn't stopped since. So many US metro areas are confined by natural geographic barriers. The area around Miami and Fort Lauderdale, for example, is bound by the ocean on one side and the Everglades on the other. Southern California borders both an ocean and a mountain range. Chicago abuts Lake Michigan. Even Austin has the Hill Country. But the land around Dallas–Fort Worth, mostly flat former blackland prairie, stretches out for hundreds of miles with no interruptions.

What we call the Metroplex has become the fourth-largest metro area in the country, with more than 7 million people. If it were its own state, it would be among the fifteen most populous in America. Some parts of the region have seen 150 percent growth for more than a decade. Depending on who is keeping track, the region could stretch as far south as Hillsboro, as far north as Denison, as far east as Greenville, and as far west as Mineral Wells.

What "Metroplex" really refers to, then, is one of the world's premier examples of urban sprawl, a vast expanse of suburbia that grows acre by acre every week of the year. Sure, the Metroplex is the neon skyline of downtown Dallas, the cow-town culture of Fort Worth, the stadiums and amusement parks of Arlington. But more and more, it's the big box stores of Frisco and Grapevine, the shopping centers of Allen and Southlake, the subdivisions named after the farms they displaced—and the web of highways holding it all together.

As more international conglomerates come to appreciate the particular form of Texas generosity known as corporate tax incentives, there are also more transplants from other states and countries. That doesn't just mean school districts with budgets of hundreds of millions a year, it means an ever-evolving tapestry of people whose wants and needs are met not just by chain restaurants but strip malls full of surprises, a cultural mix that belies all the seeming sameness. Perpetual change may not have been Harve Chapman's intent when he coined the term "Metroplex," but it might end up being the term's most enduring definition.

A BRIEF LIST OF WEIRDLY NAMED TOWNS

By David Courtney

TEXAS IS SO full of towns with funny place names that not only is there an Oatmeal, Texas, but also a Raisin, a Bacon, and a Coffee. And Coffee City. And in no particular order: Noodle, Ding Dong, Dime Box, Cut and Shoot, Gun Barrel City, Gunsight, Point Blank, Kermit, Telephone, Loco, Notrees, Best, Cool, Smiley, Sweet Home, Grit, Joy, Wink, Fink, Bug Tussle, and Turkey. And Nimrod, Uncertain, North Zulch, and Zipperlandville. Oh, Jot 'Em Down! No, don't actually transcribe this list. Jot 'Em Down is just another funny town name. When you find yourself with a little time to kill, pull out your map, zoom in close, and start reading—there are plenty more where these came from.

Borderland *Cariño*

By Katie Nodjimbadem

AROUND THIRTY YEARS AGO, as my parents disembarked at El Paso International Airport, they heard the faint notes of mariachi music. A dozen or so of my mother's friends and colleagues had gathered, some with instruments, to welcome my African father to the United States—a country he'd never visited before marrying my American mother abroad. My father embraced a new title that day. It was one that my mother had accepted just nine years before, and one that I acquired by birth a year and a half later: El Pasoan.

In a border city where the census estimates that more than 80 percent of the population identifies as Hispanic, and just under 4 percent identifies as Black, my family—a tall, lanky man from the conflict-riddled nation of Chad, a white woman with the slight hint of a Georgia drawl, and a bushy-haired kid—was unusual. Like many El Pasoans, we're bilingual, but instead of Spanish, our Romance language is French. El Paso isn't the most obvious place for a family like mine to plant roots, yet there's no place we'd rather call home.

"This culture is so open to loving you," my mother says, citing El Paso's Mexican influence and its *cariño*, a Spanish term describing affection and care. At first a reluctant transplant from the East Coast, my mother has come to adore El Paso's Chihuahuan Desert landscape, the bird-of-paradise plants that attract butterflies and hummingbirds, and the sweet acacia trees. She can't resist stopping to smell Chihuahuan sage, the shrub that sprouts purple flowers each summer. Likewise, all El Pasoans marvel at the visual blast of yellow-orange from the Mexican poppies in the spring. They cherish the thriving wildlife—rattlesnakes, geckos, coyotes, jackrabbits, mountain lions, more than one hundred species of birds—and the flawless blue skies of the city's three hundred sunny days per year.

Living so far from relatives, our family's cultural traditions became that of the borderland, the place that embraced us with *cariño*. In elementary school, that meant my classmates and me donning pink and yellow ruffled skirts to perform a *folklórico* dance to the classic "De Colores." Later, it was the quinceañeras, where I watched my friends become women as their parents gave them commemorative high heels. In high school, it was dancing *cumbia* at the Chamizal National Memorial, a park and cultural center commemorating the settlement of a century-long border dispute between Mexico and the United States. At Christmas, it tasted like red tamales from Gussie's and glowed like the thousands of luminarias along Scenic Drive. During Lent, it was the aroma of *capirotada*, the delightfully sweet and salty cheese-filled bread pudding an old friend would give my mom at church each year. In the summer, it was the harmonizing of the cast of *Viva! El Paso*, the annual musical performance recounting the city's four-hundred-year history in an outdoor amphitheater tucked away in a canyon.

Despite the predominance of *cariño*, I understood early on that my family was "other" in El Paso. Anti-Black sentiment persisted in some corners. I recall the never-ending search for a stylist who knew how to care for my dense, curly hair, and the shame I felt when more than one turned me away. I still feel the sting of the moment an elementary-school classmate called me "blackie" and the realization that it wasn't just an observation about my skin tone. Yet I know that I'm privileged as a person of color and the child of an immigrant to have grown up in a majority-minority city full of immigrants.

Toni Morrison, my favorite author, once said: "In this country, American means white. Everybody else has to hyphenate." Even though my hyphenation looked different from that of most of my friends in El Paso, I felt connected to them by our shared sense of multiculturalism and the grit passed on to us by our shared immigrant ancestry. El Paso is a nourishing place for people who don't quite fit the typical "American" mold. In our binational and bicultural identity, my family reflects the profound and unexpected beauty of this border city that bloomed in the severity of the desert.

Life in the Oil Patch

By Christian Wallace

IF YOU CLIMB THE concrete stairs to the top of Mustang Stadium, one of the highest points in Andrews, Texas, and look past the parking lot and the asphalt loop that surrounds the town, mesquite-choked fields sprawl to the horizon in nearly every direction. At dusk, you can make out gas flares blazing yellow and orange alongside the innumerable pumpjacks and tanks that dot the scenery. And as night settles in, the bright lights of drilling rigs punctuate the dark. This is the Permian Basin oilfield, my home.

Time is marked in two ways in the Permian: boom and bust. During the region's first boom, in the 1920s and '30s, company towns sprouted from the vast desert floor almost overnight. They had their own saloons, hotels, shops, and churches. The families of roughnecks and roustabouts lived in tents and simple shotgun shacks. Many of these communities disappeared just as quickly when the work dried up, and today there's scant trace they ever existed, not even ghost towns. The mesquite and prairie grass reclaimed the land long ago.

The places that have persisted—Midland, Odessa, Kermit, Pecos, Monahans, Wink, Pyote, and a smattering of other hardscrabble towns—have all been forged by the brutal cycles of boom and bust. Andrews, my hometown, is one of them.

My dad grew up on a small ranch near Andrews. Like many of his peers, he started working in the oilfield while he was still in high school. But after he graduated, the devastating bust of the eighties forced him to look elsewhere for a paycheck. He went west to Arizona and later to California, swinging a sledgehammer and gripping a jackhammer, but months after I was born, in 1988, my parents returned to Andrews. My dad took a job with the city, one of the few employers in town with steady work.

My childhood was colored by the lean years following the eighties bust. When I was a kid, people were more likely to leave Andrews than to move in. The few out-of-towners who did visit wrinkled their noses at the sour smell of gas in the air, but I grew accustomed to it. When there was a particularly strong whiff on the wind, I'd mimic the elders and exaggerate a deep breath. "Smells like money."

The "patch" was my personal playground. My friends and I shot Coke bottles in those fields. We dug elaborate trenches through the brush and lobbed dirt clods at rattlesnakes. We rode our bikes for hours down dusty lease roads and ate our sandwiches next to stock ponds or in the shade of fiberglass oil tanks.

The elementary school I attended was named after the Devonian rock formation; other schools in town were named after other oil-bearing strata.

During the summer, we watched the Midland RockHounds, a minor-league baseball team whose name is West Texas slang for the geologists who hunt for crude and whose logo depicts a dog in a hard hat in front of a gushing oil derrick. I remember on one of our drives home from Midland, Mom and Dad talked quietly about how none of the pumpjacks that lined the highway were moving. Even as a kid, I knew that when those metal horse heads weren't bobbing up and down, something was wrong.

I had no notion back then of how geopolitics affected the fortunes of Andrews—how global supply and demand fluctuations could dictate whether a local family could put food on the table. But my friends and I grew used to hearing adults discuss the price per barrel of West Texas Intermediate the way folks elsewhere might talk about the weather, and soon the meaning of those figures was not lost on us. We grew up on stories about flash floods of money in former boom times. We also heard plenty of horror tales about men killing themselves in the patch after losing everything.

But my generation saw neither the extravagant wealth nor the immediate fallout of a bust. Throughout the nineties, Midland's independent oil companies essentially plodded along, many of them getting by on steadily producing but unspectacular wells they'd drilled long before. By 1998, most of the oil majors had vacated their West Texas offices. They'd given up on the Permian. In 1999, just forty-three rigs were left working across the region. West Texas was slowly withering.

At the time, my friends and I were more concerned with other matters. In high school, we learned how to drive our trucks through the mud after a rare heavy rain (and how to dig out a stuck pickup when someone's mudding got a little too ambitious). We threw pumpjack parties, not house parties. "Meet me after the game at the Bush Machine," someone would say, and everyone knew where to go. One of these nights, a buddy of mine decided to "ride" the Bush Machine. He straddled the pumpjack like it was a bucking bull—and got bucked right off. He could've earned a lot more than a sprained wrist from the fall. But most nights passed without incident. Just a few bored teenagers, our trucks parked in a circle around a pumpjack, drinking beer we stole from ice chests left in the beds of company trucks, listening to George Strait or Tom Petty, and talking about what we were going to do when we left.

But things started to change in 2004, when the price per barrel of WTI (West Texas Intermediate) ticked up to more than $40 for the first time since the mid-eighties. Like farmers celebrating the arrival of storm clouds in a drought, West Texans rejoiced. The upward trend continued for the next four years until sweet crude peaked at an all-time high of $147.27. Around this time, oil companies in the region started using hydraulic fracturing (or fracking) and horizontal drilling techniques to tap into the vast quantities of oil that had been previously locked in porous shale formations. The shale boom was on.

Stories of the boom reached me while I was attending grad school in Ireland in 2012. I decided to return home and earn some money. I spent 2013 working for a friend's dad's oil company in Andrews. My duties included hauling parts to far-flung locations and roughnecking on a pulling unit (essentially a smaller drilling rig used to work on wells that have gone off-line). I made a good dent in my student loans that year, but after a few close calls on the rig and a few too many eighty-hour workweeks out in the elements, I eagerly traded in my OSHA-required steel-toes for a pair of civilian cowboy boots.

Oil prices fluctuated, and there were lean times, but by and large the boom went on. And on. And turned out to be the biggest one in the region's history. The Permian became the world's most productive oil field, outpacing even the Ghawar, in Saudi Arabia. Once-sleepy highways turned into twenty-four-hour traffic arteries.

Thousands of workers packed into man camps on the outskirts of small communities.

Booms are, by definition, explosive—sudden blasts of activity that can take a community by surprise. Even in the Permian Basin, which has weathered nearly a century of ups and downs, a boom like the most recent one was impossible to prepare for. And while it brought opportunity, it also posed serious problems— overcrowded schools, deteriorating roadways, and an influx of crime, to name a few. Still, to most West Texans, the difficulties of a boom always beat the heartaches of a bust.

As production continued to grow to record new heights in 2019, some officials in the region said the days of the boom-and-bust cycles were done; this boom, they said, would last. It didn't. The COVID-19 pandemic gutted demand just as Russians and Saudis got into a price war. The price of West Texas oil dropped below zero for the first time in history. Even hardened oil patch vets were stunned. In a few weeks, the mightiest boom of all time had mostly evaporated.

It's impossible to say what booms and busts will come, but as wind and solar power proliferate across the Permian today, it's clear that someday the region's fortunes will cease to rise and fall with the nodding pumpjacks. As someone who grew up with and spent time working on rigs with so-called oil field trash, it's hard not to feel sad about the dimming of this sliver of Texas culture. For West Texans, oil is not a geopolitical chess piece or an abstract financial instrument; it's an elemental substance that spatters your clothes, stains your hands, and cakes beneath your fingernails. It's the smell that lingers after a shower, even after you rub IcyHot on your aching muscles. For many, it's a deep-rooted way of life, come what may.

These Creatures Can and Will Kill You, Maybe

By Wes Ferguson

AMONG THE UNDERAPPRECIATED ACHIEVEMENTS of the acclaimed television adaptation of Larry McMurtry's *Lonesome Dove* is the healthy fear of snakes that it instilled into a generation of Texas children. "Water moccasins!" unlucky young sprout Sean O'Brien screams moments before the end of the first episode. He thrashes about in the Nueces River, swarmed by a terrifying tangle of moccasins, also known as cottonmouths—right before one bites him on his cheek and sends him to an early grave. The lesson to impressionable viewers is plain enough: the natural landscape of Texas is beautiful, yet deadly. To answer its siren call to outdoor adventures is to accept the risk of encountering one of these, the state's most dangerous creatures, along the way.

SNAKES

Even aside from those cottonmouths who got the better of poor O'Brien, several other threatening species of serpents slither about the state. Texans familiar with coral snakes remind themselves that "red and yeller kill a feller." They also watch for the copperhead and the western diamondback rattlesnake, named for its distinctive diamond-patterned markings. But it's the timber rattlesnake, also known as the canebrake rattler, that's doubly deadly. It possesses two kinds of venom: hemotoxic, which attacks the circulatory system; and neurotoxic, which attacks the nervous system, potentially paralyzing its victim.

SPIDERS

The male black widow spider is harmless, but the female, which sometimes eats the male after mating with him, strikes fear in the most stout-hearted Texans. She is jet black with a red or yellow hourglass shape on her underside. Her victim might not even notice her pinprick bite, only later feel an array of unpleasant symptoms, from cramping and convulsions to sweating, tremors, vomiting, and loss of consciousness. Woodpiles and outdoor toilets make excellent black widow habitats. Meanwhile, Texas's other species of venomous spider, the brown recluse, often hides in dark basements or garages. It's golden brown, with a dark, fiddle-shaped pattern on its back. Its venom can cause fever and chills, lesions, and restlessness.

ALLIGATORS

At night, when alligators mosey into some swampy Texas waters, their eyes poke above the surface, catching the moonlight and seeming to glow. The primordial reptiles, whose bodies can weigh close to a thousand pounds, rarely hassle people—unless they lose their fear of humans and become aggressive. In 2015, in the Southeast Texas town of Orange, a twenty-eight-year-old man became the first fatality from an alligator attack in Texas since 1836 when he allegedly uttered a few poorly chosen words—"F**k that gator"—and jumped into a bayou for a late-night swim right where a twelve-foot-long alligator lurked.

BRAIN-EATING AMOEBA

When diving into a swimming hole to seek relief from the Texas summer heat, one should also beware *Naegleria fowleri*, a nasty little single-celled organism nicknamed for its favorite pastime. Naegleria enters through the nose and shimmies up to the brain, where it destroys tissue. There's really no body of fresh water that can be considered safe from this amoeba, and it can also strike through contaminated tap water. Experts advise keeping one's head dry when wading in streams or lakes where water temperatures are warm and water levels are low. The good news? Infections are rare. Experts don't know why a few people get sick each year while millions of other swimmers don't.

SHARKS

The Global Shark Attack File reports fifty-eight unprovoked shark attacks in Texas since 1865, including five that were fatal. The last person killed by a shark in Texas, forty-year-old Hans Fix, was surf fishing in waist-deep water off Andy Bowie Park on South Padre Island in 1962 when an unknown species of shark bit his lower right leg. Dozens of species of sharks prowl the Gulf. "You'll never go in the water again," as they say.

SCORPIONS

Wise Texans shake out those boots before sliding them over their stockinged feet. Scorpion stings, while rarely fatal, can cause intense pain and swelling. The venom can trigger allergic reactions, leading to difficulty breathing and twitching muscles, as well as vomiting. (Pro tip: if one of these lobster-like arachnids ever hitches a ride to Garner State Park in the bag where you keep your air mattress, and then pricks you on the palm, immediately stop setting up camp and promptly dunk your hand in the Frio River.)

FIRE ANTS

As if Texans needed another reason to panic in the aftermath of 2017's Hurricane Harvey, viral online videos revealed giant flotillas of invasive fire ants, a species that adapted to survive frequent flooding in its native South America by forming teeming mats of up to 100,000 venomous insects looking for a dry place to reestablish their cursed colonies. As the invasive ants have spread across the southern United States since the early twentieth century, their cone-shaped mounds have damaged farm equipment and lawn mowers, rudely interrupted countless barefoot backyard moments, and even killed livestock. "Infested tracts contain upward of forty mounds per acre," *Texas Monthly* once reported. "They defend their territory by attacking in large numbers, and they sting repeatedly." And not even floods can eradicate them.

MOUNTAIN LIONS

Also known as the cougar, panther, puma, or catamount, this powerful but shy wildcat could absolutely murder the average human if it wanted to. But it doesn't want to. Only four mountain lion attacks on humans in Texas have been reported since 1980, all of them in remote areas of West Texas, and none of them were fatal. But the rarely seen cats, which can reach four feet in length and 170 pounds, have been expanding their habitat in recent years, with an uptick in sightings in the scrubby hills of more heavily populated Central Texas.

NINE-BANDED ARMADILLOS

Often oblivious to their surroundings as they noisily root around for insects and other grub, these cute little armored creatures, so often spotted as roadkill, are alarmingly common carriers of leprosy, or Hansen's disease. As many as 20 percent of armadillos carry the ancient ailment considered a curse from God during biblical times. Armadillos likely acquired the microbe that causes leprosy from humans sometime after Christopher Columbus showed up in the New World. They can retransmit it to humans and are responsible for about one-third of leprosy cases in the United States each year, primarily in Texas and Louisiana. For that reason, experts discourage the eating or handling of armadillo meat.

WHITE-TAILED DEER

A deer doesn't have to crash through a windshield at seventy miles per hour to inflict harm on humans. Whitetail attacks aren't as rare as you may think. In 2007, *Outdoor Life* magazine reported that a Texas fisherman was watching as a nine-point buck swam across the Trinity River and shook itself dry, and then its "demeanor changed from one of simple curiosity to one of pure malevolence." The buck pawed the ground and charged, smashing the angler and tossing him into the river, where they tangled in the water. When they climbed out, the buck charged again, slamming the man to the ground and stabbing his face with his antlers. The man's nephew had to slit the buck's throat to end the brutal blitz.

A PRICKLY POINT OF CONTENTION

By David Courtney

THE SAGUARO CACTUS, the largest cactus found in the United States, can reach heights in excess of seventy-five feet, may live for more than two hundred years, and really is quite a looker. Perhaps because of the succulent's ample size, or perhaps its stately pose, artists have long found it irresistible to insert saguaros into illustrations of Texas. These images, though well intended, are plain wrong. While Texas is home to more than one hundred other types of cacti, ranging in size from the thousand-pound fishhook barrel cactus to the tiny button cactus—a wider assortment than that of any other state—the saguaro ain't one of them. Rather, the Sonoran showboat grows naturally only in southern Arizona and parts of California and Mexico—and not in the Chihuahan Desert of West Texas or in any other part of the state. (While we're on the subject of desert canards, the many-limbed and very spiky ocotillo found throughout the Chihuahuan is, in fact, not a cactus at all but an unusual shrub.)

Texans have their own iconic cactus, of course. The Lone Star State is so packed with prickly pear that it is the official state plant. And prickly pear, otherwise known as nopal, is a more useful plant than the saguaro, providing Texans with delicious magenta fruit to add to margaritas, tender paddles to add to tacos, and vibrant displays of flowers to add to any landscape. If given a binary choice between the prickly pear and the saguaro, most Texans will choose the down-to-earth (literally) prickly pear every time. No matter what misinformed artists think.

Friday Night Temples

By Michael J. Mooney

IMAGINE THE OBLONG SILHOUETTE of a football as it leaves the hand of a quarterback and floats upward toward the heavens, a tight spiral cutting through the crisp, late-autumn night. For just a moment the entire world slows, and as the ball hangs there, rotating in the air, dangling provisionally above this planet, so many fates and fortunes also hang precariously in the balance.

For plenty of people on the field—and in the stands and watching with clenched fingers and teeth at home—that forward pass is a prayer. It's a wish. It's hope for something better: a happier moment, a brighter future, the unbridled exquisite joy of success. It's a reason to release a cathartic bellow, to spasm uncontrollably. It's a brief, glimmering reason to believe in something bigger than the individual.

In Texas, many of our most popular, most dramatic public rituals take place in football stadiums. Built ostensibly to showcase athletic prowess, the physical structures themselves have become prominent modern temples, holy places in the *other* religion here. In fact, an anthropologist unfamiliar with the importance, zeal, and pageantry of Texas sports could easily conclude that some of these buildings are shrines to the animal or historical figure their region holds most sacred: The Longhorn, The Bear, The Cowboy, The Angry Farmer.

The two NFL stadiums in Texas, in Arlington and Houston, and the two biggest college stadiums, in Austin and College Station, are titanic monuments to the state's favorite pastime, each drawing some 100,000 humans on any given weekend. On game days, it's not just the coliseums themselves that host the festivities. The surrounding areas, from the parking lots to the nearby homes and businesses, are filled with the orgiastic consumption of meat and ale, singing and dancing, mass chanting, and general revelry of all kinds. If you squint, it can look a little like the age-old religious festivals held in cities around the world.

On the high-school level especially, these venues truly seem like houses erected for a holy game. R. R. Jones Stadium, in El Paso, is more than 100 years old and built into the ground amphitheater-style right in front of the school. Altogether, the arrangement looks a little like the Pantheon in Rome. Some, like Darrell Tully Stadium in Houston and Mustang-Panther Stadium in Grapevine, are constructed inside giant hills reminiscent of ancient Viking burial mounds.

Like religious temples, football stadiums come in a variety of shapes and sizes. There are hundreds of them sprinkled across the state, built from different materials in different eras, each a reflection of its community.

In the dusty single-stoplight towns of the high plains in the Panhandle, for example, the assemblies are modest and simple: patchy football fields abutting warped metal grandstands under humming floodlights, old water towers on the horizon boasting of faded district championships. On Friday nights, you can hear the marching bands for miles in every direction.

In the wealthy suburbs around Dallas and Houston, high-school stadiums can be massive and ostentatious, built with cutting-edge materials and the latest technology. The newest stadiums all have oversized high-definition video boards visible from hundreds of yards away and seating for more than 10,000 people, sometimes a lot more. And the costs to the school districts are extraordinary. Prosper's stadium cost $53 million and includes the largest video board in any high-school stadium in the state. Allen High School's stadium cost a reported $60 million and includes a weight room that's more than eighty yards long. In nearby McKinney, the stadium was $70 million and has nicer locker rooms than most college facilities. Katy, just outside Houston, built a stadium that cost $72 million and it has multiple hospitality suites available for corporate sponsorship—and that was after scaling down the proposed models.

Most of these areas have seen huge population growth over the last ten or twenty years, and a lot of the school districts were poor for decades. Now that they have more money from property taxes, this is how voters and elected leaders have decided to spend it. If you ask the superintendents overseeing construction and renovation, the nice press box, the beautiful turf, the gargantuan LED scoreboard—they're all markers of prestige. They are signals that the community gives its children everything they might need to succeed.

Of course, football has the power to unite total strangers, individuals who might have nothing else in common. Football can also divide families, creating what might seem like silly strife where previously there was none. Football is responsible for alliances and rivalries that pass down, often inexplicably, through families and regions for generations. But the spaces are about more than football. They're about more than sports, about more than the school districts that build them. Most of these structures are the largest gathering places in their communities. Most host not only a year's worth of different sporting events, but also concerts, banquets, graduations. It's not rare for a school to erect a stage in an end zone and seat graduates all the way to the fifty-yard line. After a hurricane, after a tornado, stadiums become shelters and triage centers.

These buildings bear the colors and insignia of the local community, but the truth is the arenas themselves are manifestations of the values and virtues most prized in the local population. Some places in the world build towering statues of military leaders. Some build pristine palaces in which they hope their deities might dwell. Some build temples on mountains that kiss the clouds. In Texas, we build football stadiums.

As for that long, desperate prayer of a pass, floating through the night air? It's called a "Hail Mary," and every time that spiraling football gently arcs through the stadium and back down to earth—whether it's caught or not—someone's prayer is answered.

Get Lost in Texas

By Dan Oko

TEXAS WAS NEVER PART of the vision. Growing up in New York City, I always dreamed of wandering off west toward adventure, and by my twenties I managed to turn myself into one of those crazy-for-the-mountains guys with a quiver of bikes and a closet full of camping gear. I simply didn't know, until I moved to the state twenty-some years ago, that Texas held so many different opportunities to get off the grid—not only in the towering Chisos, Davis, and Guadalupe Mountains but also the action-packed Hill Country, hundreds of miles of coastline, swampy backwaters, primitive deserts, and wild rivers.

Now, after countless expeditions—alone, with my daughter, with friends—I still find myself covering new ground. Even though some 95 percent of Texas is posted as private property, there are nearly 4.5 million acres of recreational public land to explore, an amount comparable to the whole state of New Jersey. These five wildlands are among Texas's greatest treasures.

DEVILS RIVER STATE NATURAL AREA

As I paddled my canoe along the Devils River, the echo of unseen whitewater rushing ahead triggered my adrenaline and anxiety. Five friends and I were a few hours into a thirty-mile, four-day expedition, still adjusting to the river's drop-and-pool rhythm, a geological pattern alternating between constricted chutes and broad lakes of bright, green-blue water. We should have been exhilarated. But hearing the river's hydraulic growl in the near distance, I rehearsed my safety-first mantra: when you are on the Devils, you are on your own.

It has long been a mystery how the Devils River got its name, but the leading theory will ring true to anyone who has attempted to navigate it. Though early Spanish explorers named the river after Saint Peter, it's said that the settlers who followed in their footsteps regarded the waterway and its surrounding terrain as so forbidding that they thought it could have been carved by Lucifer himself. And so the gatekeeper to heaven gave way to the ruler of hell.

Beginning at the western fringe of the Hill Country and ending in West Texas, near the Mexican border, the Devils is one of the most untouched rivers in the state, hosting little more than a thousand visitors a year. It bisects a rough-and-tumble landscape dotted with cacti and patrolled by mountain lions, rattlesnakes, and the occasional black bear. During rainstorms, the aquamarine stream can rapidly transform into a raging brown torrent, hurling boulders and uprooting trees. Those looking for a place to sleep or dry out are warned not to disobey the ubiquitous "No Trespassing" signs along the privately owned banks that run along most of the river's length. There are a few official campsites, but they remain primitive.

Those willing to face such risks are in for something special, especially if they take to the Devils during the spring, when my friends and I visited. Once we got past the thick canebrakes and the first set of rapids appeared shallower than normal, our challenge became pushing and pulling our canoe and four kayaks over slick, water-carved rocks. Our reward was willow-shaded pools where dragonflies buzzed and tanagers, redstarts, and cardinals darted like flowers taking flight. When we arrived at the famed Finegan Springs on day two, tattooed with bruises and scrapes from navigating rough limestone chutes, we spent a long time admiring the cascade of crystal water tumbling over the fern-furred emerald cliff. After navigating the notorious Dolan Falls later that day—considered the true crux of any trip on the Devils—I strung my fly rod and caught (and released) a couple of smallmouth bass out of the now deep water below the froth.

There was no room to be complacent about the river's hydraulics—on day three, our canoe became pinned sideways against a rock and nearly sank—but as we continued downstream, we also found peaceful pockets of water that shone turquoise, a phenomenon caused by the pale limestone along the bottom reflecting the afternoon sunlight. On our final day, we drifted over deep pools and gaped at fish—gar, perhaps, or catfish—roughly the size of fat baseball bats. As the late sun broiled the edge of the desert, everybody stripped to the waist and let the cool water massage our weary bones.

PADRE ISLAND NATIONAL SEASHORE

Flanked by the Gulf to the east and Laguna Madre to the west, the seventy-mile-long Padre Island National Seashore restores hope for those who lament the general scarcity of pristine ocean beaches in Texas. Padre Island is the longest undeveloped barrier island in the world. And unlike on South Padre Island, where trinket shops and towering resorts dominate, the wild dunes and hypersaline lagoons of the federal seashore can offer the kind of seclusion that rivals the backcountry of Big Bend National Park—and requires the same amount of self-sufficiency.

It helps to know where to go. The North and Malaquite Beaches are popular with shell seekers, birders, and surf anglers, while Bird Island

Basin, on the bay side, is one of the nation's top windsurfing spots. To get away from it all, you can camp on the island's empty southern beaches, as I did. Most of Padre Island is accessible only by four-wheel-drive vehicle, but since I didn't have one, I simply drove south on the park's only road until I saw no sign of anyone—and then drove a mile farther. After I set up my tent on South Beach, about six miles past the end of the road, the night brought high winds and a cloudless view of the stars. I gazed up at the seven sisters of the Pleiades and Orion unsheathing his sword.

The cool morning revealed a beach decorated with the translucent, sail-like bubbles of Portuguese man-of-wars that had washed ashore. Fantastic to look at, and often mistaken for jellyfish, a man-of-war packs a nasty sting. I sipped my coffee and kept my hands to myself.

BIG THICKET NATIONAL PRESERVE

When your guide is a Vietnam veteran who lets slip that the wooded waterways of East Texas remind him of the missions he led as an elite Army Pathfinder in Southeast Asia, it pays to be ready for anything. "There was a time when you needed to be a warrior to live on this river," drawled Larry Williams, who was steering our canoe. We were sampling a ten-mile stretch of the more than fifty-mile path the wild Neches River winds through Big Thicket National Preserve. Williams (who has since passed away) was referring to the settlers who migrated here from Appalachia in the nineteenth century, lured by the plentiful timber. The Big Thicket is known as "America's ark" for its biodiversity, and I felt the sudden need to keep an eye out for alligators, cottonmouths, and black bears.

Some of the last stands of longleaf pine are found here, along with bald cypress, twenty types of orchids, and four species of carnivorous plants. "If you keep your eyes open," Williams said, "you'll always spot something new." Around us, belted kingfishers hovered over the water, an otter splashed in the distance, and pileated woodpeckers hammered old-growth snags. When we pulled over to camp, three wood ducks—a species Williams hadn't seen before—sailed down from

their roost. And after sundown, the fireflies put on a mind-blowing show.

The Big Thicket has a reputation for Bigfoot sightings that date back to the 1950s. From inside my tent in that far-reaching wilderness, where moss-draped pines darken the bottomlands, it didn't seem like such a stretch that a seven-foot, apelike creature could be hiding in the shadows.

CAPROCK CANYONS STATE PARK

Up in the Panhandle, where the Rolling Plains give way to the Llano Estacado, the historical and geological marvels of Palo Duro Canyon, otherwise known as the Grand Canyon of Texas, have been well documented. So in order to chart some new terrain, I recently lit out for the area with Caprock Canyons State Park in mind instead.

The park boasts ninety miles of trail. To find some quick elevation, I

chose the Upper Canyon route. I spent the night in the South Prong camping area, about five miles from the park's entrance. After a front-porch sunrise over the canyon, one of the Caprock's virtues immediately became clear: I had the campground to myself. It came as little surprise, therefore, that the only footprints I encountered during my seven-mile hike belonged to coyote and deer (though the Texas State Bison Herd also calls the park home).

As I stopped to rest on a steep portion of the path that rose above a set of twisted, coppery cliffs, a line came to mind from Lubbock-born Max Crawford's 1985 novel, *Lords of the Plain*, about the campaign to subdue the Comanche in their own rugged lands. "The cliffs above still caught the late sun," Crawford wrote, "the canyon walls bathed blood-red, the gypsum crystals sparkling as if the rocks were encrusted with diamonds." The Caprock canyons might not be the biggest, but they're as enchanting as they are forbidding.

BIG BEND NATIONAL PARK

Speaking of the Grand Canyon: Texans have got their own South Rim, thank you very much. Here, atop the cliffs of the Chisos Basin, along a bruising circuit out and back from the Chisos Mountains Lodge, the only hotel in Big Bend National Park, you can peer up to one hundred miles into Mexico. Taking in the mountains that stretch into Chihuahua and Coahuila is a stupefying exploit—and often private, unlike at that other South Rim, which is bounded by blacktop and gets roughly ten times the annual visitors.

I considered this while standing, very much alone, near where the southeast and southwest portions of the rim converge, ten miles into a backpacking trip. Sweat and determination are really the only way to reach these heights. I'd arrived at this overlook via the tough Pinnacles Trail. Though the fourteen-mile South Rim Loop can be conquered in a day, there are several camping areas along the way. I took my time over two days. Now, across the desert before me lay an array of strange formations, like figments of Salvador Dalí's imagination. The dun-colored prong of Elephant Tusk stood to the west, while a sliver of silver beyond the hills hinted at the Rio Grande. At 1,252 square miles, the national park itself is about the size of the state of Rhode Island. It's no surprise that sixteenth-century Spanish explorers, confronted with this vastness, labeled it *el despoblado*. The uninhabited.

The Stars at Night

By Courtney Bond

LET'S JUST GO AHEAD and get something out of the way, which is that deep in the heart of Texas, the stars at night are big and bright . . . in *some* places, like sparsely populated pockets of the Hill Country. However, the stars are big, brighter, and infinitely more numerous (or so it seems) way out at the southwestern edge of the state, deep in the dry, rocky, odd little corner known as Big Bend. And boy, are we lucky to have this pristine patch of pitch black. A truly dark sky, one free of the harsh intrusive glow of artificial light, is getting harder and harder to find. Texas Parks and Wildlife's Dark Skies Program cites a statistic that suggests that 80 percent of Americans have never seen the Milky Way. If that seems preposterous, one need only look back to the January 1994 earthquake-induced blackout in Los Angeles, when the Griffith Observatory fielded multiple calls from befuddled residents who had stepped outside, looked around, and freaked out over the dazzling swath of luminescence over their heads.

Most of us can see only a tiny fraction of the stars in the sky. That is certainly true for denizens of the Lone Star State, studded as it is with bright lights and several of the country's most populous cities. Fortunately, Texans are also blessed with plenty of places from which to escape the glare, some informal and some officially designated, most in Central and West Texas. Many are associated with beautiful landscapes that are already sanctuaries, state parks like Big Bend Ranch, Copper Breaks, and Enchanted Rock.

West Texas, impossibly distant (for most) and appropriately removed, is of course mecca, with the McDonald Observatory its shrine. A unit of the

University of Texas at Austin, created from the bequest of a Paris, Texas, banker and astronomy buff, it's a collection of research telescopes set about 7,000 feet above sea level atop Mounts Locke and Fowlkes. The temple-like domes, brilliant in white and silver, look otherworldly in the Chihuahuan Desert surrounding Fort Davis, alien portals to some of the darkest night skies in the continental United States.

When conditions are optimal, the observatory hosts its famous "star parties," which, thanks to the altitude, can be chilly affairs. It's easy to feel small and inconsequential, perched in the dark on a cold stone bench, wrapped in layers, craning your neck for a constellation here or there, maybe a meteor or two, all the while being regaled with delightful tidbits that help bring things down to earth. (Did you know that dung beetles navigate using the Milky Way?)

But it's not so bad to feel inconsequential, to get lost in thousands of pinpricks of light instead of in the minutiae of our overscheduled, overanalyzed, overly complicated lives. In fact, Texans are downright negligent if we don't, at least once a year, settle into a camp chair on the banks of the Colorado River, lie on our backs out in the middle of Big Bend Ranch, or plant our butts on a slab of stone at the McDonald Observatory and take the time to ponder the sheer scale of the universe, the massive and inconceivable machinery that births baby stars and witnesses the eons-long dissolution of the elders. To gaze at the incarnation of the galaxy we live in, shimmering like so much fairy dust. To contemplate our very own star, a middle-aged ball of hot gas. To tune our ears to a stardust melody that's always playing, ever so faintly, if we choose to listen.

The Secret Swimming Hole

By Wes Ferguson

OF ALL THE SWIMMING holes in Texas, the Holy Grail would have to be the Narrows, a semisecret wellspring of Hill Country tranquility hidden in an otherwise dry section of the Blanco River near Wimberley.

Extremely difficult to access, the Narrows begins where the rocky Blanco riverbed splits apart to reveal an otherworldly oasis below. In a canyon so tight you can almost jump across the rim of its oddly shaped limestone formations, delicate maidenhair ferns sway and droplets of spring water spill into a series of waterfalls and large potholes that seem black from a distance but, upon closer inspection, are as clear as gin. They're just that deep. The canyon itself is about forty feet tall and perhaps a quarter mile long.

If you can't secure an invitation to the Narrows from one of the riverfront owners, I can't say I recommend it. There's nowhere to park, and you can only get there via a ten-mile slog through one of the most inhospitable stretches of public riverbed in Texas, across stagnant pools and over seemingly unending jumbles of boulders. After you've finally had a chance to swim, the difficult return hike awaits, and you've completely defeated the purpose of a swimming hole: to beat the brutal heat.

Swimming holes are the saving grace of notoriously hot Texas summers. We're blessed with an abundance of them, especially in the Hill Country, where pure springs seep through porous ledges and limestone shelves, feeding into streams that keep flowing through even the driest sum-

mer months. Swimming holes don't just make the baking sun more tolerable; they make you long for those days when thermometers rise beyond ninety or a hundred degrees. That first plunge takes your breath away, and instantly, everything's better.

Swimming holes come in all shapes and sizes, depths and temperatures; creeks, rivers, and, I would argue, lakes. Some are part of official parks, like that famous West Texas oasis, Balmorhea, which require entrance fees and advance planning; others are more informal and most often frequented by locals. The best tend to be shaded by enormous trees, like the bald cypresses that tower above Blue Hole, on Cypress Creek in Wimberley, or the tall pines alongside the rock-walled pool built during the Great Depression at Camp Tonkawa Springs, outside Nacogdoches.

Longtime aficionados can get pretty cagey about their favorites, with good reason. When the secret's out, long-secluded spots can become overrun almost overnight. I've given up on some of the best, like Hamilton Pool, at a public nature preserve west of Bee Cave, where the roof of an enormous cavern fell down eons ago to reveal an enchantingly wide and deep pool ringed by cave walls and fed by a dramatic, fifty-foot waterfall. I swam often in Hamilton Pool until recently, when the growing crowds forced park employees to switch to a reservation system; my luck has run out ever since, and I haven't snagged one of those highly prized time slots.

That's okay, though, because there are so many other beautiful places to cool off. During mild spring days when I just can't wait another day for summer, I seek out waters that aren't quite as frigid, like a dammed stretch of the Blanco River upstream from Blanco State Park, where you can float to the middle of the river and prop your elbows on the concrete dam to enjoy a beer or two or three as your legs sway and your feet can't touch bottom. When the days turn off hotter, I venture out to cypress-lined rivers like the San Marcos or to the Devil's Waterhole, in an eastern cove of Inks Lake, where thrill seekers leap off pink granite cliffs. Having retired from most thrills, I now prefer to kick back in an inner tube and watch the action from a comfortable distance.

While roadtripping from June to September, I'll gladly veer an hour out of my way to cool off in more far-flung swimming holes on the Nueces and the Medina, or to venture down miles of backroads in search of beckoning scenes on the Llano, Guadalupe, or, truly, any stream that's running clear and cold. Just don't ask me to come back and spill my secrets when you can, and should, go find your own.

Miles and Miles of Texas

By Christian Wallace

BEING RAISED IN WEST Texas will warp your sense of what constitutes a long drive. The state's vastness feels a little less intimidating when you're used to driving an hour round trip to pick up a case of beer (a weekly endeavor growing up in then-dry Andrews County). Eight hours of truck time for the Houston Rodeo even seems like a fair deal.

Over the years, I've learned traveling in every season has its perks. Summer road trips typically involve some sort of water—maybe one of the swimming holes that dot the limestone-strewn Hill Country or one of the 7,000 lakes scattered across Texas. At least once a year, I steer toward the world's largest spring-fed pool at Balmorhea State Park, a miraculous blue gem in the Chihuahuan Desert. And summer in Texas means tubing: the San Marcos River or maybe the Guadalupe or the Comal or the Frio, where I met my wife, when we were just getting our feet wet in college.

In the fall, I like to drive across Texas on Friday nights, scanning the radio until I hear a drawl announcing a high-school football game—the Iraan Braves, the Lamesa Golden Tornadoes, the Mason Punchers. The smell of burning cedar and mesquite fills the air as ranchers burn brush piles cleared over the summer. It's not yet freezing, but there's a chill that means the honky-tonks feel cozy with packed dance floors, the Tyler rose gardens are blooming, and the trees in McKittrick Canyon are putting on a show of color.

After Thanksgiving, I'll often stop somewhere around Sterling City and find a tumbleweed from the bar ditch to take home and decorate for Christmas. As the holiday gets closer, many of the county courthouses are lit up red and green or pure white. Some towns go all out. Salado transforms into a Victorian Christmas spectacle, and Fredericksburg, with its tinseled German architecture and towering Christmas pyramid, feels like stepping into a Yuletide Bavaria. A fire burns in the potbelly stove at the General Store in Luckenbach, surrounded by denim-wearing guitar pickers.

Spring outings might be my favorite. The lavender pops in Johnson City. The prickly pear flaunts its yellow-orange blossoms around Sonora. Wildflowers kick up colors from Hebbronville to Pampa. The weather practically begs you to slip a canoe into the Rio Grande to marvel at the 1,500-foot walls of Santa Elena Canyon. It's also the perfect time of year to wake up early and make the pilgrimage to see Tootsie Tomanetz at Snow's BBQ in Lexington.

Sometimes the drive itself is the point. Some 314,00 miles of blacktop (the most of any state) crisscross Texas, and I've managed to collect a few favorites over the years.

THE RIVER ROAD

Farm to Market Road No. 170 (FM 170), often cited as "the most scenic" in the state, dramatically undulates through the Chihuahuan Desert just across the Rio Grande from Mexico. The "River Road," which traces the river's path between Lajitas and Presidio, has earned its reputation. FM 170 makes you want to pull over every few miles to snap a photo of the dramatic desert valley below—especially from the top of the aptly named Big Hill in Big Bend Ranch State Park—or to take a short side hike into a narrow slot canyon.

THE OLD WEST PORTAL

The fifty-two-mile stretch of US Highway 90 that connects Langtry to Lake View offers flyover views of Lake Amistad and the Pecos River, the latter of which you cross on the highest highway bridge in Texas, a steel deck truss bridge that rises 273 feet over the water. US 90 can also transport you through time. A short jaunt into Langtry drops you back off in the Old West, when Judge Roy Bean held court here at his Jersey Lilly Saloon. From the museum at the center of town, it's a few blocks to the rocky hills above the Rio Grande, where Bean once held an infamous prizefight on a sandbar in the river.

THE DEVIL'S BACKBONE

When it comes to the backroads of the Hill Country, it's hard to find a road that's *not* a great drive. Bikers know this, and, in the spring and fall, motorcycle clubs roar en masse down these curving, oak-lined two-lanes from one watering hole or riverside rest stop to the next. Perhaps no road in the region is more evocative than Ranch to Market Road No. 32 (RM 32), which snakes from just north of San Marcos up toward Blanco. The highlight of this twenty-three-mile stretch is the overlook offering views of the Devil's Backbone, a wickedly zigzagging range of hills that's as beautiful as it is rugged. It just so happens that the viewing point is a mile or so down the road from the Devil's Backbone Tavern, one of the oldest honky-tonks in the state.

THE PASTORAL IDEAL

Old No. 9 Highway, also known as San Antonio Road, also known as Old Fred Road, runs north to south between Fredericksburg and Comfort. Whatever you call it, this two-lane gem is the epitome of a bucolic Hill Country roadway. Sturdy barns and stone homes built by German settlers in the nineteenth-century sprout from groomed fields. Cypress trees tower over easygoing streams. Roll the window down, turn the music up, and cruise till you find Old Tunnel State Park, a nirvana for bat lovers. Just beyond the park lies another kind of heaven: the cheeseburger paradise of Alamo Springs Café. Those burgers are worth the drive every time.

THE UNDERWORLD

The Panhandle has no mountain passes, no winding hillscapes. The tilled cotton fields and feedlots of this tortilla-flat expanse are hardly a feast for a weary driver's eyes. Rather, the dramatic scenery here hides *below* the horizon. The canyon breaks that score this part of the state are full of secrets: valleys, mesas, and creeks. The best and most accessible example of these hidden wonders is Palo Duro Canyon. Texas State Highway 207 lends spectacular views from above, but State Highway Park Road 5 passes right through the heart of the nation's second-largest canyon. Drivers are greeted by riots of reds and pinks, ocher and rust, millennia of geologic time unfolding on the canyon walls one striation of rock at a time.

THE SPACE COAST

If cruising at sea level is more your thing, it's hard to beat State Highway 4, styled by South Texans as Boca Chica Boulevard. Not only is Highway 4 one of the southernmost roads in the mainland United States, it starts in Brownsville's southmost neighborhood, a nationally celebrated haven of cheap and delicious tacos, and connects up with Boca Chica Beach, a gloriously undeveloped stretch of sand and sea just 24.5 miles to the east. In between the tacos and the sea, Highway 4 occupies a spit of land dividing the Brownsville Ship Channel on your left and the Rio Grande on your right. Through coastal flats of yucca and cacti and just past Palmito Ranch, historic site of the final land battle of the Civil War, is an up-close view of the SpaceX launch site, where eccentric tech billionaire and newly installed Texan Elon Musk blasts rockets into the heavens. When you've reached the dunes, the pavement suddenly hits sand, and Highway 4 ends at an empty beach, where the vastness of the Gulf of Mexico spreads before you.

THE CAMINO REAL

Texas Highway 21 isn't the fastest route to pretty much anywhere, which is part of its charm. Part of what is credited as the first road across Texas and known by a variety of other monikers, namely the Old San Antonio Road and the Camino Real, or Royal Road, this winding highway stretches for more than 300 miles from the Central Texas city of San Marcos through finely aged towns such as Bastrop and Crockett, then Nacogdoches and San Augustine, not ending until it's reached the state's eastern boundary on a bridge over Toledo Bend, the largest man-made lake in the American South, where Louisiana's Highway 6 takes over. The farther east you drive on Highway 21, the more it twists and turns with little rhyme or reason, through ever-deeper forests of pine and leafy hardwood. The zigzags come courtesy of old trails not plotted by any self-respecting road engineer but likely blazed by herds of buffalo and traced for centuries by travelers on foot and then horseback. The peccadillos of the ancient route make for a serenely meandering journey, no matter the mode of transportation.

—Additional reporting by Wes Ferguson

LONG LIVE THE HIDY SIGN

By David Courtney

AS ALL TEXANS worth their collective roadkill know, the hidy sign—also known as the hi sign, the one-finger wave (not that one finger, Bubba), the Medina wave, or the Texas wave—is an effortless gesture consisting of nothing more than the raising of an index finger to salute an oncoming motorist. The rules of engagement couldn't be simpler: you give one, you get one, and vice versa. When executed properly, it is a deeply satisfying, if entirely fleeting, form of social interaction, a timeworn expression of neighborly ties. And yet this staple of Texas roadways is disappearing—perhaps because of the proliferation of distracting gizmos in the cabs of vehicles (it's a miracle today's motoring public notices anything that happens beyond the windshield), perhaps because of the proliferation of Californians and Yankees on Texas roadways. Whatever the reason for the decline, it is one more slice of a simpler time in Texas that is slowly falling away. Traditionally, the hidy sign has not been performed in urban areas (too many cars, too many tourists), but perhaps the time has come to change that. While Houston's Loop 610 at drive time may be more crowded than Texas 118 through the Davis Mountains, the commuters sealed off in their cars are usually even more lonesome. A properly executed hidy sign here and there, even when we're hurtling past each other, does a better job of connecting people than all the personal computing devices you can muster.

Planting Wildflowers in a Pandemic

By Deborah D.E.E.P. Mouton

GROWING UP, I NEVER had a green thumb. My grandmother's lush herb garden tried to teach me to prune and till. My mother even made a science project of constructing the world's largest compost heap in our backyard, the stench staining my hands. But everything I touched quickly wilted into a brown shriveled mess. In high school, I killed a spider plant that my mother had had since I was an elementary-school student. I thought maybe it was a matter of age or maturity, so I waited to see if my thumb would green over time.

By my wedding, I was willing to try again. My mother-in-love is a horticulturist, so I felt I had married into some advantage. When she gave me a small herb garden for our tiny apartment, I had visions of freshly seasoned sauces and aromatic garnishes. Unfortunately, raising a young child while juggling two jobs and a new marriage quickly took over. By the time I remembered to water the herbs, the Houston heat had scorched them into something that reminded me of what Ursula was transforming merpeople into under the sea in *The Little Mermaid*. I began to wonder if my hands would ever be enough to make something grow.

Then, we got pregnant again. But this time, things weren't as smooth. Soon complications turned into weekly doctor visits. And then there was no more reason to go. I remember sitting on the patio of my apartment, looking into a sea of plastic pots, all holding dirt and tombstones, my black thumbs having murdered them all. And I felt not equipped to hold a life inside me.

I had always dreamed of a home with bustling bluebonnets, magnificent marigolds, and wildflowers that burst through the ground every spring. The kind of home that looks alive and well. Something I hadn't felt I had been in so long. I began to think that kind of life was unattainable.

By the time we bought our home, I was resolved to hire a landscaper to make my outdoor dreams come true. But with all of our money dumped into closing and moving costs and an even newer child on the way, that seemed less feasible. So I decided to try it on my own one last time.

I bought a planter box from Lowe's and filled it high with soil. I planted cucumbers. I figured, since I had failed with flowers so many times before, maybe I should try something I could eat. I watered them every day, and before long they broke ground. Then the vines were wrapping around the trellis, and then I was watching small cucumbers stretch like balloon animals on the vine. I remember crying. Life had seemed so far away before. Here, the small seeds held possibility.

The next year, I expanded my vegetable garden, still avoiding flowers. Before long, parsley, bell peppers, and watermelon vines were stretching far and wide across my lawn. The Texas sun was beating my sweat and tears down into the soil. But somewhere in me there was still some inadequacy, a fear that I would touch something or do something wrong and ruin it all.

One thing I have learned in my fourteen years in Texas is that the bluebonnets always bloom. These flowers find a way to beat all the odds, no matter how harsh the winter or how vicious the hurricane season. When spring lifts her head to sing, the bluebonnets and wildflowers will fight through harsh soil and the uncompromising humidity. Having been trampled and picked, they will come back again and again.

So in the year 2020, with the world on the brink of losing everything as we know it, I paused my fear long enough to buy some flowers. I pushed all my worries and frustrations into my flower bed, digging and planting each marigold meticulously. I watered them every other day, between news updates and the calls of my young children; between the dismal reports of pandemic death tolls and the promises of economic stimulus. And nothing died.

I know that whatever harsh times we have in front of us, whatever I cannot control today, whatever mourning may come, the next year the ground will rattle. And something beautiful and expected will erupt and remind us all that, for a moment, we couldn't see our way out. Beautiful things were always still there, beneath the earth, waiting to live, just like us.

THE BLUEBONNET SNAPSHOT

By Suzanne Winckler

ON FINE SPRING days when the sky is blue and decked with clouds, a peculiar exodus takes place from Texas's cities. People pack their loved ones—babies, betrotheds, favorite aunts, pets—out to the nearest and best patch of bluebonnets, set them down amid the prodigious blue, and snap their pictures. Bluebonnet snapshots are a badge of place, proof of membership in the large and otherwise amorphous Texas clan. That is not to say that bluebonnet snapshots make for good art. It is notoriously difficult to take a picture of people in those flowers. The sun is invariably too bright, forcing the subjects to squint, or too high in the sky, washing out all detail. The breeze rattles the bluebonnets, so they come out blurred and vague. And the images most often fail to record the blue as vividly as one's eye does. On top of all that, there are baby cries and beestings, since both infant and insect fail to appreciate the rite in progress, and the roar of nearby traffic, since the greatest concentrations of bluebonnets appear alongside highways, thanks to the Department of Transportation sowing 30,000 pounds of roadside wildflower seed each year. If the end result is less-than-brilliant photography, that is all right, because a bluebonnet snapshot is simply one's private entrance into memory. It is the record of a day in the country, out of doors, in the fresh air. The romp is what it's all about.

Notes from a Hill Country Deer Blind

By Emily McCullar

MY DAD'S SHOULDERS HEAVED the way they do when he's stifling laughter, trying not to make a sound. It was just after dawn on a December morning, and we'd been sitting in the deer blind for the better part of an hour, waiting for a buck to wander up to the feeder. On such mornings, we often whisper off-color jokes and quote our favorite movies to pass the time, and *Dr. Strangelove*

references are a part of the routine: "You can't fight in here. This is the War Room!" It gets Dad every time.

Soon enough, a broad-shouldered buck ambled innocently from a clearing in the cedar, and Dad grabbed his binoculars. He confirmed that the animal was at least three and a half, old enough to have enjoyed a couple of ruts, or breeding seasons. In other words, a shooter. I raised the .243 I'd recently borrowed from my stepbrother and carefully chambered a round. I tried to slow my breath, just like Dad had taught me. I waited for the stag to turn broadside, then closed my left eye and focused my right through the scope, aiming for the spot just below his shoulder blade, where I knew his heart to be. I pulled the trigger on an exhale, and when the gun went off, I realized I had forgotten to put in my earplugs.

It was my third or fourth attempt to bag a buck that season. Previous hunts had been thwarted by the usual variables to which the prospective deer killer is beholden. One November evening brought a good crowd, but I didn't see a shooter, just a doe and a couple of playful yearlings. The next morning not a single mammal passed before me. Later that night I spotted a nice eight-pointer, but Dad wasn't there to verify the buck's age. He has a better eye for such things, and neither of us wants to take the life of something young.

In the fifteen or so years I've been hunting whitetail, I have yet to pull the trigger without my father present. I spend most of the weekends between early November and mid-January with him on our family's ranch outside Brady.

During these trips, we fall into a familiar pattern. We set our alarms for five thirty a.m. Dad makes the coffee and readies the rifles. Once we're dressed and sufficiently caffeinated, we gather our armaments and creep in silence to the truck, already practicing the care we'll have to show once we're in the presence of the skittish animals we're hoping to kill.

Dad drives, and we plod along on

a narrow dirt road flanked by prickly pear and cedar, scanning the brush for the orange tape identifying the turnoff to whichever blind we've chosen to inhabit that day. The land has been in our family since it was snatched up by my mom's people sometime after they left Idaho for the Texas Hill Country, in the late 1870s. The blind is cramped, roughly a four-by-six box made of some combination of plastic, wood, or metal. There, we entertain ourselves as quietly as we can until the sun rises and the feeder goes off, dropping kernels of corn to lure our prey.

After one of us takes a shot, we descend from our perch to find the body. One of us gets the truck and moves it closer, allowing for easier load-in once the field dressing is done. We each grab an end to flip the buck over. With the animal's legs thrust skyward, one of us pinches the skin above the groin, makes a cut, and slices slowly toward the sternum, careful not to puncture the organs inside. We watch the blood and steam spill out into the winter air.

At this point, it is not unusual for at least one of us to cry.

MY FATHER HAS never lived in the country but has always idealized what he refers to as "the arts and sciences of rural life." This is something he inherited from his mother. My paternal grandma was born in the twenties, on a stretch of South Texas coastland that had been in the family since they sailed over from Essex, England, in the mid-nineteenth century. Once, when her grammar-school teacher asked the class if anyone could identify the four seasons, Grandma confidently spoke up: "Deer season, duck season, dove season, and prairie chicken season."

By his own admission, Dad "was always prowling in the woods" near his childhood home in suburban St. Louis, where his family had settled after my grandfather's tire business took them from South Texas to Missouri. Dad had a .22 and would while away hours of free time searching for rabbits and squirrels. He killed his first deer the Christmas after he turned fifteen.

These days, when Dad tells the story of that first buck, he usually pauses between "there I found him" and "dead." Fifty years later, it's as if he still needs a moment to come to terms with the threshold he'd crossed. He hunted for a few more Christmases before graduating high school, joining the Marines, and calling in naval gunfire in Vietnam. He didn't hunt for nearly a decade after that, distracted by college, then a burgeoning journalism career in Austin. When he was thirty, he met my mother at a house party. Like my father, she was from a longtime Texas family who'd continued to congregate on the same patch of land for generations, even after they'd moved away. In Mom's case, it was a ranch in the Hill Country, just outside her hometown of Brady.

They fell in love, married, and had their first child, my brother, within two years. Sometime during this period, Dad began hunting again. He eased back into it by shooting dove

with both of my grandfathers. By the time I came along, three years after my brother, Dad was a deer hunter again.

My maternal grandparents had passed by then, and my mother had inherited her portion of the family tract. Dad settled comfortably into the role of ranch patriarch. He raised his two kids around the same rural "arts and sciences" that had shaped his own childhood, and though we lived in Austin, we visited the ranch as often as we could. We were a hunting family. Dad made sure of it. My earliest memories are of ranch trips, dead animals, and gamey meats. Trips to the ranch often ended with my parents up front in my grandad's old 1983 Suburban, my brother and me riding in the back with the corn, and a slack-jawed, field-dressed deer carcass in the carrier bolted to the vehicle's brush guard. When we got to the house, Dad would hang the deer from a live oak outside the kitchen window to let the blood drain out. My earliest meditations on mortality came while I stared at the limp, gray tongues dangling from the mouths of those deer.

There's a photo of me as a toddler, kneeling curiously over the body of a dead buck, while my father stands nearby. I don't look upset and likely wasn't. I don't remember being disturbed by the killing, and I know that I appreciated the spoils. My childhood breakfasts frequently featured venison sausage.

My brother stopped hunting when he was thirteen, around the time our mother lost her battle with breast cancer. After her death, Dad took on more responsibilities at the ranch. For our family, like many landowning families today, the bulk of the income that keeps us from having to sell comes from hunting leases. Dad worked with Mom's brother to manage the leases and oversee general maintenance. This includes keeping up with yearly harvest recommendations necessary to manage the population of deer. So Dad kept hunting.

When I was twelve, Dad remarried, and my new stepbrother, Nick,

who was eight at the time, started joining my dad for dove hunts in the fall and deer hunts in the winter. Sometimes they'd invite Nick's friends and their fathers out or just head to the ranch to pal around with the lease hunters, where they would grill burgers, play poker, and return home with jokes they claimed were inappropriate to share with us girls, which infuriated me. My principal interests at the time were Agatha Christie books, Red Baron pizzas, and episodes of *ER*, but the thing that mattered most was my relationship with my father. When he took my stepbrother hunting, Dad wasn't just teaching him marksmanship; he was teaching him how to be still, how to listen, how to be safe, how to provide, how to respect an animal's life even when you're taking it. I resented missing out on anything solely on the basis of gender, and I was terrified that someone might grow closer than I was to my only living parent. So, not long after I turned fifteen, I told my dad I wanted him to take me deer hunting.

SHOOTING A DEER with a scoped rifle from a blind at a corn feeder is not terribly difficult. You're hidden, you're seated, and you have a window ledge on which to rest your heavy gun.

But killing a deer quickly and humanely is a different story. The first deer I killed—on only my second visit to a blind—was an easy one. I pointed, I shot, and that eleven-pointer dropped where he stood. A fount of blood spewed roughly four feet out of the entry wound. Another year, I foolishly decided to forgo the usual pre-hunt trip to the rifle range. I shot low and to the left, shattering my target's two front legs. Dad had to put him out of his misery with the .45 he keeps on his hip, while I wept nearby.

For those first few years, I cried every time we walked from a blind to a body. Dad seemed close to tears sometimes but restrained his emotions by listing his reasons for sticking with the sport. Hunting reminded him of his childhood. It made him feel closer to his father, who had died a few years after my mom. He felt a sense of stew-

ardship for my mother's land and a duty to manage its deer population. He liked the meat. It was part of the Brady routine.

I abandoned the sport for the better part of a decade. I went to New York City for college and even half-heartedly practiced vegetarianism for a couple semesters before coming to my senses. I moved to San Antonio, then Southern California, then back to New York. But Texas called me home. I missed my dad, and it was time to start helping take care of the ranch. I was eager to establish the routines that would define my adult life in Texas.

Naturally, Dad and I headed to a deer blind the first November weekend after I moved back. It felt right to be there, on land passed down from one of my grandfathers, holding a rifle passed down from the other, and talking with my dad about them both.

AFTER TAKING A shot at that broad-shouldered stag last December, I was nervous. I was fairly certain I had hit him, but the buck had disappeared into the brush. Adrenaline can propel deer quite far, even if they're mortally wounded.

I would've been fine with a clean miss. What I worried about, in those fifteen minutes we waited for the deer to bed down, was that I'd incapacitated the animal, hitting him in the leg or the shoulder. I pictured him under a mesquite tree somewhere, unable to move but feeling everything.

We headed toward the brush to the right of the blind. Thirty or so yards from the feeder, we found the buck, dead. The shot was clean. ("Thank God," I whispered to myself.) We dragged him out of the pile of cactus into which he'd fallen, then dressed the body, loaded it into the bed of the pickup, and headed back to the house.

My older brother, who still spends weekends with us at the ranch even though he no longer hunts, met us by the cleaning station when we pulled up to the house. Though he hasn't wanted to kill a deer for over twenty years, he's always down to help when one of us does. We used a garden hose to wash out the body with water from the well. Then my brother and dad hoisted the animal up to the A-frame, where he'd hang for the rest of the day until we moved him to a walk-in cooler.

We headed inside to make tacos and sausage rolls. On the way, my brother talked about wanting his future kids to go hunting but not wanting to take them himself. I gave it some thought and then promised that I'd take them when the time came.

HOW TO TALK LIKE A HUNTER

By Emily McCullar

MOST YEARS, AROUND 5 percent of Texans hold hunting licenses. So to most folks in the state, a sentence like "Billy boogered everything so we went home to watch horn porn" sounds like nothing more than salacious gobbledygook. Unless, of course, you have the benefit of the following brief glossary.

BALDIE An antlerless deer, such as a doe or fawn, or a springtime buck that drops its antlers after the rut.

BAWL The haunting shriek a deer makes when wounded or afraid.

BLOW (SNORT) The nasal harrumph a deer uses to alert other deer when suspicious of its surroundings. Often accompanied by the raising of the deer's white tail. May indicate that someone has boogered the grounds.

BOOGERING When some dumbass in the hunting party makes too much noise and spooks the game.

BOONE AND CROCKETT CLUB The wildlife conservation club founded by Theodore Roosevelt in 1887. Its whitetail scoring system is the accepted standard for trophy deer. The score accounts for antler pattern, number of points, tine length, spread width, and beam circumference.

BUCK FEVER The shaky hands and racing heart experienced by hunters when they spot a large deer within shooting distance.

FIELD DRESSING The extraction of a dead deer's organs at the site of the kill.

GROUND SHRINKAGE The phenomenon of approaching a bagged buck and realizing it's much smaller than it appeared from the blind (the ensuing sinking feeling comes from knowing that its Boone and Crockett score won't impress one's friends).

HORN PORN A thriving industry of DVDs and YouTube videos featuring very big bucks.

MANAGEMENT BUCK A buck with stunted antler development that hunters are encouraged to remove from the gene pool.

RATTLING A technique used to lure bucks during the rut, in which the hunting party bangs antlers together, mimicking the sound of two bucks fighting over a doe.

RUT Deer-breeding season, which varies by location and from year to year. In most parts of the state, the rut peaks in early to mid-November.

TINES The forks on an antler.

WALL HANGER A big fellow with a nice rack that's worth shoulder mounting and displaying prominently.

III

Arts & Entertainment

The Texas Western, Redefined

By John Spong

I'M NOT SURE WHAT I expected when I went with my dad to see John Sayles's film *Lone Star* in an Austin arthouse theater shortly after its release in June 1996. I know I'd read a couple of the universally glowing reviews, so I was aware that Kris Kristofferson's performance as a corrupt small-town sheriff was viewed as a completely unexpected career resurrection. As an earnest fan of Texas songwriters, I was down with that. I knew too that critics were predicting that Matthew McConaughey's small role, as Kristofferson's chief adversary, would be his last layover on the way to full-fledged stardom with the release later that year of *A Time to Kill*. As a lucky attendee of the Austin world premiere of Richard Linklater's *Dazed and Confused* three years earlier—and as a friend of a bunch of guys who'd been McConaughey's fraternity brothers at the University of Texas—I felt a little hometown pride as well.

Beyond that, all I would have known was what was laid out in *Lone Star*'s trailer. And that was a complete misdirection, not so much a bait-and-switch as a flat-out lie. Or rather, two lies. One was small and subtle. The preview was backed by an instrumental version of "Wake Up Dolores," a moody, Latin-psyche stomper by Los Angeles–based Chicano roots-rockers Los Lobos. But Sayles's film was set squarely on the Texas border, and the writer-director had been meticulous in filling it with genuine Texas conjunto and old R&B. There's a Los Lobos snippet in the film, but it's an acoustic version of an old Norteño song, "Anselma."

The second lie was the bigger one. The trailer teased *Lone Star* as a murder mystery built on one of the state's great icons—the solitary law man. But the movie I ended up seeing not only eschewed the customary hagiography, it presented a withering critique of it, a depiction of the way everyday Brown, Black, and white Texans were still dealing with the state's cruel racial history. *Lone Star* wasn't a murder mystery set in Texas. It was a story of real Texas—one that I'd not seen on-screen before—that happened to be set in a murder mystery.

But let me back up. I was between gigs that summer. Or maybe it would be more accurate to say between lives. A couple months earlier I'd abruptly quit a lawyering job at a small Austin litigation firm, leaving the career path I'd been on since giving up my original, little boy's plan to be a cowboy. But while that first dream had been a fantasy born of a strict diet of John Wayne movies, the second had been an all-too-real, unfulfilling slog. After two years at the firm, all I had to do was look at a stack of discovery documents and I'd fall asleep at my desk.

But I didn't know what I'd do next and was of an uneasy mind. I had the idea that I wanted to write and had announced as much to my dad. An Episcopal priest with a counseling practice, he was a thoughtful, compassionate man, but he didn't spend much energy skirting hard truths. "Writing is hard," he said. "What if you're not good enough?" I thought my comeback was strong—"Do people actually pay you for that kind of advice?"—but he had a better answer ready. "Well, they don't pay me to lie to them."

Vitally, though, he had another hat he wore as a seminary professor. He taught a class called Film as an Occasion for Prophecy and Perception, in which his students watched and reviewed movies with an eye out for spiritual lessons. Right about the time I started leaning away from the law, he began inviting me to watch and discuss films he might add to his syllabus. So we saw Woody Allen's

Crimes and Misdemeanors and talked about why bad things happen to good people. We watched Peter Sellers in *Being There* and talked about why people search for a savior. Turning over questions like that grabbed me in a way law school had not. I'd loved working through complicated legal theory passed down by the professors. But this exercise with my dad was actually going out into the world—into art—and finding big-picture meaning in movies I would have previously merely enjoyed.

I'd always been curious prior to that, but more to shore up ideas than challenge them. In undergrad at UT in the mid-eighties, I'd spent a year working as a tour guide at the state capitol. The script we recited for visitors was a mini-Texas history lesson, kind of a highlight reel from the state-mandated seventh-grade class on the subject. As a standard-issue Texas white boy, I'd loved that class, and this was a chance to dive in deeper. I found the script's source material in the legislative library: T. R. Fehrenbach's *Lone*

Star: A History of Texas and the Texans. It was the state's accepted history, a decidedly Great Man version. I raced through the chapters celebrating the unflinching Anglo badasses who saved Texas from the Mexicans and Native Americans, absorbing a notion of Texan Exceptionalism that I trumpeted at every frat party I crashed for the rest of college. Fehrenbach's description of the Texas Revolution may have shot a few factual holes in John Wayne's *The Alamo*, but Davy Crockett and crew still came off as heroes, and Wayne could have played any one of them. He was also my mind's image for the men in other books I found, like *Rip Ford's Texas*, the memoir of a noted Texas Ranger and Confederate army colonel, and *The Raven*, Marquis James's Pulitzer Prize–winning biography of Sam Houston. It's worth noting that another book I fell hard for in those years, Larry McMurtry's *Lonesome Dove*, had begun as a screenplay, and McMurtry originally had Wayne in mind for the character who became Woodrow Call.

So maybe it was a new set of inquisitive eyes and shifting priorities. Or maybe the act of redefining myself had finally opened me up to rethinking the world around me. Whatever it was, *Lone Star* hit theaters at the exact right moment.

THE FILM OPENS with two middle-aged, white guys wandering through an abandoned rifle range in remote South Texas brush country, one cataloging cacti, the other looking for old bullets with a metal detector. Both are career soldiers stationed at fictional Fort McKenzie, an army base at a border town that Sayles named Frontera. They discover the remains of a long-dead body, plus a Mason's ring and a crusty sheriff's badge. A cold-crime whodunit is set in motion.

But hints come quickly that the film is headed elsewhere. The camera cuts from the sun-bleached skull to the opening credits, and while a late-fifties jukebox hit by Rio Grande Valley legends Conjunto Bernal, "Mi

Unico Camino," plays in the background, the actors' names appear, not with the big stars first but in alphabetical order. This is an ensemble film, a dissertation on life on the border. But if there's a thought the history might be harmonious, it's dispelled when the Bernal brothers fade out, and the law shows up. Sheriff Sam Deeds, played by Chris Cooper, is an unlikely lawman, his reluctance evident in perpetually pursed lips and soft, distant eyes. He surveys the scene and warns the two men not to jump to any conclusions about who might have died or at whose hand. "This country's seen a good number of disagreements over the years," he says with a resignation that dogs him throughout the film.

His comment sounds vaguely like an apology, and it is. Sam's aware that the most tragic of those disagreements were instigated by one of his predecessors as sheriff, a vile racist named Charlie Wade. According to local legend, Wade was run out of town forty years earlier, not for mistreating any-

one but for unprincipled graft. When Sam realizes that the dead body is Wade's and starts digging into his disappearance, harrowing flashbacks show just how awful Wade was. Kristofferson plays him as bigoted evil incarnate, beating up a Black waiter for not paying him proper deference, shooting a Latino in the back for bringing undocumented Mexicans into his county. And the most terrifying thing about him isn't the satisfaction he takes at humiliating people who don't look like him, nor even in his outright murder of them. It's the hand he keeps on his gun and the star on his chest. He is the law.

The flashbacks are clues to more than a crime. *Lone Star*'s great technical achievement was the way Sayles wove in his time travel. There's no fade to black to connote memory. Rather the camera pans in one shot from the present to the past, sometimes across the scrubby landscape, sometimes from one side of a restaurant to another. The implication is that life on the border has not changed as much as one might think. The impact of past injustice is still being felt.

The characters dealing with it now are descended from the people Wade wronged. Three families comprise the focus of *Lone Star*, one Black, one Brown, and one white. There's a Black colonel who has just taken over Fort McKenzie, who struggles to help Black soldiers fit into the army and the border. He happens to be the estranged son of the waiter Wade beat up, and that waiter, Otis Payne, now owns the town's only Black nightclub. There's the Latina high-school teacher who fights to include Mexican contributions to state history in her class. Her mother, Mercedez Cruz, was married to the man Wade shot, and Mercedez, who long ago crossed into Texas illegally herself, now owns the busiest restaurant in Frontera. She also speed-dials the border patrol when she sees Mexicans on her land.

And then there's Sam. His father is the revered Buddy Deeds, the deputy who stood up to Wade and later succeeded him as sheriff. Buddy, now dead, is only physically present in three brief scenes, and as portrayed by a young McConaughey, he's a little too good-looking and a little too cocksure to be entirely believable. But it's Buddy's memory that looms in the film. He's the murder's prime suspect, and Sam's ambivalence when townsfolk talk about him in sanctified tones at first suggests a typical father and overshadowed-son dynamic. But as Sam learns more, we learn more. Buddy also took a cut from the Black-owned businesses. He forced Kickapoo families off their land to make way for a development he was investing in. And he had a strict edict against interracial dating in town.

And that points to the relationship at the heart of the film. In high school Sam was in love with Mercedez Cruz's daughter, Pilar, and in a flashback, Buddy tries to all but beat that desire out of him after catching the two in the back seat at a drive-in movie. When Sam and Pilar rekindle late in the second act, the scene provides one of the film's few grace notes.

They meet after-hours in Mercedez's darkened restaurant. Pilar drops a quarter in the jukebox, and they dance to "Since I Met You Baby," a 1956 R&B hit by Ivory Joe Hunter, a piano player from Kirbyville, Texas. But the jukebox doesn't play Hunter's version. Instead, it's the one Sam and Pilar would have heard on the radio in high school, a Tejano take by Freddy Fender, sung in Spanish and renamed "Desde Que Conosco." Finally, they're together. Maybe there's hope yet.

I REWATCHED *LONE Star* recently to see if it held up, if it rhymed with my memory. Largely, it did. I'd understood Sayles's theme to be that borders, whether they're geographical, cultural, generational, or even cinematic—like a cut to a flashback—are arbitrary lines that can blind us to our common humanity. While some of the dialogue, like Sam's line about the years of disagreements, sounded a little heavy-handed, it likely wouldn't have if Sayles's theme weren't in the front of my mind. And I was stunned all over again when Charlie Wade's killer was revealed. The murder-mystery plot was not what had stuck.

I wondered how true to life Sayles's take on border life had been, and how novel. So I called Charles Ramírez Berg, who teaches a class at UT called Latino Images in Film. "Historically," he said, "if you crossed the border in a movie, it was for booze, drugs, prostitution, or to escape the law. When *Lone Star* showed up, it was great. The border was not a place for escape, moral or criminal. It was a place where people live."

Ramírez Berg, who grew up in El Paso, with a mom from Mexico and dad from Kansas, said he was amazed that Sayles, a guy from New Jersey, captured the border, and the people who live there, so accurately. "He saw things we couldn't even see ourselves. Maybe that's because we are in it, on one side or the other." Even all these years later, Ramírez Berg's only real issue was with the way Sayles ended the film, a sequence that had always vexed me as well. It opens like a quiet coda, then abruptly turns into the film's true reveal.

After Sam learns Wade's killer, he meets Pilar back at the long-shuttered drive-in, and they sit side by side on the hood of his car. Slowly, he tells her his investigation's other discovery: Buddy and Mercedez were longtime lovers. He and Pilar are half-siblings. He curses his dad—their dad—while she takes in the news, and then she tells him she can't have kids. They decide to stay a couple, to forget the history and start all over. The camera pulls back to show the dilapidated drive-in screen as a scratchy recording of "I Want to Be a Cowboy's Sweetheart," the 1935 hit by Patsy Montana, starts to play. And then the credits roll.

That ending was what always came to mind when someone mentioned *Lone Star* to me. It was unsettling in 1996, and it still is. Sayles had made a point on the arbitrariness of borders that people needed to hear. The prohibition against incest is a different kind of line.

But Sayles was also talking about the damage those borders can do. Sam and Pilar didn't invite their situation. It was the consequence of an oppressive culture, the entirely too possible by-product of hypocrisy. Ramírez Berg agreed. "If you pull away and consider it as the theme, we are in fact all intertwined in ways we don't even know, closer to each other than we think."

Essential Texas Movies

By David Courtney

This is Texas—mighty colossus of the Southwest. A land of infinite variety and violent contrasts; a land where today's ranch hand can become tomorrow's multimillionaire. But more than a state, here is a state of mind: manners, morals, emotions. Of people who are often as exhilarating, exasperating, exciting as the land they belong to. Out of this fabulous and tempestuous panorama comes a story of magnificent scope and great personal charm, a cavalcade that spans a quarter century . . . A mighty monument of memorable entertainment.

THAT SLAB OF GRANDIOSE verbiage comes from the official trailer for George Stevens's 1956 three-hour-and-change star-studded epic *Giant*, but it aptly describes why there have been hundreds, if not thousands, of films made about Texans and Texas, going all the way back to the likes of the earliest Texas-set films such as 1903's *The Dance of the Little Texas Magnet*, of which no copy is known to exist, and *Old Texas*, a silent 1916 self-produced biopic of sorts starring legendary cattleman Charles Goodnight that has grainy footage of actual Kiowa Indians hunting bison in Palo Duro Canyon.

Of the twenty movies that follow, a couple may not be the greatest examples of filmmaking you've ever seen, but, rest assured, each of them, in its own way, is indeed a mighty monument of entertainment that elucidates the potent mythos—good, bad, and ugly—behind Texas. They remind us of who we were, or are, or who we thought we were, or *think* we are.

Red River, **1948.** The grand Howard Hawks cattle-driving Western starring John Wayne, Montgomery Clift, Walter Brennan, and Joanne Dru has Wayne in one of the darkest roles of his career, that of Texas rancher Tom Dunston, whose stubborn single-mindedness incites a mutiny on the trail and almost costs him his herd—and, indeed, everything.

The Searchers, **1956.** Another iconic John Wayne western, directed by John Ford and based on the real-life 1836 Comanche abduction of young Texan Cynthia Ann Parker, this one casts Wayne in *the* darkest role of his career.

Giant, **1956.** Portraying a changing Texas spurred by the arrival of oil, the sweeping Western based on the Edna Ferber novel also dares to show the greed and bigotry of Texas society. The film's stunning shots of the Trans-Pecos region (as well as of Rock Hudson, Elizabeth Taylor, and James Dean) went a long way toward putting Marfa on the map.

The Alamo, **1960.** The historically suspect telling of one of the most pivotal moments of the Texas origin story cast John Wayne (Who'd you expect?) as Davy Crockett, Richard Widmark as James Bowie, Frankie Avalon as a young Alamo defender, and Seagoville native Chill Wills as the bumbling Beekeeper. Not everybody loves it, but every Texan has seen it.

Hud, **1963.** As the titular Hud Bannon, star Paul Newman clashes with his rancher father, chases after the family housekeeper, and makes for an impeccable cowboy rounder in this anti-western Western based on Larry McMurtry's novel *Horseman, Pass By*.

Bonnie and Clyde, **1967.** The action-packed biographical drama follows the lives and bullet-ridden deaths of Texas's first couple of crime, played by Warren Beatty and Faye Dunaway, who were considerably more glamorous than their real-life counterparts.

Brewster McCloud, 1970. Houston's Astrodome, once billed as the eighth wonder of the world, is the central location in this absolutely bonkers farce—involving a string of murders and piles of bird shit and featuring a young Shelley Duvall in her first big-screen appearance—from director Robert Altman.

The Last Picture Show, 1971. The desolate, dusty, small-town coming-of-age story, directed by Peter Bogdanovich and based on Larry McMurtry's semi-autobiographical novel, stars Jeff Bridges, Timothy Bottoms, Cybill Shepherd, and Ben Johnson.

The Texas Chainsaw Massacre, 1974. Featuring a murderous chainsaw-wielding cannibal known as Leatherface, the low-budget horror flick shocked critics and defined a genre.

Urban Cowboy, 1980. The unlikely John Travolta vehicle launched Debra Winger's career and brought Texas honky-tonk culture and mechanical bulls to the masses. Trivia: the choreography was handled by Houston-born dancer Patsy Swayze, mother of Houston-born actor Patrick Swayze.

Tender Mercies, 1983. The Horton Foote–penned story of down-on-his-luck country singer Mac Sledge, played by Robert Duvall, who did all his own singing for this role, is a stirring tale of love and redemption in quiet rural Texas.

Fandango, 1985. San Antonio–born director Kevin Reynolds made his comedic drama debut in this cult favorite starring young Kevin Costner, young Judd Nelson, and young Sam Robards. *Fandango* shows us that West Texas road trips are sometimes silly, sometimes poignant, and always a good idea, even if spontaneous and not very well thought out.

The Thin Blue Line, 1988. Errol Morris's groundbreaking documentary investigation of the shooting of a Dallas police officer led to the over-turning of the capital murder conviction of Randall Dale Adams.

Lone Star, **1996.** This John Sayles–directed drama involving sheriffs, corruption, murder, and Matthew Mc-Conaughey brought nuance to border politics and family secrets.

Selena, **1997.** Bronx-born Jennifer Lopez, in her breakout role, portrays Lake Jackson–born Tejano star Selena Quintanilla Pérez with a surprising fidelity that makes her murder, just as she was launching the once-regional genre into the mainstream, all the more shocking.

Friday Night Lights, **2004.** The film inspired by the Buzz Bissinger book about the Permian Panthers of Odessa—which later inspired a popular TV series—showed the world that high-school football in Texas is so much more than just high-school football.

No Country for Old Men, **2007.** Joel and Ethan Coen's crime thriller version of the Cormac McCarthy book stars San Saba native Tommy Lee Jones and Josh Brolin and represents the best of the five McCarthy adaptations. Javier Bardem won an Oscar for the unforgettably cold hit-man Anton Chigurh.

Bernie, **2011.** Austin auteur Richard Linklater based this deeply weird, dark, and comedic East Texas murder mystery on the 1998 *Texas Monthly* story "Midnight in the Garden of East Texas." Starring Jack Black as the most unlikely of killers, the film reminds us that, in the right hands, Texas crime and criminals can be so damn entertaining.

Dallas Buyers Club, **2013.** Long-view's own Matthew McConaughey won a Best Actor Oscar for his portrayal of real-life Dallasite Ron Woodroof, who contracted HIV in the eighties, when the virus was tantamount to a death sentence and, in true Dallas fashion, found an entrepreneurial solution to helping himself and others prolong their lives.

Boyhood, **2014.** In his most groundbreaking film, Richard Linklater incorporated the aging of his cast over twelve years into this chronicle about growing up. From Houston to San Marcos to Austin to the final gorgeous moments at Big Bend Ranch State Park, Texas plays an indelible supporting role.

The *Dallas* Effect

By Max Marshall

FROM 1978 TO 1991, the world capital of mergers and acquisitions, greed, consumption of champagne and whiskey, cuckoldry, and plot twists was a midsize horse farm east of Plano. Behind its wood rail fence stood a white frame house that wouldn't have looked out of place in any luxury cul-de-sac. Three generations of billionaires shared that home, and for a long stretch of the eighties, they were the most popular television family in the world.

The *Dallas* miniseries premiered on Sunday, April 2, 1978, with a bombastic earworm theme song. Helicopter shots of glittering towers, grazing cattle, and oil derricks panned across the title sequence. The plots centered around Bobby, a reformed playboy in love, and Pamela, a reformer of playboys. The soap-operatic plots, fistfights at discos, and oilman villainy turned off some early viewers. But then, on March 21, 1980, millions watched Bobby's brother, J. R., work late at his desk, answer a ringing phone only to be greeted by silence on the other end, get up to refill his coffee mug, hear footsteps down the hall, take two gunshots to the stomach, and fall to the floor as the credits start to roll. The CBS Marketing Department soon launched a promotional campaign built around the tagline "Who Shot J. R.?" and America—and a good chunk of the rest of the world—lost its mind.

It's hard, from the vantage point of our era of Netflix and HBO, to grasp why *Dallas* caused such a global ruckus. In 1980, the show was arguably the hottest pop culture entity in existence; about as many Americans tuned in to find out who shot J. R. as voted for president. But today it looks like a relic of the era "before TV got good." After families like the Sopranos and the Drapers ushered us into the Golden Age of Television, critics started grading series in terms of filmic scope and literary ambition. By those metrics, the Ewings have been tossed into the bin of trashy, campy pop culture, right next to the cast of *The Love Boat*.

That's partly because *Dallas* was, by its own estimation, trashy and campy. The Ewings were more operatically miserable than any other family on TV, they slept around more, and many of them were single-mindedly devoted to ruining their associates' lives, for money or just for sport. Inside their all-American house lurked murder schemes, secret relatives, rare diseases, and an entire season that was all a dream. The show upended our common logic—our moral codes, our sense of cause and effect—with a J. R. Ewing smirk.

But to criticize a nighttime soap opera for absurdity is to miss the point. *Dallas* leaned into its absurdity and in the process defined an era and transformed its namesake hometown. Two years before Ronald Reagan became president, and nine years before Oliver Stone's *Wall Street* accidentally turned "Greed is good" into a mantra, the Ewings already knew what the eighties were going to be about. The Ewings celebrated excess, and they saw the boardroom, ballroom, and bedroom as overlapping war zones. Questions of virtue and civility were dissolved in J. R.'s certainty that "All that matters is winning."

Spoken by a less deliciously malicious actor, that line might have seemed like a pretty bleak way of looking at things. But when Larry Hagman said with a smile that "A conscience is like a boat or a car: if you feel you need one, rent it," it sounded like a jingle. When he ruined some poor fool's life, hundreds of millions of viewers cheered.

While *Dallas* was selling a new American ideal—not to mention official *Dallas* aftershave, deodorant, commemorative dishes, twenty-four-karat-gold Southfork belt buckles, and J. R. Ewing Private Stock beer emblazoned with the slogan "If you have to ask how much my beer costs, you probably can't afford it"—to fans at home and abroad, it was also selling them a new vision of Dallas and Texas. Like the Texans portrayed in *Red River* and *Giant*, the characters on *Dallas* were full of swagger. But they didn't just rope cattle and strike oil; they orchestrated coups against Communist regimes in Southeast Asia that threatened their oil interests and wore Valentino dresses while they fell off the wagon.

The corporate dealmaker may have lacked the romance of the Texas Ranger, but he was, in many ways, an accurate update. By 1978 80 percent of Texans lived in urban areas, and its cities were booming. The Wild West had become the Sunbelt, and the region needed a new myth. Even if *Dallas*'s interiors were shot in Los Angeles and its geographical specificity was blurry enough that it could've just as easily been titled *Tulsa*, the show turned Texas into the home of the modern Western, where, instead of

dying in the town square, the villain NetJets into the sunset after unloading shares in a new company called Enron.

As the show *Dallas* went global, so did the city. High-priced oil and cheap loans attracted more new residents and construction cranes to town. "You could see the difference very quickly," says David Paulsen, a writer, producer, and director for *Dallas*. "If you look at the original *Dallas* title sequence, there's only a handful of buildings downtown. When we changed the intro [in season eight], all these buildings had suddenly gone up."

The word "Dallas" took on a new meaning. "We're the place that killed JFK," said Susan Howard, who played Donna Culver Krebbs. "That stigma remained. And then, suddenly, Texas is where everybody wanted to go. They wanted to see the Cowboys. They wanted to see Southfork. And it was like all that stuff just washed away. It was over, it was gone, and we were forgiven."

As the show entered its later seasons, the TV landscape got crowded with *Dallas* semi-impostors. In response, *Dallas* ratcheted up the eighties camp, delving into outlandish plots about international intrigue and relegating its female characters to lame story arcs. With chances to capitalize on their fame elsewhere, some of the show's stars decided to leave. As often happens to prime-time shows nearing their double-digit birthdays, *Dallas* began to lose millions of viewers.

Four decades later, the Dallas skyline is still filled with cranes. The city of Dallas has since turned from J.R. and Bobby toward other mythical figures, like Mark Cuban and Jerry Jones. But when we watch TV to-day, we're visiting a house that *Dallas* helped build. Back in 1978, it was rare for a show's stories to bleed from one episode to the next, for each season to end with a cliff-hanger, and for scripts to foreground a morally compromised protagonist. Today that's a standard blueprint for prestige television. "You can draw a straight line from J.R. Ewing to Tony Soprano to Walter White," argues Matt Zoller Seitz, the television critic for *New York* magazine, who grew up in Dallas while the show was airing.

In short, for all their resemblance to the cast of *The Bold and the Beautiful*, the Ewings changed Dallas, changed Texas, changed America, and changed the medium of television.

Why McMurtry Matters

By Skip Hollandsworth

IN 1970, WHEN I was a junior-high-school student living in the North Texas city of Wichita Falls, I rode one afternoon with a friend and his older brother to the town of Archer City, twenty-five miles away. There, a movie called *The Last Picture Show*, about some teenagers trying to find happiness in a desolate Texas town, was being filmed by director Peter Bogdanovich. Rumor had it that one of the actresses in the movie, Cybill Shepherd, a young model who was Bogdanovich's girlfriend, was going to be doing a nude scene that day. My friend's older brother told us we had to be there. There was a chance, he said, that we would get to see Cybill Shepherd's breasts.

When we arrived at Archer City, we gathered with other onlookers at the end of a street. We watched as the film crew moved equipment from one building to another. For the next hour, nothing else happened. Cybill Shepherd did not appear. We figured our trip was a waste of time. But just before we headed back to our car, the adults in the crowd began buzzing. One of them pointed at a thin young man quickly crossing the street. He had thick, tousled black hair and he was wearing Buddy Holly–style glasses.

"That's Larry McMurtry!" a woman exclaimed. Seeing the baffled look on the faces of my friends and me, the woman explained that McMurtry was an Archer City rancher's son who had written the novel *The Last Picture Show*, upon which the movie was based. "Hey, Larry!" someone else yelled. McMurtry turned and gave us a brief wave. I had no idea that a writer could be famous.

I went home, came across a worn-out paperback edition of *The Last Picture Show*, and devoured it. I read about Sonny Crawford, a high-school senior who plays football for Thalia High, hangs out at a pool hall, drives a butane gas truck for his boss, Fred Fartley, and obsesses about having sex with girls in town, including his class-mate Charlene Duggs, who kisses him "convulsively, as if she had just swallowed a golf ball and was trying to force it back up." I couldn't believe that someone had written a novel about teenagers just like ones I knew in real life. Nor could I believe that such a book—set in the same plains where I'd grown up, with a character named Fred *Fartley*, of all things— was being praised as a literary masterpiece. "A performance rarely equaled in contemporary fiction," read one critic's quote on the cover of the paperback. Although I had no earthly idea then what good literature was, I knew I had stumbled onto something. The prose was both dramatic and slapstick funny, and the dialogue—pages and pages of it—was curiously riveting in its plainspokenness. I read almost all of it in one sitting.

Months later, I sneaked into a Wichita Falls theater to see the movie, which was rated R and being condemned by local pastors for its obscenity largely due to a skinny-dipping party scene in which Shepherd did indeed disrobe and bare her breasts. Around that time, I heard a rumor that she had left the dashing Bogdanovich for the bespectacled McMurtry.

In my early twenties, I decided to compose my own McMurtry-ian novel about a boy coming of age in Texas. "How hard could it be?" I asked myself, leafing through *The Last Picture Show* for the hundredth time. After learning that McMurtry wrote five double-spaced pages of fiction on his manual typewriter every day of the week, just after breakfast, I vowed that I would do the very same thing before going off to my job as a reporter at a Dallas newspaper. I never got past the second chapter.

IN AMERICAN LETTERS, McMurtry, who died in March 2021 at the age of 84, is something of an icon—winner of both a Pulitzer Prize (for the novel *Lonesome Dove*, about a cattle drive in the 1870s) and an Oscar (for the screenplay to *Brokeback Mountain*, about two sexually conflicted modern-day cowboys). For more than fifty years, he wrote novels—thirty in all, plus fourteen books of nonfiction and more than forty teleplays and screenplays. His storytelling has been compared to that of Charles Dickens and William Faulkner, and even the famously self-absorbed novelist Norman Mailer—himself a winner of two Pulitzers—once confessed his admiration. "He's too good," he said, explaining his resistance to McMurtry's novels. "If I start reading him, I start writing like him."

Nowhere is that writing as fiercely cherished or as deeply felt as in Texas, the setting for the majority of Mc-Murtry's work, and which the author by turns elevated and eviscerated with the kind of marrow-piercing observations only ever allowed native sons. That his voracious curiosity and his ability to spin yarns were forged on the empty flatlands of rural Texas makes either no sense at all or all the sense in the world. He spent his early childhood on a small ranch fifteen miles outside Archer City, where his father had him riding a horse by the age of three and herding cattle at four. There were no books in the house—until a cousin heading off to World War II dropped off nineteen boys' adventure books with such titles as *Sergeant Silk: The Prairie Scout*. After devouring those, young McMurtry bought pulp novels from the paperback rack at Archer City's drugstore. When he was in Fort Worth one weekend for a high-school track meet, he took a city bus downtown just so he could wander through Barber's Book Store. He read *Don Quixote* and *Madame Bovary*. He even leafed through the *Bhagavad Gita*.

Anything he could get his hands on to escape what he called "the drabness of Archer City."

His first novel, 1961's *Horseman, Pass By,* combined two short stories he'd conceived in a creative writing class at North Texas State College (now the University of North Texas), in Denton, just under two hours' drive from Archer City. Set in the fifties, the book tells the story of a noble but financially struggling North Texas rancher named Homer Bannon; his coarse, unscrupulous stepson, Hud; and his earnest teenage grandson, Lonnie. The book opens with a lovely description of the Texas plains in April "after the mesquite leafed out." In a subsequent chapter, Lonnie describes a horseback ride across the high country with his grandfather. "There below us was Texas, green and brown and graying in the sun, spread wide under the clear spread of sky like the opening scene in a big western movie."

At the same time, the novel is starkly unsentimental about rural life as the golden age of ranching is coming to an end. A state veterinarian orders Homer to destroy his herd of cattle over fear of hoof-and-mouth disease; among the cattle he must kill are two old longhorn steers he loves. ("I been keeping 'em to remind me how times was," says Homer.) Hud is a restless, violent man who sexually assaults the family's cook. Driving home one night from a rodeo, Hud accidentally hits Homer, who is crawling, senile, on the side of the road, and Hud decides to put the old man out of his misery with a .22 rifle. At the end of the novel, a disillusioned Lonnie climbs into a cattle truck and heads toward the lights of Wichita Falls.

McMurtry expected *Horseman, Pass By* to sell "maybe a handful of copies and disappear," and, in fact, the novel was hardly a best seller. But shortly after it was published, *New York Times* critic Charles Poore declared McMurtry, then just twenty-five years old, to be "among the most promising first novelists who have appeared this year." Impressed in particular

with McMurtry's descriptions of the "gnarled pastoral side to Texas life," Poore hailed him for offering a new understanding of Texas. "The material he has at his command as a descendant of Texan generations is usable in all kinds of new ways. We say that, obviously, in view of the narrow range in which [Texas] has been exploited so far in our literature. Mostly boots and saddles, or oil rigs and billionaires."

The rights to *Horseman, Pass By* were snapped up by a Hollywood producer, who turned it into the movie *Hud*, a kind of revisionist Western starring Paul Newman. Released in 1963, *Hud* was a critical and commercial success, nominated for seven Academy Awards and winning three. In the meantime, Harper published McMurtry's second novel, *Leaving Cheyenne*, which follows the lives of three more rural North Texans through the first half of the twentieth century. Again, critics were impressed. "If Chaucer were a Texan writing today, and only 27 years old, this is how he would have written and this is how he would have felt," wrote Marshall Sprague in the *New York Times*. Though McMurtry was not yet convinced he could make a living as a writer—he supplemented his income by teaching, first at TCU, then Rice—he decided to write one more novel, and in 1966 he published *The Last Picture Show*. The movie version, released in 1971, won two Oscars after being nominated for eight. Jack Kroll, *Newsweek*'s veteran film critic, went so far as to proclaim *The Last Picture Show* the best American movie since *Citizen Kane*.

That his books translated so well to the screen would, over the next several decades, propel McMurtry to stratospheric fame—especially as he made a seemingly effortless shift from rural to citified subjects, ranchers to socialites. If before his work had caught attention for its unsparing portrayal of the state's agrarian identity, now he was lauded for so easily embracing Texas's emerging modernity. In the 1975 novel *Terms of Endearment*, the protagonist, Aurora Greenway, makes

dramatic pronouncements ("The success of a marriage invariably depends on the woman"), juggles a bevy of suitors (among them, a wealthy oilman who lives in a Lincoln Continental that's parked on the twenty-fourth floor of a parking garage he owns in downtown Houston), and takes care of her daughter, Emma, who over the last sixty pages of the book dies of cancer. The movie version became a blockbuster hit in 1983, receiving eleven Academy Award nominations and winning five. The *New York Times* critic Janet Maslin was so impressed at McMurtry's ability to capture the inner lives of women that she would later seek to credit him as the father of chick lit.

MCMURTRY ATTEMPTED TO distance himself from other Texas writers, including the great J. Frank Dobie, skewering them publicly for ignoring the realities of an evolving state, with its rapidly sprawling suburbs, in favor of nostalgic historical novels. In an essay published in the *Texas Observer* in 1981, McMurtry lambasted these Old West novels for being nothing more than "Country-and-Western literature," overly romanticized stories about honorable cowboys and the joys of the open range. Still, he could not escape the state's own hold on him: even in the narratives set outside Texas, his characters often had to contend with the state in one way or another. In one comic scene in *Somebody's Darling*, two screenwriters, Elmo Buckle and Winfield Gohagen, steal the director's master print in hopes of secreting it away to Texas. "Texas is the ultimate last resort," says Gohagen. "It's always a good idea to go to Texas, if you can't think of anything else to do."

And then McMurtry himself chose to go to Texas in a way no one could have expected. He began writing an old-fashioned Western about a cattle drive. McMurtry saw the Old West not as a romantic frontier but as a shatteringly lonely and often barbaric place, where few people found any happiness at all. Now he set out to prove this, opening his novel with two retired, hard-bitten Texas Rangers in the forlorn border town of Lonesome Dove.

The ex-Rangers, Augustus "Gus" McCrae and Woodrow Call, lead a cattle drive to Montana with a ragtag team of cowpokes, which includes a Black cowboy, a bandit turned cook, a piano player with a hole in his stomach, a young widow, a teenager who is Call's unacknowledged son, and a prostitute. On their journey, the group encounters psychopathic outlaws, vengeful Indians, buffalo hunters, gamblers, scouts, cavalry officers, and backwoodsmen. They endure perilous river crossings, thunderstorms, sandstorms, hailstorms, windstorms, lightning storms, grasshopper storms, stampedes, drought, and a mean bear. There are plenty of shootings and a few impromptu hangings. The prostitute, Lorena, is gang-raped. In the end, after McCrae is mortally wounded by Indians, he asks Call to bury him in a little peach orchard by the Guadalupe River near San Antonio, where he was once in love with a woman. Call dutifully carries his partner's half-mummified body back to Texas.

When *Lonesome Dove* was released, in 1985, it grabbed hold of the public's imagination like no Western of its time, selling nearly 300,000 copies in hardcover and more than a million in paperback. Readers raved over McMurtry's precisely drawn characters, his depictions of place, his ear for frontier idioms, and his action-packed set pieces. They memorized lines of dialogue ("The older the violin, the sweeter the music"; "Ride with an outlaw, die with him"; Call's unforgettable declaration after beating a surly army scout to a pulp in front of shocked onlookers: "I hate rude behavior in a man. I won't tolerate it"). And they reveled in the details, whether about food eaten on the cattle drive (beans laced with chopped rattlesnake) or, say, medical treatment (a cowboy bitten by an angry horse is given axle grease and turpentine

for his wound). For Texans, went one joke, *Lonesome Dove* had become the third-most-important book in publishing history, right behind the Bible and the Warren Commission report.

The book was awarded the Pulitzer the following year, and when it was inevitably adapted for the screen—CBS aired a four-part miniseries in 1989, starring Tommy Lee Jones and Robert Duvall—a staggering 26 million viewers tuned in. Together, the novel and miniseries were arguably more influential in shaping Americans' vision of the Old West than the movies of John Ford.

Decades later, in 2016, when I asked a then eighty-year-old McMurtry about *Lonesome Dove*'s success, he shrugged. "It isn't a masterpiece by any stretch of the imagination," he said. "All I had wanted to do was write a novel that demythologized the West. Instead, it became the chief source of western mythology. Some things you cannot explain."

His fame grew all the more: Annie Leibovitz took his photograph;

universities invited him to lecture. If McMurtry was impressed by all the attention, however, he didn't show it. As a joke—or maybe it wasn't a joke—he sometimes wore a sweatshirt imprinted with the words "Minor Regional Novelist."

Was he right? Perhaps it was true that the next generation of readers, an increasingly diverse swath of globalized and digitized consumers, would know little of McMurtry or his work. But it was also true that McMurtry had forever shaped the way people see Texas, with all of its past, all of its stories, all of its changes. As Mark Busby, a professor of English at Texas State University and a leading McMurtry scholar, told me, "What no one can deny is that McMurtry has made Texas feel very real. His books have taught people that Texas is not just a curious part of the country but an unforgettable piece of the American experience."

I still own that paperback of *The Last Picture Show*. It sits on a bookshelf in my house—a reminder, in some ways, of all the stories there are to tell, and that remain to be told, about Texas.

Essential Texas Books

By Rose Cahalan

SELECTING THE BEST TWENTY books by Texans and about Texas is a little bit like trying to single out the best bluebonnets along a highway in April: an impossible task, as the field teems with too many stellar choices. This wide-ranging list, which spans genres and decades, seeks not to anoint any winners but rather represent the state's diversity of voices. Reading these volumes will expand anyone's understanding of the Lone Star State today.

Amigoland **by Oscar Cásares, 2009.** No one writes about life on the Texas-Mexico border as vividly as Oscar Cásares does. This poignant, melancholy novel centers around two grumpy but tenderhearted old men, brothers who reunite for a road trip into Mexico after years of estrangement.

Big Wonderful Thing **by Stephen Harrigan, 2019.** The adjectives in the title describe not only the state but the book itself. At nearly one thousand pages, and with Harrigan's knack for distilling complicated historical events into clear and compelling personal dramas, *Big Wonderful Thing* comes as close to a single definitive history of Texas as exists.

Blood and Money **by Thomas Thompson, 1976.** A true crime tale for the ages, this story of a high-society murder gets more unbelievable at every turn. It's also essential to understanding Houston's potent mix of oil money and overinflated egos.

Bluebird, Bluebird by **Attica Locke, 2017.** The first volume in Locke's Highway 59 mystery series finds Texas Ranger Darren Mathews investigating two racially charged murders in his East Texas hometown. The sense of place is as thrilling as the tale: you can practically hear the wind whispering through the Spanish moss on the cypress trees.

The Boy Kings of Texas by **Domingo Martinez, 2012.** Too often, writing about the Texas-Mexico border reduces the region to "poverty porn," flattening a wide range of experiences into the same tired tropes about drug violence and immigrants searching for the American dream. Martinez's memoir of childhood in Brownsville explores those subjects too, but they're just part of a more complex story—one that is consistently funny and wry, even as it plumbs the darkness.

Empire of the Summer Moon by **S. C. Gwynne, 2010.** The legendary Comanche chief Quanah Parker comes alive in this vivid, meticulous history of the battle between white settlers and those indigenous to the Texas Panhandle. *Texas Monthly* called it "a tale of radical hope."

Everyone Knows You Go Home **by Natalia Sylvester, 2018.** A family saga set in a Texas border town, this luminous novel recalls the work of Isabel Allende in its use of magical realism and exploration of multigenerational trauma, grief, and resilience.

Friday Night Lights by **H. G. Bissinger, 1990.** The book that spawned a movie and a beloved TV series remains one of the best examples of immersive reporting on small-town life in Texas.

Goodbye to a River by **John Graves, 1960.** Part travelogue, part essay, Graves's masterpiece traces hundreds of years of history and the muddy banks of the Brazos. A poignant ode to the state's vanishing wild places, this tale hits even harder when read through the lens of the climate crisis.

***Homelands* by Alfredo Corchado, 2018.** A longtime journalist who covers Mexico for the *Dallas Morning News*, Corchado complicates the myth of the American dream in this deeply personal reflection on his own immigration story and those of three friends. He blends reporting skills, geopolitical analysis, and intimate memoir in this genre-defying work.

***The House on Mango Street* by Sandra Cisneros, 1984.** This perennial best seller paved the way for a generation of Latina writers to share their stories, and there's a reason it's still taught in classrooms across the country. Cisneros tells a lyrical coming-of-age tale that feels timeless.

***Lonesome Dove* by Larry McMurtry, 1985.** Required reading if you want to understand the Texas myth, *Lonesome Dove* is also one of the greatest platonic love stories ever told; if the decades-long friendship between cowboys Gus and Call doesn't move you to tears, you might be made of stone.

***Lot: Stories* by Bryan Washington, 2019.** Washington's debut is a love letter to Houston that's written in granular detail, teeming with street names—Waugh, Memorial, Washington, Montrose—and vividly centering the experiences of queer, working-class men of color. Perhaps more than any other young author today, Washington captures the complexity of the nation's fourth-largest city.

***Monday, Monday* by Elizabeth Crook, 2014.** The 1966 University of Texas Tower shooting was the country's first mass campus murder; American life was never quite the same after the tragedy. Crook's propulsive novel imagines how that fateful day played out for three students who were there, as well as how it reverberated for the rest of their lives.

***Pale Horse, Pale Rider* by Katherine Anne Porter, 1939.** Based on the author's experience as a survivor of the Spanish flu of 1918, this blistering novella will change your understanding of the coronavirus pandemic. The late, great Texas literary critic Don Graham praised Porter as "the best writer the Lone Star State has produced"; she deserves to be much better known.

***The Son* by Philipp Meyer, 2014.** A sweeping family epic, *The Son* follows three generations of the McCullough family from the mid-1800s, when they clashed with the Comanches, to the near-present day, when oil and gas wealth has transformed their lives. Meyer spent five years researching how Texas settlers and Native Americans lived—once going so far as to drink buffalo blood.

***Texas* by James Michener, 1985.** Spanning 1,400 pages and four centuries, this behemoth of a book is nearly as big as the state itself. But that's kind of the point: Michener's fictionalized history encompasses Texas in all its contradictions, complexities, and larger-than-life characters. Notably, *Texas Monthly* wasn't a fan when the book was first published, awarding Michener a Bum Steer of the Year Award for his "hackneyed" work. Tens of thousands of readers disagreed, as the book promptly sold out its first run of 750,000 copies. It continues to be a popular and polarizing tome.

***Thursday Night Lights* by Michael Hurd, 2017.** Long overdue and compassionately told, this is the story of Black high-school football in Texas during segregation. Since white teams reserved stadiums on Friday nights, Black teams played on Wednesdays and Thursdays—and overcame countless barriers along the way.

Trick Mirror **by Jia Tolentino, 2019.** The sharp, funny, feminist essays in this book draw on the author's youth in suburban Houston. One standout chapter seamlessly interweaves megachurch culture, hallucinogens, and the music of DJ Screw. Tolentino has drawn comparisons to Joan Didion for her edgy blend of journalism and memoir.

With His Pistol in His Hand **by Américo Paredes, 1958.** Using an innovative blend of folklore, journalism, and historical research, Paredes was the first to expose the racist underpinnings of the work of Walter Prescott Webb, dean of Texas history. By doing so, he set an example for the new Texas histories that were to come.

Rewriting History

By John Phillip Santos

FOR SO LONG, IN a distant simpler time, it seemed there was only the one true history of Texas, and everybody knew it. It was veritable scripture for those of us born and raised in San Antonio, where the Alamo, the ageless limestone shrine of Texas liberty, stoically stood at the very center of our city. The hallowed story was like a reboot of the war for American independence, only this time it involved a triumphant Anglo colonist uprising against *Mexicano* tyranny, after which the Texas Republic, and later the state, were established.

We were taught that we were lucky to be born into this noble saga. One elementary-school field trip for a guided tour of the Alamo, followed by a screening of the 1960s John Wayne film of the same name, and we were all in.

I didn't know it then, but my ancestors had come into the story of Texas by very different roads from those the celebrated Anglo settlers had taken. I eventually learned that telling our story required reaching farther back than 1836. San Antonio had been founded in 1718, and the earliest expeditions into the region began in the sixteenth century with the wanderings of Cabeza de Vaca through South Texas. There was no border yet, it was still all one land: one that had been settled by indigenous peoples for thousands of years.

My mother's ancestors were early colonizers of northeastern New Spain, arriving in the 1620s, a hundred years after the conquest of Mexico. Roughly one hundred years later, they were among the founders of the *pueblitos* of Mier, Camargo, and Revilla (known today as Guerrero Viejo) on the southern banks of the Rio Grande. At some time during their centuries-long settlement in those lands, Texas and the border appeared. By the time my mother was born in

1925, the family was living in Laredo, Texas.

My father's family had fled Coahuila in 1914, fearing the upheavals of *la Revolución* in their village of Palaú. As our elders recalled, San Antonio felt familiar, like the larger Coahuilense towns of Múzquiz, Sabinas, Nueva Rosita, and Piedras Negras they left behind. DNA tests of that lineage reveal myriad indigenous, Iberian, and Jewish ancestral sources, the mixed origins of a mixed people, finding their way with everyone else to Texas. My father was born in San Antonio, and the Santos family's story has unfolded from there ever since.

I grew up in the shadows that the Alamo cast across my modern American hometown. Ironically, this scene of legendary defeat for the Anglo insurrection against Mexico became the symbol of their eventual triumph over Mexico. Just in case we should forget, San Antonio's annual spring Fiesta celebrates that victory, yet is deliriously embraced by most of the city's Mexican American community. As a Mexicano Texan, I was nurtured in the conflicted epicenter of this greatest myth of Texas history.

Illustrating just how deep the mythic history of Texas can reach into you, in one of the first studio photographs of me, age four, I appear in full Western regalia—jeans tucked into my boots, bolero hat cocked to one side, two six-shooters strapped to my waist. It's a snapshot from my short-lived, open-carry phase, clearly staking my lot with the triumphant cowboys.

You didn't have to be a scholar of the canonical history of the Lone Star State to be seduced by its audacious sagas, vainglorious martial chronicles, and knee-slapping tall tales. Long-revered Texan myths of the cowboy's fortitude and uprightness, of solitary rugged individualism, of pugnacious and stalwart insurgencies in pursuit of liberty, were like breath itself to us Texas-born. You didn't have to read a single book. With Hollywood films, TV shows, and popular culture this mythic history found its way deep into the bloodstream of the collective American imagination. Texas became the apotheosis of America.

Lionized Texas historians such as Walter Prescott Webb and T. R. Fehrenbach played central roles in proffering these mythic *crónicas*, spinning out with formality and gravitas the preeminence and inevitability of the physical, intellectual, and moral excellence of the Anglo settlers over the savages. Webb saw in the origins of Texas a "conflict of civilizations," which he epitomized in the triangle of "Indian Warrior, Mexican Vaquero, and Texas Ranger."

"Without disparagement," Webb wrote, ". . . it may be said that there is a cruel streak in the Mexican nature, or so the history of Texas would lead one to believe." He wrote that in 1935, just fifteen years after the so-called Hora de Sangre, concluding a decade during which as many as 5,000 Mexican Texans were killed by Anglo mobs in the borderlands, many with the acquiescence or complicity of the Texas Rangers. Webb's observation

on "Mexican nature" used historical scholarship as a way of granting the white Texas colonists impunity for their lashing out at others. There are still lecture series and endowed university chairs named in his honor.

Although we can't change the past, the rewriting of Texas history has been underway for some time. In his 1958 book debut, folklorist Américo Paredes took the first shot at Webb, responding to his observation about a cruel streak in Mexican culture with the reply, "Professor Webb does not mean to be disparaging. One wonders what his opinion might have been when he was in a less scholarly mood and not looking at the Mexican from the objective point of view of the historian."

In the decades since, historians of Mexicano or Tejano Texas, such as Frank de la Teja, David Montejano, Andrés Tijerina, and Monica Muñoz Martinez, among many others, have been especially effective in broadening the narrative of the state's history. By confronting the violent suppression of the Tejanos, these historians also initiated a chronicle of that community's resilience, perseverance, and fortitude.

And they challenge us to seek out other excluded or ignored histories of Texas. As early as 20,000 years ago, archaeological evidence reveals, the first peoples were already migrating and settling, especially along the verdant riverbanks, across the broad landscapes of what would become Texas. We know there was extensive contact among them, with great cultural and linguistic diversity. The very term "Texas" is said to be derived from a Caddo word signifying "friend" or "ally." And ancient Mesoamerican civilizations held stories of how their ancestors migrated from the north to the south, into central Mexico.

These migrations and many more that were to come, voluntary and enslaved, unleashed the murderous clashes between strangers that have shaped the history of Texas. But they also brought about unexpected exchanges and mixtures.

Writing in 2019 about a few recently published works on Texas history, esteemed Texas-born historian Annette Gordon-Reed speaks of three forces—cotton, slavery, and empire—that were integral in forging early Texas yet scantily treated in the once-respected histories. As she writes, ". . . situating the state in 'the West' and not 'the South,' buries huge, defining swaths of Texas history and culture . . . What would Texas literature look like if more of its writers had, over the years, mined this rich but tragic terrain instead of focusing on the blinkered mythology of the cowboy—a mythology that excluded the large numbers of cowboys who were black?"

In addition to the work of these historians of Mexicano/Tejano Texas, books such as Stephen Harrigan's 2019 *Big Wonderful Thing: A History of Texas*, and Doug Swanson's 2020 *Cult of Glory*, a history of the Texas Rangers, are making the state's history ampler and more inclusive.

Meanwhile, by the 1970s, following

decades of migration, San Antonio was once again a majority Mexican American city. By 2004, the state itself became "majority minority." Despite its white supremacist origins, Texas may be the American state that has the most cosmic story to tell about the mixing of races and cultures. Comanche mastery of the horses brought here by the Spanish. The wide adoption of Mexican regalia by many Anglos and Blacks. Tex-Mex *música*, absorbing the accordion into Mexican song tradition. Freddy Fender, aka Baldemar Huerta, dedicating "Wasted Days and Wasted Nights" to his soul partner Sir Doug Sahm. Pastrami tacos. Sushi tacos.

For centuries, Texas was regarded at the edge of Mexico, at the edge of the United States, a frontier place where law and culture barely mattered. But borderlands are also the places where strangers can meet and exchange tools, histories, ideas, music, and food, and by this process become something new. That's the story of Texas becoming Texas.

Houston, Art City

by Rainey Knudson

IN THE HEIGHTS NEIGHBORHOOD of Houston, the artist Bill Davenport runs a longtime, much-loved storefront selling oddball items alongside fantastically inexpensive art by himself and others. The crowded shop is all the more likable and fun if you know that Davenport attended the prestigious Rhode Island School of Design before moving to Houston as a Core fellow at the Museum of Fine Arts, Houston. He cast aside that pedigree, which was grooming him for art-world fanciness, to set up shop in a run-down 1929 building and sell his brilliant trompe l'oeil paintings for a few hundred bucks a pop. He calls his store Bill's Junk.

The mystery of Houston's hold on artists like Davenport can be difficult to pin down. Faced with the city's undeniable homeliness, its lack of cool factor or even an identifiable personality, one hems and haws and falls back on the old cliché: artists like Houston because it feels like a place where they can do whatever they want. At its best, Houston is about freedom. Freedom from dogma, freedom from style, freedom from the weight of history. The rules don't apply here, for better and worse.

Part of that sense of freedom comes from the fact that Houston flies well below the national radar, oddly so for a city of its size. It's not so much that people elsewhere dislike Houston, it's that most of the time Houston doesn't even occur to them—and that is the unlikely source of its attraction for a lot of artists. For art lovers, Houston has all the goods: rich museums with intriguing collections of objects from all over the world; lively nonprofit spaces that hit more often than they miss; a busy gallery scene; and—most crucially—a large and affable community of artists who pursue their work with as much seriousness and grit as they do a sense of play. It adds up to an art city that's something of an art-world secret.

For many years, the artist Tierney Malone has documented Houston's musical roots with an ongoing, nomadic project called the Jazz Church of Houston, placing his own elegant artworks of hand-lettered text alongside ephemera from local musicians in rotating venues. Malone is just one example of Houston artists who, rather than making discrete works of art in a studio, create "social sculpture," ambitious meta-projects that impact their communities. Downtown, Jim Pirtle runs Notsuoh (Houston spelled backward), a bar/gallery/performance venue that is an extension of Pirtle's long history of wildly experimental performance art. In the Fifth Ward, Emily Sloan has a delightful space called Mystic Lyon, which commissions murals, mounts exhibitions of neighborhood artists, and hosts classes in a space humorously titled the Center for Centering.

By far the longest-running and most influential social sculpture in Houston is Project Row Houses. Founded in 1993 by a group of Houston artists in the Third Ward, including MacArthur "genius grant" winner Rick Lowe, and internationally recognized for its inventive reuse of shotgun row houses as contemporary-art galleries, PRH also hosts reading series and festivals and provides affordable housing and mentoring for young mothers.

Artists who buck the establishment are the foundation of any great art scene (think of the Impressionists and their Salon des Refusés), and Houston's legendary twentieth-century art patrons, the late Dominique and John de Menil, knew this well. The Menils were famously friends with artists, and they built one of the most unconventional and visionary collections of art in the world. The Menil Collection opened in 1987 and was designed by the architect Renzo Piano (another example of the de Menil's vision). The building still represents arguably Piano's finest work: seamlessly integrated into a Montrose neighborhood of 1920s bungalow houses, the Menil Collection's cypress siding and interior dogtrot hallways invoke southern architecture without satirizing it. Over the years the Menil campus has grown to include several other buildings, most recently a lavish Drawing Institute devoted to the medium. Nearby, the celebrated Rothko Chapel, also commissioned by the de Menils, underwent a restoration in 2020, with fresh plaster walls and a new skylight to show off its permanent installation of fourteen somber, monochromatic paintings by Mark Rothko.

Though the Menil still enjoys the widest reputation for a Houston museum, the Museum of Fine Arts Houston has more recently become the more daring institution, especially since the 2020 opening of its Kinder Building, which houses its impressive collections of modern and contemporary art. The MFAH can also claim the title of second-largest museum in the United States in terms of square footage and endowment size (behind New York's Metropolitan Museum of Art). Exuberantly defying outworn conventions of "tasteful" museum display, the curators responsible for the Kinder's inaugural exhibitions packed the galleries with objects from the collection not seen in years (including over a dozen paintings from the MFAH's holdings of Brazilian abstract art, a weird bird painting by René Magritte, and a 1972 "Flying Carpet" chair by Ettore Sottsass). Best of all, works by a wide and diverse group of Houston artists were included without comment throughout the galleries, not shunted aside in an all-Texas ghetto. The MFAH was already a powerhouse museum, but with the addition of the Kinder Building, it became a national force.

Catty-corner from the MFAH, in a distinctive 1972 metal building, the Contemporary Arts Museum Houston has presented legendary shows of contemporary artists for many decades, but in recent years it has gotten a run for its money from a trio of university spaces (the Blaffer Art Museum at the University of Houston, the University Museum at Texas Southern University, and the Moody Center for the Arts at Rice University) as well as the Houston Museum of African American Culture, which opened in 2012. The renowned and ramshackle Orange Show Center for Visionary Art is yet another pillar of the scene, thanks among other things to its hosting the massive annual Art Car parade, easily the largest single art event in Houston. The parade itself began in the early 1980s, when art students at the University of Houston used cars to make mobile sculptures, playfully celebrating the almighty automobile while poking fun at the notion of art as a holy relic to be set on a pedestal.

Yet for the survival of many Houston artists, it's the commercial galleries that matter most. The city has a surprisingly large group of dedicated galleries, some of which, like the Texas, Moody, McClain, Sicardi, Inman, and Devin Borden galleries (to name a few), have been selling art for decades. It is not an easy business, but galleries survive through boom and bust thanks in part to a large base of collectors in Houston. Because along with freedom, you need money for a great art scene. And Houston certainly has money.

It's not just any money. The pragmatic nature of the city's dominant energy business makes for a pragmatic culture. There's an impatience here, a lack of fussbudgeting, a willingness to skirt the rules of tasteful urban planning that has allowed this strange, flat, swampy expanse to sprout clusters of skyscrapers. Houston is a city whose very existence is an act of will: it's a port city, but only because we dredged a ship channel fifty miles inland from the Gulf of Mexico. That willfulness manifests itself in the most underrated and exciting art scene in the country. Outsiders may hear about Houston mostly in the context of natural disasters or, if you're really paying attention, the phenomenal food culture. But the Houston art scene, like Houston itself, has its own rough magic. Long may it live.

ALL THE UNDERRATED
ART TOWNS

By Rose Cahalan

AS HOUSTON HAS quietly amassed its worldly collections and Austin and Marfa have basked in creative-class stardom thanks to their outsize national media profiles, two of Texas's less conventionally buzzy cities have stirred up the art world with unexpected museum and gallery scenes.

FORT WORTH

FORGET THE WEARY stereotype that Fort Worth is all about cowboys. In the vibrant cultural district west of downtown, you can walk to no fewer than six major museums, three of which house world-class art. The Modern's five glass pavilions appear to float atop a reflecting pool; walk inside and discover some three thousand works, including by Picasso, Warhol, and Pollock. At the Amon Carter, which was beautifully renovated in 2019, Frederic Remington's nostalgic paintings of the Old West share space with stark shots from contemporary photographers. And around the corner, the Kimbell has a small but mighty collection that spans the globe, from Michelangelo's first-known painting to Japanese ceramics and West African sculptures.

SAN ANTONIO

SAN ANTONIO HAS always punched above its weight art-wise, with a diverse art community more focused on creative freedom than on winning awards. The world finally took notice in 2019, when Ruby City opened. The idea for this striking red building came to the late Linda Pace, of the Pace salsa fortune, in a dream; it's since been named to *Time*'s list of the World's 100 Greatest Places. With an eclectic, growing contemporary collection, it's a must-see. So are the McNay Art Museum, set on the sprawling grounds of a Spanish colonial-style mansion; the San Antonio Museum of Art, which houses one of the nation's largest Latin American collections in a repurposed brewery; and the Briscoe Western Art Museum, where you can marvel at Pancho Villa's saddle. A thriving creative community centers around the galleries of the historic Southtown neighborhood.

Long Live the Honky-Tonk

By Christian Wallace

THERE WAS A TIME, not so long ago—after World War II but before Willie moved to Austin—that most Texans would have shared a common, if working, definition of "honky-tonk." But nowadays, many seem to have the wrong idea about what qualifies. Part of what makes the term so tricky to nail down is the fact that there are certain ineffable qualities that a true honky-tonk must possess. Some historic venues lose it over time, and some brand-new joints have it from day one.

A honky-tonk, for one thing, is not a dance hall. Many of Texas's most beloved dance halls were built by German and Czech settlers in the second half of the nineteenth century. They are often beautiful structures, originally constructed to host social clubs and other family-friendly affairs. Honky-tonks, by contrast, tend to have roots as shallow as tumbleweeds'. Few can trace their history back more than a few decades. The ceilings are low, the walls cinder block and windowless, the lighting neon. A honky-tonk is also not a restaurant. The fare is typically limited to the kind you'd find at a Little League concession stand: Frito pie, nachos, nuts, and various fried or pickled items. These are not places to take small children.

While groups like Texas Dance Hall Preservation have taken steps to save the state's handsome dance halls, the dingy honky-tonk hasn't inspired the same kind of conservation effort. As a result, the honky-tonk is now endangered. This is a shame, because honky-tonks serve an important role in their communities: they are places where a person can unspool a troubled mind, pursue or nurture romance, drown their sorrows, or shake their limbs to a country song. Those that remain—my favorites are listed below—are mostly welcoming places. So long as you don't get too out of line or come in proselytizing for veganism.

ARKEY BLUE'S SILVER DOLLAR, BANDERA

To enter this honky-tonk heaven established in 1968, you must go down. Down a wooden staircase behind a red metal door on the main street of Bandera, down into the cool darkness beneath the town's general store. A local woman will greet you at the bottom of the stairs. You'll give her $5 (if it's a Saturday night) and she'll hand you a ticket to this neon kingdom.

Your eyes will need a moment to adjust to the dim light, at which point you'll take in your surroundings: The ceiling is low and made of red pressed tin. There's a small stage to your right, and the bar beckons at the far end of the room. The air smells of popcorn, beer, and tobacco. The dance floor is blanketed with sawdust. Arkey Juenke, the owner, was a young songwriter and guitar picker when a record producer took to calling him Blue, because of his tendency to write and sing sad songs. The name stuck. Arkey opened the Silver Dollar in 1968, and ever since Arkey Blue and the Blue Cowboys have been playing tear-in-your-beer tunes every Saturday night.

LONESOME ROSE, SAN ANTONIO

Although it bills itself as "the oldest honky-tonk on the St. Mary's Strip," the Lonesome Rose has been open only since 2018. Despite its relative infancy, the Rose feels like a classic honky-tonk, albeit with a few modern touches. There's Texas craft beer, for instance, but there's also a jukebox impeccably stocked with vinyl 45s. Local musician Garrett T. Capps handles the booking, and under his curation, the bar has hosted a range of acts, from honky-tonk traditionalist Weldon Henson to San Antonio conjunto legend Santiago Jiménez Jr. It's the San Antonio vibe that really sets the Lonesome Rose apart. One Saturday night, a handful of dancing couples glided in front of the stage while a mirror ball not much bigger than a grapefruit spun above them, and the lead singer of the 501's slipped references to the Spurs into a Tim McGraw cover as the ace accordion player added a layer of conjunto to the country sound. When the band launched into the Texas Tornados' "Guacamole," whoops of "¡Órale!" went up from the tattooed crowd.

TEXAS ROSE BAR, LA FERIA

Afternoon in a good honky-tonk can be as fine a time as a Saturday night, though for inverse reasons. A stillness settles over the bar like a saddle blanket. The jukebox plays softly, pool shooters circle their felt battlegrounds with quiet contemplation, and conversation, when it comes, flows in slow, easy currents. If you've ever stepped inside the Texas Rose at midday, you know what I mean. Situated about a mile off the interstate on a quiet road between La Feria and Harlingen, the Rose is one of the last watering holes on what was once a bustling strip of them. Railroad tracks and a grazing pasture sit across the street, and there's a caliche-pad RV park to the rear. Inside, tabs are kept by hand on slips of paper next to the register. Beer is fished out of a cooler. White wine is poured over ice into plastic cups. While I was hanging out one Saturday afternoon, a local picker with a Walt Whitman beard sat onstage playing a tobacco-stained guitar. His sneakers were kicked off to the side, and he worked his guitar pedals in white-socked feet, singing "Make the World Go Away," which is exactly what you're aiming to do in a honky-tonk at three p.m.

NEON BOOTS DANCEHALL & SALOON, HOUSTON

Neon Boots Dancehall & Saloon is a welcome sight amid the industrial sprawl on Houston's northwest side. The building has been a mainstay of this part of town since 1955, when it opened as the Esquire Ballroom and went on to host dozens of legendary honky-tonk acts in addition to being Willie Nelson's place of employment in his early songwriting days (he composed "Night Life" about working at the bar). The Esquire closed for good in 1995, and the building hosted a string of short-lived ventures (boxing venue, quinceañera hall) before six Houstonians stepped in to give it a new life as the state's largest LGBTQ country bar, in 2013. Today Neon Boots represents the future of southern music: H-Town rapper Megan Thee Stallion held an album release party here and rode in on a literal white horse. Such soirees may push the boundaries of what is accepted by purists, but this joint is no stranger to transgressive acts. Decades ago, the Esquire was among the first country bars to host African American country crooner Charley Pride.

TEXAS STAGECOACH SALOON, EL PASO

When this small stone bar was built on El Paso's northeast side some forty years ago, it was called the Connection. Later it was known as the Outpost; after that, the White Stallion; and since 2012, the Texas Stagecoach Saloon. No matter, it has always been a honky-tonk. Thanks to its proximity to Fort Bliss, many of its habitués are GIs, a fact that is reflected in the decor. Flags from the 1st Cavalry and 82nd Airborne Divisions hang on the wall. Dollars dangle from the ceiling like suspended confetti, and some of the names scrawled on the bills belong to servicemen and -women who didn't make it home.

DEVIL'S BACKBONE TAVERN, FISCHER

The Devil's Backbone Tavern sits atop one of the most beautiful vistas in Texas. At nearly 1,300 feet, the hill it's perched on offers a clear view of the zigzagging limestone ridge that gave the bar its name. Native Americans once camped on the hilltop, no doubt admiring the rugged terrain below. The handsome stone building that now houses the tavern was built in the thirties to serve parched souls traveling between then-dry Hays County and its wet neighbor Comal. Eight decades later, it continues to offer bibulous locals and wayward pilgrims a chance to relax, wet the whistle, and listen to music—or some ghost stories. The tavern and the entire rocky outcrop it sits upon are rumored to be haunted.

BROKEN SPOKE, AUSTIN

When it comes to great honky-tonks, Austin's mug runneth over. But the granddaddy of them all is the Broken Spoke, considered by many to be the greatest in Texas. It's a miracle the place has survived. Austin has radically changed since James and Annetta White opened the doors, in 1964. No longer does the joint sit alone on the far edge of town. The wide-open field that once surrounded it is now covered in hulking apartment buildings.

Yet the squat, red structure stands proudly and preposterously out of time. Inside the Spoke, hardly a thing has changed in fifty-five years. The speckled ceiling tiles still hang so low that a tall cowboy has to doff his hat. Chicken-fried steak is still served with steaming white gravy. And twirling couples still waltz, shuffle, and polka on the polished-concrete dance floor.

Essential Texas Songs

By Andy Langer

AMERICAN MUSIC CAME FROM Texas. Not in 1776, when Texas was still ruled by a Spanish king and run by the Comanche. But as America developed its own culture, and as blues and swing and rock and roll and conjunto came into being, Texas musicians had more to do with our national music than anyone else. There is no one place in human history that has resulted in so much great music.

Part of this is because of geography, part is because of historical accident. Anglos from Tennessee, Mestizos from Mexico, Czechs from the Old Country, Cajuns from Louisiana, and African Americans, brought as slaves, from the South, mixing, marrying, learning one another's songs, changing them up. Hispanics transforming the polka. Anglos studying the blues. African Americans picking up the fiddle. That's the history.

But one's only hope of knowing Texas music begins with respecting its past as well as reveling in its present. Here's the rub: both then and now are too big, too broad, too significant to hope to properly make an even remotely definitive list, let alone rank 'em. So what follows isn't a list of the "best" Texas songs, whatever that means. Nor the "most important" or "most influential." But if you want to understand Texas—the real Texas, the full picture—these thirty-six songs from Texas artists past and present are a great sampling of the breadth and depth of Texas music. Start here and venture forth. There's a lot to explore.

"Dark Was the Night, Cold Was the Ground," Blind Willie Johnson, 1928. The groundbreaking Pendleton-born singer, guitarist, and evangelist recorded thirty songs between 1927 and 1930, among them the definitive takes on the call-and-response classic "John the Revelator" and this nineteenth-century crucifixion hymn, an instantly unsettling fusion of guttural moans and bottleneck guitar.

"New San Antonio Rose," Bob Wills and His Texas Playboys, 1940. Though it's still a honky-tonk standard today, the King of Western Swing's all-time best seller was in its day a controversial outlier: the song is entirely free of pedal steel and fiddle and hinges instead on saxophones and trumpets. What looked like a concession to big-band pop of the day was a Trojan Horse: it wound up making Wills (and his music with fiddles on it) internationally famous.

"That'll Be the Day," Buddy Holly and the Crickets, 1957. A punchy and letter-perfect merging of swagger and invention. These two minutes changed rock and roll forever.

"Lonely Woman," Ornette Coleman, 1959. The Fort Worth titan titled his 1959 album *The Shape of Jazz to Come*, but it's not bravado if you can back it up. The album is a cornerstone of the avant-garde canon, and this opening number—a melodically lush meditation on solitude—is widely recognized as a legitimate standard.

"Only the Lonely (Know the Way I Feel)," Roy Orbison, 1960. A sad song for sure, but it's sung like the legend-making triumph it would become: it was the first of many memorable hits for the Vernon singer and marked the arrival of his glorious, downright singular, near-operatic range. Also unforgettable: the big finish.

"Waltz Across Texas," Ernest Tubb and His Texas Troubadours, 1965. It's probably intentionally unclear whether Tubb's love for Texas or for the young lady with whom he'd like to waltz across it was stronger, but there's plenty of time left to venture a guess: to this day, darken the doorway of any real Texas dance hall and you're still likely to hear this song at least twice, one from the band, once from the jukebox.

"You're Gonna Miss Me," 13th Floor Elevators, 1966. Opening with the one-two of a sputtering electric jug and front man Roky Erickson's exquisite scream, this unapologetically raw but super-trippy debut single from these Austin-based pioneers stands as an early—and enduring—blueprint for psychedelic music.

"Tighten Up," Archie Bell & the Drells, 1968. A 2004 *Texas Monthly* accounting of the 100 best Texas songs asked, "Has there ever been a greater party record?" Nope. Its legendary bass line, syncopated guitar riff, and Bell's immortal intro ("Hi, everybody! I'm Archie Bell and the Drells, of Houston, Texas . . . We just thought of a new dance called the Tighten Up")

never get old. This scorcher from 1968 is still the king.

"Me and Bobby McGee," Janis Joplin, 1971. A Texas twofer: Port Arthur's Janis sings Brownsville's Kristofferson. Her extraordinary vocal control and phrasing made this an instant classic, though tragically she didn't live long enough to see its release.

"Pancho and Lefty," Townes Van Zandt, 1972. Thanks largely to Willie and Merle's 1983 version, this betrayal ballad first released in 1972 is the uber-influential Fort Worth troubadour's best-known song. Line for line, the narrative is so richly rendered ("The dust that Pancho bit down south / Ended up in Lefty's mouth") it alone would've made Townes one of the tiny handful of modern singer-songwriters who actually deserved being called a poet.

"La Grange," ZZ Top, 1973. This raucous ode to a house of ill repute from the Little Ol' Band from Texas isn't just the consummate example of a perfect meld of blues and boogie, it also might be the most intrinsically Texas-sounding recording on this list. Have mercy!

"Desperados Waiting for a Train," Guy Clark, 1975. Before Clark cut it himself for his 1975 debut, Jerry Jeff Walker featured a version on his legendary *¡Viva Terlingua!* album. Later, the Highwaymen would release their take as a single. But Clark's already weathered and weary voice perfectly suits this meticulously detailed account of an elderly Texas wildcatter's mentorship.

"Mammas Don't Let Your Babies Grow Up to Be Cowboys," Waylon Jennings and Willie Nelson, 1978. This entire list could be three words long, "See: Willie Nelson." With that understood, this number is here just for fun and because Waylon is on it too. And while the pair didn't write it, they crawled inside every line, made it their own, and rode it to the top of the country charts.

"Amarillo by Morning," George Strait, 1982. Country music's most consistent hitmaker has forty-four number one singles, and this rodeo ballad isn't one of them. It's one of his signature songs anyway, maybe because it's one of his most authentic vocal deliveries. Every weary breath and delicately twanged-out annunciation conscientiously serves the cowboy's story.

"Pride and Joy," Stevie Ray Vaughan and Double Trouble, 1983. This chunky Texas shuffle— the first single from Stevie Ray's first album—single-handedly revitalized the blues. Its dazzling and dizzying solo section, rendered even more jaw-dropping on the first of the artist's two *Austin City Limits* appearances, is still one of the best how'd-he-do-that moments in modern music.

"True Love Will Find You in the End," Daniel Johnston, 1984. This two-minute slab of wobbly and deceptively simple-sounding outsider genius originally appeared on a 1984 edition of the hand-made *cassette tape series* Johnston handed out to friends and strangers across Austin. There's a nominally slicker 1990 rerecording—and Beck and Wilco have also recorded terrific versions of the song—but for the real gut punch, stream the original.

"Ay Te Dejo en San Antonio," Flaco Jiménez, 1986. Conjunto Tejano was forged in South Texas at the end of the nineteenth century, so there's nearly a century's worth of stylistic history baked into this zesty ranchera. Originally written and performed by conjunto pioneer Don Santiago Jiménez, this souped-up 1986 version from his legendary accordionist son helped Flaco win a long overdue Grammy for Best Mexican-American Performance.

"If I Had a Boat," Lyle Lovett, 1987. Although "That's Right (You're Not from Texas)" might be the more obvious choice, this early-career, deftly spun fantasy about putting a pony on a boat went a long way toward putting Lovett's name into every conversation about Texas's finest all-time singer-songwriters.

"(Hey Baby) Que Paso?" Texas Tornados, 1990. This accordion-drenched sing-along cemented the Tornados's (Flaco Jiménez, Augie Meyers, Freddy Fender, and Doug Sahm) standing as the Tex-Mex Traveling Wilburys, or, more to the point, Texas's most important supergroup ever.

"Mind Playing Tricks on Me," Geto Boys, 1991. Once described by NPR as "the first vulnerable gangsta rap song," this highly quotable paranoia anthem details a series of hallucinatory visions triggered by post-traumatic stress. It's a landmark document not just for Houston's Fifth Ward or Texas hip-hop, but for rap itself; it was a permission slip for subsequent generations of artists to talk openly about their feelings.

"Como La Flor," Selena, 1992. Selena's first real hit in the United States, this gorgeous ballad about love and loss—and more specifically, a particularly dramatic and dynamic performance of it at her final televised concert—has been inextricably woven into the narrative of her tragic death.

"Walk," Pantera, 1992. Unrelentlessly bombastic and unapologetically antagonistic, this is the signature song from the Metroplex's biggest metal export ever. It's never been played in a yoga studio.

"Merry Christmas from the Family," Robert Earl Keen, 1994. "Mom got drunk and Dad got drunk." While Willie's *Pretty Paper* may be Texas's best Christmas album ever, this goofy tale of a dysfunctional margarita-swigging family Christmas is line for line the most inherently, unmistakably Texas Christmas song of all time.

"June 27th," DJ Screw, 1996. This snapshot of Houston's still-burgeoning underground rap scene was released as a thirty-five-minute mixtape titled *Chapter 012: June 27th*. It stands today as the seminal example of "chopped and screwed"—the slowed-to-a-crawl remix technique that the late DJ Screw is credited with inventing. June 27 is still widely celebrated as an unofficial holiday in Houston.

"Tyrone," Erykah Badu, 1997. Dallas's Badu—an early architect of R&B's "neo-soul" movement—released this not-so-gentle breakup song on her double-platinum *Live*. A clever punchline—instructing her lover to call his pal Tyrone to help him pack up his stuff and go—is enveloped by a slinky funk/jazz fusion. If true, her claim years later that the performance was "totally freestyle" makes it even more amazing.

"Goodbye Earl," The Chicks, 1999. Before the country music establishment betrayed them, the then-named Dixie Chicks were testing the form's boundaries. On what was both a surprise radio hit and a source of controversy, the band drizzled pop sheen over a traditional bluegrass murder ballad. Earl had to die, but at its core, it's a tale of two women who most definitely have each other's backs.

"Your Hand in Mine," Explosions in the Sky, 2003. These Austinites became what *Texas Monthly* once called "Texas's most subliminally recognizable export," thanks to this tune from *Friday Night Lights*, a gorgeous, evocative, and sprawling instrumental that definitively answered the question, "What might West Texas sound like?"

"I Turn My Camera On," Spoon, 2005. Since 1996, the beloved Austin rockers have put out a new album every two years or so, allowing them in 2019 to distill the best into one of the tautest, most filler-free greatest hits records in Texas music history. Spoon's sound has always been indefinable but instantly identifiable, but

if you still need an introduction, this snappy, tightly wound anthem is as good as any.

"Int'l Players Anthem (I Choose You)," UGK featuring Outkast, 2007. A big part of Houston's Underground Kingz (Bun B and Pimp C) legacy might be how well they played with others; they traded verses with Jay-Z on his "Big Pimpin'" and followed it up by sharing the spotlight on what's now widely regarded as the Best Texas Rap Song Ever with Outkast's André 3000 and Big Boi. All four verses of this paean to hustling are legendary, and every rap fan has a favorite, but to Texans it's pretty easy to narrow it down to two.

"Merry Go 'Round," Kacey Musgraves, 2012. This super-relatable debut single paints a bleak portrait of small-town Texas life (a subject Musgraves knows intimately, as a product of tiny Golden) but employs a light touch; there are splashes of cleverness around every corner, most memorably, "Mama's hooked on Mary Kay / Brother's hooked on Mary Jane / Daddy's hooked on Mary, two doors down."

"Coming Home," Leon Bridges, 2015. The debut single that made this supple-voiced Fort Worth soul singer an overnight sensation was designed to sound timeless, with its shamelessly Motown-modeled production. But it also surprises, with one of modern R&B's most Dylan-esque lyrics: "The world leaves a bitter taste in my mouth, girl / You're the only one that I want."

"Formation," Beyoncé, 2016. A funky outcry of pride and protest, this track launched a national conversation because it's about so many things at once: among them, Black positivity, southern resilience, and Black femininity. It's also about Black migration and the Knowles family's journey: "My daddy Alabama, Momma Louisiana, You mix that negro with that Creole make a Texas bama."

"Masseduction," St. Vincent, 2017. Sultry, rocking, and innovative, Dallas native Annie Clark is too experimental, too artistically restless, for two songs, let alone albums, to sound alike. This one sounds like Prince in all the right ways.

"Sicko Mode," Travis Scott, 2018. Basically a half dozen songs in one, this herky-jerky pastiche of disparate tempos and beats is held together by Scott's finesse for delivering perfect phrasing and cadence. In addition to cementing Scott's place in the pantheon of hip-hop greats, it helped keep current Houston's reputation for upending the genre.

"This Land," Gary Clark Jr., 2019. Not content to be this generation's anointed blues savior/guitar hero, Clark released this statement piece about racism in America at the height of the Trump era. The music is funky and incendiary, the lyrics brimming with defiance and condemnation. His declaration at the end of each chorus that "I'm America's son, this is where I come from" is chilling.

"Savage Remix," Megan Thee Stallion (featuring Beyoncé), 2020. You've probably got a favorite line from "Savage," but ours is when Beyoncé declares "Texas up in this thang," as

if there were any mistaking that either half of this icon/upstart Dream Team could be from anywhere but Houston. It's plucky and unflinching, breezes by, and yet is probably more than we deserve. Classy, bougie, ratchet? For sure.

The Sound of Humanity

By Michael Hall

WHEN NASA LAUNCHED TWO Voyager spaceships back in the summer of 1977, each carried a message in a bottle to the stars: a phonograph record, made of copper and plated in gold, created to last forever. The record offered an audible and visual slide show of all things earthly: words (greetings in fifty-five languages), sounds (a train, a kiss, a barking dog), pictures (mountains, dolphins, sprinters), and ninety minutes of music. There were panpipes from Peru, bagpipes from Bulgaria, and drums from Senegal. And at the very end, summing up the power and the pathos of humankind, were two singular pieces of music by two singular men who couldn't have been more different. One was a deaf German whose song was recorded by a string quartet in a professional studio. The other was a blind Texan who played his song on a cheap guitar in a Dallas hotel room. The German was Ludwig van Beethoven, and he closes the album, befitting his reputation as the greatest composer ever.

Leading into his work was a song recorded and played by a twentieth-century Texas street musician, Blind Willie Johnson. "Dark Was the Night, Cold Was the Ground" was a largely wordless hymn recorded in 1927 and built around the yearning cries of Johnson's slide guitar and the moans and melodies of his voice. The two musical elements track each other, finishing each other's phrases; Johnson hums fragments of the melody, then answers with the fluttering sighs of steel or glass moving over the strings. There's no meter or rhythm. In fact,

"Dark Was the Night" sounds less like a song than a scene—the passion of Jesus, his suffering on the cross, the ultimate pairing of despair and belief. Occasionally Johnson's slide clicks against the neck of the guitar, and you remember that this was a man playing a song in front of a microphone. You can hear the air in the room. You can hear the longing in his voice. This is what it sounds like to be a human being.

This recording made by this particular human being—as well as the other twenty-nine Johnson made in his life—would change American music over the next century, especially that made by young men with guitars, from Black blues players such as Elmore James, Mance Lipscomb, and Muddy Waters to white guys including Duane Allman, Eric Clapton, and Jimmy Page. Johnson's music would be dissected and played by scores of musicians, including Bob Dylan, Bruce Springsteen, and Jack White, all of whom tried to revive the emotion he brought to life in his singing and playing—the *feel*. Where, they wondered, did it come from?

Johnson is believed to have been born in tiny Pendleton, just north of Temple, on January 25, 1897, to Dock and Mary Johnson and grew up in Temple and Marlin, thirty-five miles to the north and east. Blinded at a young age (according to one story, an angry stepmother threw lye in his face at age seven), he did what a lot of young blind men did to earn a living: he became a musician. Poor, blind, Black, and living in rural Central Texas—where African Americans were treated as second-class citizens—he got very good at his trade.

Johnson played the streets of Marlin, with its genteel mineral baths and grimy brothels, but he also performed at local churches. He'd head to nearby Hearne on Saturday afternoons, when the cotton farmers and their families came to town to socialize and buy provisions. "He'd get on the street and sing and pick the guitar and they would listen and would give him money," remembered a preacher.

"Every Saturday, he wouldn't hardly miss." Johnson had a tin cup tied to the neck of his guitar with some wire. The preacher remembered days when Johnson would play on one corner and Blind Lemon Jefferson (from nearby Coutchman) on another. This part of the Texas cotton belt produced many great musicians, most of whom played blues. (The cotton-picking areas of West Texas produced country and swing players). Jefferson was a bluesman, and he played songs about drinking, dancing, and "That Black Snake Moan."

Not Johnson. He sang spirituals, songs about the love of Jesus and the hope of salvation but also the wrath of God; Johnson believed in the fire and brimstone. He sang in two voices—one clear and high, the other deep and raspy, the better to get attention and rise above the street din. He occasionally sang a topical or "message" song—but no blues.

Johnson began venturing further east to towns such as Brenham and Navasota. Songster Mance Lipscomb said in his oral autobiography, *I Say Me for a Parable,* that he saw Johnson play in front of Tex's Radio Shop in Navasota in the late teens. "He just had people from here to the highway. Just hundreds of people standing right on the streets, white and Black. Old colored folks and young ones as well. Listenin' at his voice."

Johnson loved to play the streets, singing his songs of faith and feeding off the energy of the listeners. He spent the next twenty years going from town to town, corner to corner, church to church, revival to revival. Occasionally he'd alight for a while—Marlin, Temple, Houston (in the red-light district of that city's Fourth Ward), Galveston, Corpus Christi. He married three times, had a daughter, and recorded thirty enduring songs. Some were older tunes, including "Dark Was the Night" and "Let Your Light Shine on Me." Some he wrote, like "Soul of a Man" and "Motherless Children." He played slide guitar on some and strummed on others. He used both of his voices, the clear tenor and the rough street voice. In a photo taken from one of his late-twenties recording sessions (the only one we know of), he's straight backed and well dressed, wearing a coat and tie and sitting at a piano bench. His eyes are closed and he's lost in the music.

Johnson eventually made it to Beaumont with his third wife. He lived at the House of Prayer and kept playing his music on vibrant Forsythe Street and at churches, including Mount Olive Baptist. One witness later remembered him as "a tall, heavy man, not dark in color; a dignified man and a magnificent singer." He died on September 18, 1945; his death certificate said the cause was malarial fever.

Johnson's raw, potent music reflected the life he lived as well as the lives of the people who gathered to hear him sing and play. It came from the very ground they stood on. And while many Texas music greats have monuments to their lives erected in the earth—Stevie Ray Vaughan and

Willie Nelson have inspired statues in Austin; Jim Reeves has one just outside of Carthage and Lightnin' Hopkins one in Crockett—Johnson has nothing of the sort. But his music is being honored billions of miles away, rushing through the heavens, ready to show the universe what kind of creatures we really are.

Willie and Me

By Doyin Oyeniyi

OVER THE TWENTY-TWO YEARS I've lived in Texas, I've only, until recently, heard snatches of song titles and lyrics by Willie Nelson. It's not that I didn't think Nelson was a good musician; I just didn't think about him, mostly because country music wasn't my thing.

There was one exception: Dolly Parton. Her 1994 album *Heartsongs: Live from Home* was a staple of my childhood in New Jersey and Dallas. It was also an outlier in my parents' collection of Nigerian artists, gospel music from across the Black diaspora, and the collected works of Bob Marley and Michael Jackson. *Heartsongs* was such a fixture in my childhood that, to this day, if I start to sing the first line of "In the Pines" around my siblings, at least one of them will join in.

I'd always assumed that someone had given the Parton album to my parents when we immigrated from Nigeria in 1996, as a kind of "Welcome to America" primer, and that, not finding it too objectionable, they'd put it in our musical rotation. But then, listening to the 2019 *Dolly Parton's America* podcast, I learned more about the Black origins of country music; one guest even made the case that Parton created "immigrant music." The show made me more curious about how *Heartsongs* made it into our lives. In February, my mom came to visit me in Austin, and one night she left her phone in my room blasting country music on Spotify. Turns out that my mom has loved country music since her teenage years in Nigeria, and she's the one who added *Heartsongs* to our family collection.

A couple months later, when my mom was back home in Mesquite, I texted her to ask why she loved country music. She explained that she found it relatable and loved the distinct voices of musicians like Parton, Don Williams, and Willie Nelson. When I called her to hear more, we talked for over two hours. I got to hear about how my teenage mother would dance to pop music at parties but gravitated toward country music in quiet moments of solitude. Our conversation moved to the Nigeria of her youth, which had a sense of safety and freedom she still misses, and my parents' lives before they were my parents.

Country music has always been personal for my mom. When artists like Nelson sing about their lives, loves, and losses, my mother has seen herself in their lyrics. Nelson has been through his fair share of trials and tribulations, and so has my mother. It's what makes his music relevant to her. As she explained with a Nelson lyric (from "Shotgun Willie"), "You can't make a record if you ain't got nothing to say."

After we got off the phone, I played the two Willie Nelson songs that my mom told me were her favorites: "Mammas Don't Let Your Babies Grow Up to Be Cowboys" and "On the Road Again." To be honest, I only half listened to "Mammas," but I was a few bars into "On the Road Again" when the lyrics caught my attention. It was April 16, 2020, just over a month since I'd started social distancing. I had been looking forward to so many things that year, but now there would be no flights to LA or New York to visit my favorite Texpats, no road trips with friends for concerts, no large celebration for my sister's graduation from UT. Up until that moment, I had barely allowed myself to acknowledge these pandemic losses, let alone mourn them. I began to cry.

I'd long avoided country music (except for Parton) because it didn't seem like it was for me. From the outside looking in, the genre seems dominated by white men glorifying a kind of cowboy culture that has all but erased the Black cowboys and musicians who made country what it is. Listening to

"Shotgun Willie," in which Nelson makes a casual joke about somebody profiting by selling sheets to the Ku Klux Klan, certainly didn't help that. There's still a long way to go to make country music more inclusive. But my mom had always just heard the lyrics that resonated with her.

You've got to live a lot of life to make 143 albums, good and bad. Getting a bit more familiar with Nelson has made me think more critically about what I know about Texas, country music, and the role of Black Americans in both. I also marvel that this eighty-seven-year-old country star has helped me feel a lot closer to my mother.

A FEW MORE WORDS ABOUT WILLIE

By David Courtney

DEVOTION TO WILLIE Nelson is a trait, like pride or carnivorousness, that many Texans learn from an early age. For virtually all of us, Willie has always been here, like springtime wildflowers or the sunrise over the Gulf. Even a severely abridged accounting of his accomplishments would include that he threw a wrench in the Nashville country-music machine by rejecting its typical sweetening, grew his hair out, tossed away his razor, cavorted with bikers and hippies, and sang about sitting around in his underwear. He cofounded Farm Aid. He helped make marijuana mainstream. And he assisted in the integration of the lily-white country genre by championing African American crooner Charley Pride, once going so far as to lay a big wet kiss on Pride's lips on a Texas stage at a time when such an act was far out of the norm, much less at a honky-tonk. All of which led to Willie's selling millions of records to shitkickers, longhairs, and the country-club set, who rarely found common ground about anything. And thankfully, like spare guitar picking and clouds of pot smoke on a warm Hill Country night, Willie's example will waft through the Texas ether for eternity and probably beyond.

A Voice for the Voiceless

By Michael Hall

DJ SCREW GOT FAMOUS by derailing rap's usual flights of wild, aggressive, beat-driven fancy. He took music apart and put it back together again, slowing it so that time itself seemed to slow as well. Listening to his tapes and CDs is like being in a fever dream. At first it sounds like something is wrong. Everything seems to be dying—voice, beat, scratches, melodies. It's like a retreat into a whole new world.

Indeed, Screw, who lived and worked on the south side of Houston, created something altogether new, a "chopped and screwed" style. With it, he and his collaborators became regional rap stars in the nineties as they delivered a message to the world: this is what Houston sounds like. Their slurred words and languid beats were tokens of identity, linked with the hairstyles, car culture, and even the humid feel of the city. After his death in 2000 at age twenty-nine, his sound grew even more influential.

Screw was born Robert Earl Davis in Bastrop, thirty-four miles east of Austin. He was a shy kid who loved music and learned to deejay as a teenager. He got his nickname for taking a screw and defacing tracks on LPs he didn't like. The nickname took on a new meaning after he moved to Houston. According to a friend, one night when Screw was manning the turntables in his south side apartment, he accidentally hit the pitch button, slowing a record from 45 to 33 rpm. Screw began making tapes featuring this new sound, and people began buying them. Soon his name became a verb: to slow something down.

Young men in his neighborhood angled for an invitation to rap on Screw's tapes. He'd make the beats, working the turntables and going back and forth between recorded hip-hop songs (by Dr. Dre, Tupac, Ice Cube), slowing them down, chopping up sounds, doubling and tripling beats or syllables, scratching. His friends would freestyle over the resulting instrumentals, rapping all night. Some of them—Fat Pat, Big Moe, Lil Keke—were intent on music careers. Others just liked to play with words and tell stories. Screw acted like a conductor, directing and cajoling his friends, taking the mic to introduce them or just talk about something on his mind.

Then he would take that tape, run it into another deck, and slow the whole thing down. You didn't just hear this music. You felt it, hypnotized by the slow beat, heavy bass, slurred words, and repeated sounds and syllables. To some listeners, the experience felt like being high on marijuana, which Screw loved. Codeine, though, became the drug of choice for Screw and his friends, who ritualistically mixed it with soda in Styrofoam cups and called it "lean," because imbibing enough made you tilt.

Screw's tapes got so popular that people would drive hundreds of miles to his Houston home to buy them. Cars waited in lines down the block. No one knows how many he recorded—at least 300, maybe a thousand. They were endlessly copied and bootlegged and passed around. He started his own store, Screwed Up Records & Tapes, which sold only his music. His friends—known as members of the Screwed Up Click—launched their own careers, touring and making CDs of chopped and screwed music, which was spreading throughout Texas and the South; some sold tens of thousands of albums. Several members of the SUC later said the vocation that Screw gave them had kept them out of prison.

Screw himself was an unassuming hip-hop star. He was short and overweight with wide eyes and a reserved demeanor. He didn't care how he looked; he displayed little jewelry and would wear the same pair of shoes until they fell apart. He didn't like to spend money. He didn't like to go out, preferring to stay in his Houston studio and work, sometimes falling asleep with his hands on his machines. Unfortunately, his work ethic, mixed with the drugs, junk food, and a sedentary lifestyle, took its toll. On November 16, 2000, he died of a codeine overdose.

And then his sound went nationwide. Artists from the north side of Houston like Slim Thug and Mike Jones "screwed" their own releases, to huge success. Mainstream stars released screwed songs and albums. Drake and Beyoncé did it. So did Travis Scott and Megan Thee Stallion. Houston deejay OG Ron C and the Chopstars even produced a screwed version of dad-rock band Wilco's album *Yankee Hotel Foxtrot*. Screw's techniques found their way to the ambient electronica of "vaporwave," the mellowed hip-hop of "cloudrap," and then "slowed and reverb," a fad where songs are digitally slowed and drenched in echo. These modern versions are smooth and easy, produced by computer programs. As Screw's

defenders are quick to point out, he did everything by hand and feel.

His influence extended beyond music. When the Contemporary Arts Museum of Houston held an exhibit in early March 2020 called "Slowed and Throwed," it featured Screw's old LPs and photos but also works by fifteen local visual artists who took their cue from Screw's techniques to create collages and fragmented images and videos. "He's an avant-garde artist," the exhibit's curator said. The line to get in snaked around the museum, as members of Houston's moneyed elite stood next to young men who had never been in an art museum before.

Screw's archives are kept at the Special Collections at the University of Houston Libraries, where his papers get requested for perusal more than any other collection. His Screwed Up Records & Tapes is still in operation, and fans make pilgrimages there to buy hoodies and CDs. Screw's fame only grew as the twentieth anniversary of his death came and went. A young filmmaker made a series called

All Screwed Up. A podcast was planned for 2021. A biography was scheduled for release in 2022 by the University of Texas Press.

The pervasiveness of his influence has been revealed in unexpected ways. When, in late 2019, convicted murderer Lydell Grant was released from prison after being exonerated by DNA evidence, it turned out that he had been a Houston rapper in his youth, inspired by Screw. After videos of the May 2020 killing of George Floyd went viral and galvanized millions to protest, it was revealed that as a young man in the nineties, "Big Floyd" had been a constant visitor at Screw's house, rapping on a half dozen Screw tapes.

Floyd and Grant were like so many young Houstonians who heard the sounds and words of those Screw tapes and dreamed of what they would say if they got their chance. Screw gave a voice to the voiceless; he brought pride to people on the south side of Houston. Screw's sound was their sound.

"Always be yourself," Screw said once in a documentary not long before he died. "Don't try to be like the next man, know what I'm saying? Be you." The words resonated, but what was more important was his example, living his life so single-mindedly and giving others who followed a road map to do the same.

Selena's Immortal Performance

By Cat Cardenas

IN FEBRUARY 1995, SELENA Quintanilla Pérez rode into the Houston Astro-dome in a white horse-drawn carriage, ready for the performance of a lifetime. She looked like a princess, sporting a now-iconic glittering purple jumpsuit and a dazzling smile as she waved to the more than 60,000 fans in attendance.

To watch footage of the concert now is to see an artist in peak form. Her fourth solo album, *Amor Prohibido*, was released the year before and proved to be a smash hit, going on to win Album of the Year at the 1995 Tejano Music Awards (among countless other awards, including a Grammy) and becoming the best-selling Latin album in the country. Her first English-language album was due out in the fall. This would be her third time performing at the Houston Livestock Show and Rodeo; she had already set attendance records there and had grown more popular than ever. And yet it is also devastating to watch. Just a little over a month later, the twenty-three-year-old would be dead, killed by her fan club president, Yolanda Saldívar.

Selena was at home onstage. After starting her hour-long set with a seven-minute disco medley beginning with Gloria Gaynor's "I Will Survive," she settled into a tight succession of fast-paced love songs; cumbias; and slower, heart-wrenching ballads. As she made her way around the stage, her joy was palpable. The wide-flared hem of the jumpsuit she designed accented her dance moves, twirling around her ankles and revealing her silver boots as she turned. She addressed the audi-ence in English and Spanish, urging them to get up and dance and saying "muchas gracias," after each song.

Midway through the concert, glistening with sweat, she transitioned into "No Me Queda Más," a mournful, down-tempo song about heartbreak. Though she spent much of the earlier half of the performance moving around the stage, now she was slower, more deliberate. She assumed the role of a woman whose lover has told her that he never loved her at all. At the song's climax, she closed her eyes and clenched a fist as she reached for the soaring notes, inhabiting the grief and anger rather than putting on a brave face. For at least a few moments, the performance was just for her.

As with other aspects of life, Selena's singing was unapologetic. In everything from her fashion to her stage presence, she won fans' devotion by pouring herself fully into any given moment. Young Latinas were desperate for a star like her, someone who embraced (and shared) their sensuality, their curves, their brown skin and dark hair. Even telenovela stars were often white and blond. But here was Selena, confident in herself, dominating the male-centric world of Tejano.

It's hard to imagine the heights Selena could have reached if not for her untimely death. But it was this performance that cemented her rising stardom for so many others who came after her. Though Selena was still relatively unknown to mainstream white audiences at the time, record-breaking attendance and higher ticket sales than well-established artists like George Strait and Reba McEntire made everyone pay attention.

At the time, the Houston Rodeo's annual Go Tejano Day was only a few years old. By 1995, it was drawing steady crowds (six out of the ten highest-attended Houston Rodeo paid events in history have been Go Tejano days). Rising stars and established artists alike have since paid tribute to Selena, recognizing the invitation to perform at the Houston Rodeo as a rite of passage because of her. Kacey Musgraves and Becky G each per-formed a cover of "Como La Flor" during their sets, while Cardi B told her fans that seeing a photo of the singer backstage was all she needed to calm her nerves and get out on stage.

By the end of the set, Selena's trademark red lipstick covered her microphone. When she introduced her final song, "Como La Flor," one of her best-known singles, she made sure to dedicate it to her fans, the ones who made it her first big hit in the United States and Mexico. What was originally a three-minute song became a six-minute performance. Moving her hands as gracefully as a ballerina's, she reached up to frame her face as she leaned into the drama of the first line: "Como la flor con tanto amor / Me diste tú, se marchitó" "Like a flower that with so much love / you gave to me, withered." As the final notes of the song rang out into the stadium, the embers of dozens of fireworks rained down around her. Then she climbed into a convertible car and waved to the crowd as she made one final victory lap around the stadium.

The New York Intellectual Massacre

By John Bloom

LEGEND HAS IT THAT, on a certain evening in October 1974, *The Texas Chainsaw Massacre* was sneak-previewed at a theater in San Francisco, where half the audience got sick and others pelted the screen, yelled obscenities, and demanded their money back. Fistfights broke out in the lobby, and the film became famous. The reality is probably less dramatic. The most credible version is that several San Francisco politicians had gone to a special screening of the movie *The Taking of Pelham One Two Three*, and it was a coincidence that *Chainsaw* was being sneaked as a second feature. The politicians were outraged by what they saw, and therefore the press heard about it. There's a good possibility that the whole thing was staged by the film's distributor to create a controversy. At any rate, a myth was born that night—that there was not only a horrific new movie but a new kind of movie, a docudrama so nauseatingly and relentlessly gory that it tested the very limits of what the First Amendment allows.

Chainsaw was the first real "slasher" film, and it changed many things—the ratings code of the Motion Picture Association of America, the national debate on violence, the Texas Film Commission, and the horror genre. The film itself, involving five young people on a twisted drive through the country, is a strange, shifting experience—early audiences were horrified; later audiences laughed; newcomers to the movie were inevitably stricken with a vaguely uneasy feeling, as though the movie might have actually been made by a maniac. Its scruffy, long-haired hippie director, Tobe Hooper, and his friend and screenwriter Kim Henkel, thought of the film as an updated Hansel and Gretel story. To create the modern version of a witch who likes to cook and eat children, they studied the then-scant literature on real-life cannibals and serial killers. One of them was Edward Gein, a handyman in Plainfield, Wisconsin, who liked to dig up fresh graves, cut the skin off corpses, and wear it on various parts of his own body.

Chainsaw was an overnight hit. Bryanston Distributors had done a masterful job of marketing and releasing the film, beginning with the classic poster. "What happened is true," it announced with classic exploitation-film showmanship. "Now the motion picture that's *just as real.*" No one will ever know precisely how many people saw it, but in its first four days in Texas alone, the film grossed $602,133. Extrapolating from that, a national release would have earned anywhere from $5 million to $10 million in its opening week—enough to make it the number one release of that month.

Then it would ascend into a different stratosphere as the critical firestorm began. Johnny Carson made disapproving jokes about it. Rex Reed called it "the scariest movie I've ever seen, the *Jaws* of the midnight movie." The *Los Angeles Times* called it "despicable . . . ugly and obscene . . . a degrading, senseless misuse of film and time." But the bad reviews helped just as much as the rare good one. By the time it reached New York, it had become as notorious as *Deep Throat*, if somewhat less popular with the Hamptons set. Meanwhile, Bryanston pulled off the coup of getting the film accepted by the Un Certain Regard section of the Cannes Film Festival in May 1975. Cannes was not widely understood at the time, so many people thought *Chainsaw* was one of the twenty-four films actually accepted for competition. It was instead part of a two-week showcase of new directors, a showcase famous for highlighting the offbeat, if not the downright bizarre. Cannes organizers treated *Chainsaw* not unlike a Ugandan documentary on female circumcision— a sort of "Get a load of what we found" entry—but spin is everything in the world of movie promotion.

Noting how angry people became

when the film was praised by intellectuals, Bryanston further stoked the fires by making a gift of a perfect print of *Chainsaw* to the film collection of the Museum of Modern Art in New York. The gift was hardly noticed at the time, but when MOMA started turning up in Bryanston's advertisements ("Part of the permanent collection of the Museum of Modern Art!"), reporters called the museum, where a spokesman confirmed that, yes, the film had recently been cataloged. Especially offended by this was Stephen Koch, a friend of Andy Warhol's and the author of a book on Warhol's films. He called *Chainsaw* "a vile little piece of sick crap" and part of a growing "hard-core pornography of murder" that should best be compared to snuff films.

"It is a film with literally nothing to recommend it," he wrote in *Harper's*. "Nothing but a hysterically paced, slapdash, imbecile concoction of cannibalism, voodoo, astrology, sundry hippie-esque cults, and unrelenting sadistic violence as extreme and hideous as a complete lack of imagination can possibly make it . . . We are here discussing something close to the absolute degradation of the artistic imagination . . . André Breton said the simple surrealist act would be to take a revolver into a crowded street and fire at random. They seem to have read Breton down in Texas."

Of course, with a major New York intellectual weighing in against the film, there was bound to be a backlash of support, especially since the phrase "pornography of violence" would become the operative term in the future debate. Roger Greenspun made a kind of backhanded defense of the film in *Film Comment* (the magazine of the Film Society of Lincoln Center!), and Lew Brighton, writing in *Film Journal*, curiously described it as "the *Gone with the Wind* of meat movies," comparing it favorably to *Night of the Living Dead*, *Cannibal Girls*, *I Drink Your Blood*, *I Eat Your Skin*, and *Soylent Green*.

The problem with all this so-called debate is that every commentator made some kind of basic factual error about what is actually in the film. Koch thought the movie was made in the Panhandle. Brighton, strangely enough, thought the movie had something to do with trespassing on the property of country rubes. "As far as I know," he wrote, apparently seriously, "Texas is the only state in the Union where it's legal to shoot trespassers, merely for stepping on one's lawn." The idea that the story could take place *only* in Texas informed a lot of the more hysterical articles, ignoring the fact that the principal source material was from medieval German folklore and Wisconsin court archives. If you read enough of the reviews, in fact, you start to think that the scariest word in the title was neither "Chainsaw" nor "Massacre" but "Texas."

"Texas itself," wrote feminist critic Mary Mackey, "is the land of male violence par excellence. In American folk mythology, Texas, more than any other state, embodies the cowboy ideal of the lone male who carves out a place for himself with his trusty Colt .45 . . . For years Texas was famous for being the only state where a man who caught his wife in bed with her lover had an automatic right (you might even say duty) to shoot her, while a woman who shot her husband under similar circumstances could almost be sure of being convicted of murder. Women have never counted for very much in Texas, and in the lives of the slaughterhouse family they don't count at all . . . One of the functions of violence against women in the cinema (and in real life, for that matter) is to reduce them to just such a state of total compliance. To the men in the audience this fantasy of having absolute power over a woman is no doubt sexually exciting, and one of the reasons for the popularity of the film."

In fact, as Berkeley professor Carol Clover would later show in her book *Men, Women, and Chain Saws: Gender in the Modern Horror Film*, the young males watching the film identified not with the cannibal family at all but with the remarkably resilient Sally. They did have fear and loathing of a female character, but that character

Arts & Entertainment

was the chain-saw-wielding, longing-to-be-a-woman Leatherface, and this constant gender confusion is what has given the slasher film its peculiar power throughout its thirty-year history. Adolescent boys could feel vulnerable by identifying with the woman, while the fearsome forces in their real lives were transformed into psychotic, asexual dragons to be slain. In *Friday the 13th*, *Halloween*, and *A Nightmare on Elm Street*, the survivors were tomboyish girls and the predators were sexually confused males.

All this would come later, though. In the first few remarkable months after the film's release, the cast and crew back in Austin were suddenly transformed into celebrities.

Teri McMinn—the actress who played Pam, the fearful, astrology-obsessed cutie in short shorts immortalized when she was impaled on a meat hook—was driving her Volkswagen bus from Austin to Houston when she and her girlfriend decided to pick up a hitchhiker. He turned out to be talkative and said he'd been to

a drive-in the previous evening and that they "wouldn't f—ing believe this movie I saw." He then proceeded to tell the whole story of *Chainsaw*, until McMinn couldn't wait any longer and said, "Do you recognize me?" "I thought he was going to have a coronary," she says. It was the first time she realized the movie would have an actual life outside Austin.

Jim Siedow—whose leering, cock-eyed visage, as the "cook," would become famous the world over—took his wife and two of his three children to a downtown Houston theater to watch it after someone told him it was "the worst movie they'd ever seen." "Later on," he once said, "we saw it again at a drive-in, and I made a point of letting the people in the next car see who I was. As they drove away, the girl in the car said, 'You were horrible!' But the way she said it, she meant the character was horrible, so it was a compliment." Ed Neal, who played the "hitchhiker," watched the movie repeatedly at the Village Theater in Austin, where he would scare unsuspecting patrons by tapping them on the shoulder while he was acting crazy on-screen: "They finally asked me not to come back anymore."

In its first eight years of release, as *Chainsaw* continued to play drive-ins, overseas territories, and midnight-movie houses (often on a double bill with David Lynch's *Eraserhead*), the $60,000 hippie horror movie grossed upward of $50 million, according to figures cobbled together by the *Los Angeles Times*. After an eight-year censorship fight in France, the film opened on the Champs-Élysées in 1982 and had grosses like those for *Superman*. For a 1981 rerelease by New Line Cinema, the gross was more than $6 million, an unheard-of amount of money for a seven-year-old film that had already been released on video. *Chainsaw* would end up being seen in more than ninety countries, sometimes dubbed, sometimes subtitled, sometimes marketed in an almost unrecognizable way. (In Italy it was called *Non Aprite Quella Porta*, or *Don't Open That Door*.) Its appeal, for better or worse, was universal.*

* *Excerpted from "They Came. They Sawed," originally published in* Texas Monthly *in November 2004.*

IV

Food & Drink

Hot, Melty Goodness

By Patricia Sharpe

EVERYBODY WHO VISITS TEXAS has an idea about Texas food: It's lusty, festive, and rowdy. It's famously fried or seductively smoked. It can speak with a western twang, a southern drawl, or a Spanish lilt. All of this is true. Except that there's no one such thing as "Texas food."

The state is a 268,596-square-mile melting pot, with six distinctive major cities, including the border jewel of El Paso and one of the most diverse metropolises in the country, Houston. Texas itself has been changing and growing with each passing decade. And as its economy and culture have evolved, it has gradually but undeniably grown in diversity and in sophistication. Two decades into the twenty-first century, the state's homey and well-loved dishes still occupy their traditional place of honor, but the melting pot is boiling faster than ever, and more ingredients, both familiar and new, are being tossed into the mix with each passing year.

And, simultaneously, Texas has evolved into a star player on the national scene, with name chefs, destination restaurants, and awards from prestigious national culinary organizations. It's one of the most exciting and exhilarating culinary destinations in the country.

Where and when did this melting pot first begin to bubble? To take the very long view, it was centuries ago and a thousand miles south, when horse-riding, sword-wielding soldiers from Spain conquered the similarly bellicose but militarily overwhelmed Aztec Empire. Much of that civiliza-

tion was laid waste, but the cuisine adapted and survived. The Aztec people's chiles, corn, and beans, not to mention wild turkeys, ducks, frogs, and chocolate went into dishes whose descendants we know today: tamales and supple tortillas, hearty maize gruels, fiery chile sauces, frothy drinks. For their part, the Spanish introduced cows and pigs, wheat and sugarcane, cheesemaking and distilling. That conjunction ultimately produced a magnificent cuisine, which spread in every direction, adapting as it went, until it ended up in the most northerly outpost of all: Texas.

Throughout the many decades that Mexican food was moving slowly north, forces were also at work elsewhere on the continent creating the second great pillar of Texas food: the resonant traditions of the American South. At first the movement of people was a trickle—adventurers and ne'er-do-wells, debtors and dreamers—hoping to acquire land from whichever entity was in charge at a given time: Spain, Mexico, the

Republic of Texas, the United States. When Texas joined the union in 1845 and English became the dominant language, the trickle increased to a stream and southern dishes began to take their place as the dominant cuisine in the new, English-speaking state. That's why on the Texas table today you'll find dishes with roots in Western Europe, the British Isles, and Africa (many of the new arrivals were or had been enslaved). Sentimental favorites include pulled pork and fried chicken, biscuits and black-eyed peas, fried okra and baked sweet potatoes, corn bread and all manner of greens.

If Mexico and the Old South anchor two parts of Texas's historic foodways, the Wild West rounds out the trio. In terms of image, it may be the most important of all. Texas was hard at work building vast cattle empires by the mid-nineteenth century (the King Ranch, to cite only one, began in 1853). When the Civil War ended, the state was well positioned to take advantage of a burgeoning national appetite for beef. In a little

more than two decades, various go-getters rounded up hundreds of thousands of animals that were roaming wild across the state and drove them to railheads in Kansas and other states, following the intricate tributaries of trails like the Chisholm and the Goodnight–Loving. It was a monumental undertaking, numbering more than 5 million animals overall, and it solidified the legend of the Texas cowboy. Everything about the era of the cattle drives was mythologized: the hats, the boots, the spurs, the gear. (Oddly enough, one thing that did not share in the glory was the chuck wagon. The ingenious mobile kitchen was invented by Texan Charles Goodnight but was too primitive to make a serious contribution to the state's culinary history.) That aside, the lasting legacy of those years was a glorification of beef and the cattle business, with its ranches, feedlots, and packinghouses, which in turn supplied steakhouses, burger stands, and barbecue joints. Even today, when many of the great

Texas ranches are shadows of their former selves and when Big Beef is under fire from environmentalists and dieticians alike, the image of Texas as beef country remains as secure as ever.

To understand where we are today, it helps to know a little about the recent past, in particular about an all-but-forgotten but seminal period in Texas cuisine that made its appearance in the mid-1980s. It started innocuously enough when a handful of up-and-coming young Texas chefs got together to hang out and see what everybody else was up to (remember—this was long before the rise of social media or even the Internet). It ended with the creation of a feisty, spicy cuisine that captured the nation's imagination and changed the course of American culinary history.

The Big Bang of this influential period can be precisely dated: 1984 was the year when these ambitious chefs—there was an initial cast of around ten, working in some of the leading Texas restaurants of the day—discovered that they were on a strikingly similar path. Quite independently of one another, they had each gravitated toward the earthy, vibrant cooking of interior Mexico. And each in their own way was in the process of creating new dishes to titillate adventurous diners. And what might those dishes be? Goat cheese quesadillas with cilantro pesto. Grilled antelope with cactus-pear glaze. At one Dallas restaurant, lobster tacos and jazzed-up tortilla soup became a sensation. Today, chefs don't think twice about mixing and matching culinary traditions, but back then diners were dazzled by the novelty—the idea of making pesto with cilantro instead of basil was wild and crazy. Soon the movement had a catchy name: the New Southwestern Cuisine.

The Texans were in the right place at the right time. Soon chefs around the country were taking notice and food writers were calling and showing up to report on the phenomenon.

Restaurant critic Craig Claiborne wrote glowingly about a groundbreaking Dallas restaurant for the *New York Times*. Famed cookbook author Julia Child visited a Houston restaurant to see what one of the celebrated young women chefs was doing. Then-fledgling chef Bobby Flay traveled to Texas to work in the kitchens of the Texas masters, who were barely older than he was. Many of the charismatic young cooks were featured in the PBS television series *Great Chefs*, which was the *Top Chef* of its day. Ultimately attention zeroed in on a trio of individuals who had become good friends and also happened to enjoy the spotlight: Stephan Pyles of Dallas, Robert Del Grande of Houston, and Dean Fearing of Dallas—in recognition of their groundbreaking work, the James Beard Foundation, the country's leading culinary organization, bestowed its coveted Best Chef: Southwest award on each of them in 1991, 1992, and 1994, respectively. The recognition signaled a nascent era in Texas:

a cadre of chefs had put the state on the national stage for something besides chili con carne and chicken-fried steak.

As Texas entered the national culinary spotlight, the state experienced full-throttle growth mode. Its relatively low cost of living and pro-business stance had always been serious inducements, and people were pouring in from all over the country and around the world. Between 1980 and 2011, the population of Texas grew nearly 80 percent, more than double the rate of the nation as a whole. In 2010, five Texas cities were among the fifteen largest in the country—Houston, San Antonio, Dallas, Austin, and Fort Worth. In terms of livelihood, the Texas newcomers were a mixture of professionals and workers attracted by jobs in tech, medicine, the petrochemical industry, aerospace, agriculture, and food service. In sheer numbers, the growth of Hispanic residents outpaced that of all other demographic groups. But some parts of Texas also had the largest-growing Black populations in the country. And the Asian population, while relatively small—on the order of 5 percent—was growing rapidly.

For the state's foodways and culinary traditions, this meant that with each passing decade, Texas was becoming more diverse. As the newcomers arrived, mostly settling in the larger cities, they brought the flavors and traditions they knew from home. Ever so gradually, the food scene was expanding. Whereas the predominantly white and Hispanic Texans of previous decades had gravitated toward chili, chicken-fried steak with cream gravy, meatloaf, and enchiladas, newer arrivals had a broad outlook. By their very presence, they were showing the old-timers how to become fluent in sushi, soba noodles, curries, tabouli, *fattoush*, and injera. A perfect example of the new reality occurred in Austin in 2015 when a popular three-year-old Japanese restaurant named Ramen Tatsu-ya offered a new specialty: brisket ramen. The crowd spilled out onto the sidewalk waiting to get in.

As time went on, travel writers began to tout Texas for its dining as well as its dude ranches and to lavish attention on Texas chefs in a way that hadn't been seen since the glory days of Southwestern cuisine. Word got around—via social media and traditional media—of an exciting new scene. Austin especially became a food media darling, thanks to the global exposure that came with hosting more than a quarter-million attendees each year to the South by Southwest Conference. No two ways about it, the Texas food world was on a roll again.

And as it had been a generation earlier, the new reality was validated by awards. Between 2011 and 2017, six Texas chefs won the Beard Foundation's Best Chef: Southwest award. In the nineties, all the stars were doing Southwestern cuisine. In the new millennium, the cuisines were so varied they were hard to describe:

creative Japanese, Nordic-influenced vegetable-centric fare, an impossible-to-pin-down global smorgasbord, modern Oaxacan, and superlative Texas-style barbecue. In 2019, after dominating its region for years, Texas received the ultimate recognition when the Beard Foundation declared it a stand-alone region. The only two other states with the same status? California and New York. Texas had arrived.

For generations, Texas's culinary identity has been rooted in nostalgic dishes with irrefutable historic provenance: yellow cheese enchiladas, pickled okra, jalapeño corn bread, kolaches, guacamole, biscuits and gravy, and dozens more. They remain the foundation of our foodways; they grace the table the nation expects us to set. But Texas's legacy is not static. A broader, more expansive culinary scene is in the making, proceeding rapidly in large cities, gradually in smaller towns. Brisket ramen and Viet-Cajun crawfish won't gain wide traction overnight or even in a generation, but one thing is certain. As the melting pot grows more and more global, Texas food will be lustier, rowdier, and more festive than ever.

MULTICULTURAL MUDBUGS

By Courtney Bond

LOUISIANA MAY HAVE a lock on boiled crawfish, but Houston happens to be home to a variation on that bayou tradition that makes people go cray: Viet-Cajun crawfish, a love child of two Gulf Coast communities whose penchant for highly seasoned aquatic creatures is just one of many things they have in common (fishing culture, rice farming, the French connection). About twenty years ago, the strip malls of Texas's multicultural megalopolis became ground zero for Vietnamese eateries offering this distinctive preparation, in which the boiled crustaceans get a bath of butter, a shower of garlic, and a table-side dunking in eater-improvised "cocktail" sauces. Come crawfish season, the plastic-sheathed, paper towel–littered tables of these joints groan under mountains of the disembodied decapods. Every crawdad chef has his own for-mula, and this recipe makes no claim to satisfy that bugbear "authenticity." All I know is that my pot crew and I ended up with a mess of sweet crawfish infused with earthy spices, aromatic citrus, and pungent garlic. We killed an afternoon drinking beer and cracking critters, sucking the piquant brew out of the head and popping off the tails for the nubbin of lobster-like meat. Fusion doesn't get any more festive than that.

Viet-Cajun Crawfish

Serves 6 to 10
This recipe made 30 pounds in a 30-quart pot in three batches.
Measurements are loose; customize to your taste.

30 pounds crawfish

6 cups seafood boil, like Zatarain's or Louisiana

5 heads garlic, halved horizontally, plus 2 heads, chopped, for garlic-butter sauce

4 sticks unsalted butter, plus 4 more for garlic-butter sauce

5 pounds Yukon Gold or red potatoes, cut in half if large

24 ears of corn, halved

Cajun seasoning, to taste

2 or 3 oranges, sliced

Aromatics of your choice, such as lemon, ginger, bay leaves, lime leaves, sliced jalapeños, and smashed lemongrass

Fish sauce and/or beer (optional)

Rinse the crawfish with fresh water (in a cooler or maybe a kiddie pool) 2 or 3 times, until the water runs clear.

Fill the pot with water, about one-third to halfway up the side (you want just enough to cover the bugs), and turn the heat on high. As the water starts to get warm, throw in 2 or 3 cups of your preferred seafood boil mix, 2 sticks of butter, and the garlic halves, plus your preferred aromatics, fish sauce, and/or beer. Bring to a boil. If you're cooking potatoes and corn too, now is the time to put those in, the potatoes first (give them a head start, about 15 minutes) and then the corn. Cover the pot and cook for 10 minutes, or until the potatoes are tender. Remove the veggies from the pot, sprinkle with a little Cajun seasoning if you like, and keep them warm.

Next add 2 or 3 more cups of boil mix, a few handfuls of orange slices, and a couple more sticks of butter. Return to a boil, then dump in a third of your crawfish. Give them a hearty stir, cover the pot, and let cook for 5 to 7 minutes. When they're done, use a wire-mesh skimmer to scoop them out and dump them into a big cooler. Continue with the next two batches. Meanwhile, make your "Cajun beurre blanc" by mixing a lot of melted butter and chopped garlic; season to taste with some combination of any or all of the following ingredients: Old Bay, Cajun seasoning, lemon pepper, paprika, cayenne, hot sauce. Serve restaurant-style—shake about half a cup of the butter sauce and a few handfuls of crawfish in a plastic bag—or just toss some crawfish and sauce together in stainless-steel bowls.

Popular condiment combos include a mix of mayo, cayenne, and ketchup; lemon juice and cayenne; and salt, pepper, and lime juice (*muối tiêu chanh*).

So Far Away, So Close

By Priya Krishna

IS IT STRANGE THAT I can still remember, with such perfect clarity, the first time I ever tried cheese enchiladas?

I was seven years old, perched at a booth at the Mi Cocina location in the Dallas Galleria overlooking the ice rink. My family had gone out to dinner—a rarity for us because we were vegetarian and constantly worried about menus not having meatless options. We settled on Mi Cocina, a Dallas-based chain, for its proximity to our house. I had never eaten Tex-Mex food before, but I was aware, at least vaguely, that my home state was known for this hybrid cuisine.

The plate of cheese enchiladas arrived on an oval platter, a red, brown, and orange assemblage; it was unclear where the enchiladas stopped and the rice and beans began. It all oozed together, crowned with thick layers of cheese, onions, and a brick-colored sauce. My mom took her fork and knife and cut me a piece of an enchilada, topping the bite with some rice and beans. Growing up eating mostly Indian food, we had this understanding that everything on the plate was meant to be mixed together—that the perfect bite was always a combination of the textures, flavors, and colors of various dishes.

This was certainly true of the enchiladas. I remember gasping upon my first taste. Yes, I gasped. This *was* the greatest thing I had ever eaten. It was familiar to me. The beans were like a richer version of the hearty dal we ate at home, the cumin-spiked rice not a far cry from the basmati my mom made to accompany each meal. Even the corn tortilla had the same chew as the rotis we enjoyed. Before this experience, when my family ate out, it was usually at Italian places, where we always got the spaghetti with marinara sauce—fine, but nothing compared with the sense-awakening flavors coming out of my mother's kitchen. These enchiladas matched the bold, spice-laden character of the Indian food I knew, but it was still different and exciting. And because kids are programmed never to appreciate how good their parents' cooking really is, I saw these enchiladas as a huge upgrade. Like Indian food, but with more cheese. My mom watched with a mixture of shock and surprise as I quickly scarfed up the three enchiladas plus the sides, using my fork to scrape the bottom of the plate to make sure I got all the crispy bits of rice.

Right then, I declared my lifelong allegiance to enchiladas. I was the reason my family started making weekly outings to have Tex-Mex, my mom, dad, and sister ordering a tortilla soup or vegetable quesadillas, while I went all in on my enchilada platter. Over the years, I perfected my order, always asking for extra salsa *roja* to dump on top and brighten the flavors. Sometimes I would double the rice because

I liked to use it as a crust on the tortillas; other times, I would request a side of well-done onions to give my enchiladas a sweet and crispy edge. Sure, I did eventually learn that the reason the beans and the rice and the enchilada sauce tasted so good had a lot to do with lard and the ground beef in the chili gravy; but I was okay living in pretend ignorance.

Texas contains such a deep sense of identity—the cowboys, the bluebonnets, the barbecue. Even the shape of Texas is unmistakable. But when you grow up in the suburbs of Dallas, in a family with no ancestral connection to the state, it's hard to feel that sense of place, like you truly belong there. Enchiladas were the first time I ever felt that deep tie to Texas. That's because the version of enchiladas that you'll find at Tex-Mex restaurants is singular—a true representation of how a dish as old as the Aztecs traveled across the Mexican border, got smothered in chili gravy and cheese, and emerged as something wholly unique and wholly Texan. My family was like an enchilada, I remember thinking. They had immigrated to a new place, adapted to the new setting, and come out the other side changed, yet mostly themselves. When the image of a "Texan" portrayed on television was never someone who looked like me, enchiladas were this marker of Texas pride that I could bring everywhere I went. When I went to college in New Hampshire, I could regale my northeast friends with mouth-watering descriptions of cheesy, gooey Tex-Mex enchiladas that you can find only in Texas. When I moved to New York and a so-called Tex-Mex restaurant would open up, I'd be the judge among my work peers of whether it was actually any good.

I have never gone to a Tex-Mex restaurant without reflexively ordering the cheese enchiladas (*and* the queso *and* the nachos—I love them all). It's just one of those dishes that anchors me, even when it's not that good. It re-minds me of where I come from and of the evocative power of food. One dish can bring out so many emotions. One dish can remind you that you are part of something so much bigger than yourself.

Last Christmas, I was in upstate New York with my partner for the holidays and I decided to make—for the very first time—Tex-Mex cheese enchiladas just like the ones from my childhood. I hadn't ever made them because it is a pretty involved process to make them completely from scratch: you have to shallow fry the tortillas, toast the chiles, make the sauce, and grate a *lot* of cheese. (I should mention that I am no longer a vegetarian so I had no issue sizzling onions in pork fat and browning crumbled beef to make the chili gravy.) My enchiladas, while solid, were a mere facsimile of the superlative versions. Still, I polished off my plate. I was 1,500 miles from Texas, but feeling right at home.

ENCHILADAS FOR THE SOUL

By Courtney Bond

THOUGH ENCHILADA VARIETIES are endless, the basic cheese version allows the focus to remain in the right place: on the chiles. *Enchilar*, after all, means "to season with chile." How exactly that happens is a matter of personal preference, whether you favor the piquant, rusty-red Tex-Mex puree of reconstituted peppers, like anchos and guajillos, or so-called chile gravy, an American concoction that combines a roux with a passel of dry seasonings. In either case, the result—fragrant corn tortillas rolled around gooey cheese, lavished with an earthy, spicy sauce, and sprinkled with toothsome diced onion—is manna from heaven.

Cheese Enchiladas with Chili Con Carne

Serves 4 to 6

FOR THE CHILI CON CARNE:

6 dried ancho chiles, stems and seeds removed

1 tablespoon vegetable oil or lard

½ medium yellow onion, chopped

2 cloves garlic, chopped

½ tablespoon ground cumin

½ teaspoon dried oregano

¼ teaspoon ground allspice

¼ teaspoon ground cinnamon

¼ pound ground beef

2 cups beef broth

Salt, black pepper, and cayenne, to taste

FOR THE ENCHILADAS:

1 tablespoon vegetable oil or lard

12 corn tortillas

4 cups grated cheddar cheese (16 ounces)

½ medium yellow onion, diced

In a dry skillet heated on high, toast the ancho chiles on each side for about 10 seconds or just until they start to puff. Fill the skillet with enough water to cover chiles. Leave the heat on until the water begins to boil and then turn off the heat and let the chiles soak until soft, about 30 minutes. Once hydrated, discard the soaking water and rinse the chiles. Place in a blender.

In a large pot or Dutch oven, heat the vegetable oil or lard, and cook the onions, occasionally stirring, until translucent, about 5 minutes. Add the garlic and cook for 30 more seconds. Place the cooked onions and garlic into the blender, along with the cumin, oregano, allspice, cinnamon, and 1 cup of water. Blend until smooth.

In the same pot you used to cook the onions and garlic, on medium heat, brown the beef, stirring occasionally, about 10 minutes. (If you like, you can drain the extra fat once the meat is browned.) Add the chile puree and the beef broth, heat on high until boiling, and then turn the heat down to low and simmer for 30 minutes, stirring occasionally. After 30 minutes, adjust the seasonings, add salt, black pepper, and cayenne to taste.

To make the enchiladas, first preheat the oven to 350°F and grease a large baking dish. In a skillet, heat up the oil or lard on medium-low heat. One at a time, heat up the tortillas in the hot oil. Keep them warm in a cloth or tortilla warmer until all of the tortillas are heated.

Take a heated tortilla and use tongs to dip it into the sauce. Shake off most of the sauce but be sure that it's moist enough to be pliable. Lay the tortilla on a plate or clean cooking surface, add $^1/_4$ cup of the grated cheese down the center of it, along with a few diced onions. Roll the tortilla. Place the rolled enchilada in the greased baking dish and repeat with the remaining tortillas. Pour the sauce over enchiladas and top with remaining grated cheese and diced onions. Bake for 15 minutes or until the cheese is lightly browned and bubbling.

From The Homesick Texan Cookbook *by Lisa Fain,* © *2011, by Hachette Books. Used with permission from the author.*

A Hard-Earned Drink

By Christian Wallace

THE SINGLE WORST CULINARY misadventure I've ever had was inspired by my college roommate, Sam, declaring one Saturday morning of our junior year at Texas State that he had a hankering for the sweet, sweet taste of prickly pear.

We had decided, soon after waking, to greet the day with margaritas. As fully devoted practitioners of the university experience, this seemed to us perfectly reasonable. But rather than go with any old tequila-and-lime standby, Sam—moved by nostalgia, perhaps, or a desire for novelty in the face of another plodding semester—proposed that we try a variation he'd recently discovered in far West Texas, where he had spent the summer working as a river guide. The outfit that had hired him was based in Terlingua, and as one is wont to do after long days shepherding tourists down the Rio Grande, he had developed an appreciation for the Starlight Theatre, a local restaurant and watering hole. There, over many evenings on the stone porch, swapping songs and tall tales with leathery locals and whoever else happened to blow in, Sam had come to love the Prickly Pear'ita, a margarita flavored with the juice of the cactus fruit and stirred to an icy, glistening crimson-red.

"It's the best drink I've tasted north or south of the Rio Grande," said Sam, who besides his own leathery tan had also returned with hippie-length hair and a decidedly more Edward Abbey–esque worldview. Despite his tireless research at the bars around San Marcos, he continued, he had yet to find its equal, which meant that there was no remedy but to re-create it ourselves—from scratch. "First," he announced, "we're gonna need some prickly pear."

After recruiting my girlfriend, Lauren, to help us, we armed ourselves with a pocketknife, kitchen tongs, leather gloves, and a plastic bucket and set out for where we imagined we might find the appropriate cacti: Purgatory Park, on the outskirts of town. Our quarry, we'd learned through a hasty Internet search, was the fruit of *Opuntia engelmannii*, otherwise known as cow's tongue cactus or Texas prickly pear. For centuries it served as the lifeblood of indigenous cultures across the region, its water-rich ovate pads, or nopales, a salvation for many a parched tongue. Its egg-shaped fruit, called a *tuna* in Spanish, is sweet but not overly so, like watermelon with an earthier undertone, so delicious that it has become a darling of both confectioners and mixologists.

The plant is also, of course, prickly, as a cactus should be, which presents some challenges for harvesting. But empowered as we were by our Internet knowledge, we had not given this a whole lot of thought. Instead, after parking in a caliche lot and heading down a path into the wilderness, we considered our newly acquired facts, like that the cactus blooms in spring but can take up to five months to ripen, and that the rind and flesh mature from melon-green to dark-purple, and that the fruit twists off easily when it's ready, and that using a set of tongs lowers one's odds of being stuck by the long spines that radiate out from every pad. We had brought the tongs, so what was there to worry about?

Searching among the cedars and grass, we soon found a healthy cluster of cacti and set about carefully detaching the tunas one by one, filling half our bucket. Satisfied with this bounty, we returned to the house, where Sam consulted the Internet again to study up on how exactly to process our crop. Meanwhile, Lauren and I shucked our gloves and began scrubbing the tunas in the kitchen sink. This seemed like an obvious place to start, because *of*

course you wash fruit that you've picked in the wild.

It was a matter of minutes before we realized our terrible mistake. Though we had outmaneuvered the nail-size spikes on the nopales, we had not yet learned that tunas too have a defensive shield: glochids, which, if your botanical lingo isn't up to snuff, are "the barbed bristles on the areoles of some cacti." These near-microscopic needles hardly sting on contact, but once they sink in, they burn like hellfire—a sensation we felt first in our hands, as a constellation of blisters spread from our fingers across our palms. Next, strangely and awfully enough, our faces erupted, an unnatural rouge sweeping across our cheeks. I looked up at Lauren, the pain of our folly provoking tears. Her expression of horror was somewhere between post-aftershave Macaulay Culkin and the haunting visage in Edvard Munch's *The Scream.*

And scream we did. Or at least that's how I remember it. Lauren and I abandoned the crusade and retreated to the couch, while Sam—an expert on all things prickly pear after a few minutes of Googling—shook his head at us and pressed on, donning his gloves to load the fruit into a pot of boiling water. (This, it so happens, is the standard and much safer method for knocking loose those tiny horticultural terrorists.) While the tunas steeped in hot water, Sam taught us the ancient river-guide trick of using duct tape to rip out embedded cactus spines. Lauren and I would spend the next few days taking turns yanking tape off each other's skin.

Sam then moved the boiled tunas to a blender, pureeing the fruit until it became a vibrant-hued slush of pulp, seeds, and juice. Since some glochids, stubborn little devils, can occasionally remain, the next important step was to strain the slush—except that our paltry collection of kitchenware did not include a fine-mesh strainer. Having read that cheesecloth could be used instead, Sam, in a flash of inspiration (or maybe it was the tequila he'd started taking nips of), decided

he would solve this problem with a pillowcase. This worked beautifully, until, pleased with his savvy improvising, Sam turned to move the pillowcase into the sink, and toppled the mixing bowl he'd been using to collect the treasured juice.

A bloodred stain blossomed across the carpet like a Rorschach test. Sam, staring in anguish, as if he'd just had to put Old Yeller down, was as low in that moment as I'd ever seen him— and I've known him since the third grade. But there was still some juice left in the pillowcase. Rallying, Sam squeezed it into a small saucepan, added some sugar, and simmered the mixture until he had a few ounces of rose-pink syrup. He poured the final product into a waiting margarita glass. There was enough to make one drink. He took a sip—and wrinkled his nose. It wasn't nearly sweet enough. He'd skimped on the sugar. "Not the best margarita I've ever had," he recalled recently.

In the years since our culinary folly, I have gone on to master other, safer Texas classics: chili, guacamole, chicken-fried steak, gringo enchiladas. Should I ever wish to repeat our endeavor, there are YouTube videos that teach one how to harvest and cook prickly pear with minimal trauma. I have also learned that you can go online and just *buy* prickly pear syrup— like, in a bottle, for $10. I'm not sure I'll ever go for a reprise, though every once in a while, when the plum-colored pods are ripening on the wild cacti that grow around the property where I now live, I get to thinking out loud that a prickly pear margarita sounds mighty fine. Lauren, who de-spite our trials agreed to marry me, reminds me about all the duct tape.

Sam, for his part, makes it a point to stop by the Starlight every time he's in Big Bend. He hasn't tried to replicate the Prickly Pear'ita again, a decision shaped as much by our travails that morning as by a final botanical retribution wrought by Purgatory Park: the day after our quest, Sam awoke to find his body covered in a rash so severe it made Freddy Krueger look like some kind of lotion model. During our hunt for tunas, apparently, Sam had brushed against some poison ivy. His left leg still bears the scars.

CACTUS JUICE COCKTAIL

By Christian Wallace

THE STARLIGHT THEATRE Restaurant & Saloon has been serving its cactus margarita for so long that no one can recall its exact origins (wilder explanations involve cameos by Native Americans and Pancho Villa). The key ingredient, says owner Lisa Ivey, is Pure Prickly Pear Syrup, a proprietary concoction that can be purchased at the restaurant or the Terlingua Trading Company next door, or from various other producers online. However the drink came to be, here are Ivey's instructions for making your own. No harvesting required.

The Prickly Pear'ita

½ cup sugar

1 cup fresh lime juice (4 or 5 medium
   limes)

¼ cup Pure Prickly Pear Syrup

Good quality silver tequila

Lime wedges, for garnish

In a medium saucepan, bring $\frac{1}{2}$ cup water to a boil and add sugar, stirring to dissolve for 2 to 3 minutes. Cool to room temperature, then add lime juice, Pure Prickly Pear Syrup, and 1 cup water. Stir well and chill. The recipe yields 2 $\frac{3}{4}$ cups of Pear'ita mix, which is good for about 7 drinks. To make a single Pear'ita, pour $1\frac{1}{2}$ ounces tequila and 3 ounces of the mix over ice, stir, and garnish with a lime wedge. *¡Salud!*

Calling Dr. Chilton

By David Courtney

UNTIL JUST A FEW years ago I had never even heard of, much less enjoyed, a Chilton, the simple and citrusy adult beverage that every Lubbockite, every Texas Tech alumnus, most every resident of the vast South Plains, and a scant few others have been imbibing for as long as they can remember. It was a Lubbock-area native and Tech alum coworker who introduced me to the Chilton's tart and crisp effervescence, and the drink's relative obscurity stirred my curiosity.

The Chilton's origin story, as told on the Internet, is short, sweet, and completely unsubstantiated by way of any concrete documentation. In some unspecified year, a person known only as Dr. Chilton asked a bartender at the Lubbock Country Club to salt the rim of a highball glass; fill it with ice, the juice of two lemons, one and a half ounces of vodka, and enough soda water to top it off; and then stir it gently, garnish it with a lemon wheel, and serve it to them. Ladies and gentlemen, meet the Chilton cocktail. That's it. There's nothing more.

Who, I wondered, was this Dr. Chilton? What kind of medicine did he or she practice? Exactly when did this occur? Is Dr. Chilton still alive? Would it be possible to send a note of thanks? I headed to the Hub City on a gumshoe mission. First stop: the venerable Lubbock Country Club. On a beautiful May afternoon, I bellied up to the alfresco bar (named, naturally, Chilton's) with the club's general manager, who explained that the drink's origin was a bit of a mystery even there at its supposed birthplace. Everyone knew the story, but nobody knew who Dr. Chilton was. Curiously, there is no record of a Dr.

Chilton having been a member of the club—though it should be noted that membership rolls go only as far back as the early fifties.

Though stymied in my research, I did manage to work my way through two tall Chiltons during the conversation—one a classic rendition and one a more recent twist on the concept. Chilton varietals have become a thing in Lubbock, I learned, and this one utilized Deep Eddy Ruby Red Vodka in lieu of the plain stuff. On the way out, I chatted up the club receptionist, Cleetta Hatchett, who has been with the LCC for thirty-nine years. Hatchett started out as a bartender and recalled quite clearly that the club was serving Chiltons back when she began—the earliest sighting of the Chilton I have been able to document. She was, however, unable to corroborate the story of the drink's creation.

My next stop was Chimy's Cerveceria, a watering hole across from the Tech campus. Though I didn't see a lot of Chiltons being drunk, the young bartender didn't skip a beat when I placed my order. "Serve a lot of these?" I yelled at her. "Huh?" she said. "Do you serve a lot of Chiltons?" "Oh, yes. Lots! They're a Lubbock thing." From Chimy's I made my way over to the Lone Star Oyster Bar. It had been recommended as one of Lubbock's best purveyors of Chiltons, which it serves in large, remarkably affordable schooners. From there, I made my way to Café J, where an efficient bartender named Kinny McKinney served me an excellent pork chop (and a Chilton). McKinney had little to add to my Chilton knowledge base, but he suggested I visit nearby Flippers Tavern. He did not mislead. At Flippers, as stylish a pinball-themed bar as I have ever stumbled into, the barkeep recommended a novelty Chilton made with Sweden's Svedka Cucumber Lime Vodka. It was a heck of a libation—the subtle cucumber nicely complementing the salt and lemon—but I left, slightly wobbly, without scoring any answers.

All the lemon juice was beginning

to take its toll on my tummy, and it was time to call it a night. But the lobby bar at my hotel was buzzing. "May I have a Chilton, please?" "Tito's?" the bartender asked. "Sure. *Hic!* Excuse me." Good night, Dr. Chilton, whoever you are.

I popped up the next morning feeling surprisingly chipper. But the mystery I had come to Lubbock to investigate remained unsolved. So, on my way out of town, I stopped by the Lubbock public library to peruse some old city directories. Because the Lubbock Country Club was established in 1921, I began around that time and went on up through the decades, looking for Chiltons involved in the medical profession. 1928: an oilman named Chilton. 1933: a traveling salesman. 1940: a foreman. And then another salesman, a carhop, a brick

mason, a student, and so on. Lubbock has almost always been populated with Chiltons, but I never found one who was listed as a physician, or even a professor.

I believe it was the tennis star Arthur Ashe who said, "Success is a journey, not a destination. The doing is often more important than the outcome." Cheers to that. In the end, despite my best efforts, the only thing I actually got to the bottom of during my time in Lubbock was a bunch of Chiltons. Hardly a failure.

On the road back to Austin, my mind turned to ranch water. It's sort of like a Mexican Chilton, made with tequila, lime juice, and Topo Chico. It's said to have been born somewhere in the Trans-Pecos, maybe in Fort Davis, or maybe at the Gage Hotel, in Marathon. I wonder.

The Texas Tacopedia

By José R. Ralat

TEXANS LONG AGO LEARNED that the taco is the perfect food: satiating, portable, and endlessly adaptable. But a good taco has to be prepared correctly, and that starts with the three basic elements, which I refer to as the Taco Holy Trinity: the tortilla, the filling, and the salsa. Because it serves as the foundation, the vessel of all this greatness, the tortilla is the most important of the trio: without a great tortilla (corn or flour), you can't have a great taco. This doesn't mean homemade necessarily—the state is full of local tortillerias that produce high-quality tortillas. Even H-E-B, Texas's beloved grocery chain, makes its own.

While the basic tortilla-filling-salsa framework is a fixed constant, the taco in Texas continues to change in new and exciting ways. Just look at the many types now available across the state, where the twin forces of tradition and modernization keep things interesting. Tradition is sustained in the rural areas, with their decades-old homey Mexican diners and cafés. In Texas cities, chef-driven restaurants and freewheeling pop-ups are experimenting, sometimes subtly and other times with abandon, often incorporating elements from other global cuisines.

To know how to taco in Texas, you need to be familiar with at least a few of the many types available. Some are more regional than others, but they all show what you can do with those three basic elements. Here are twenty to know.

Al Vapor. In Texas, *tacos al vapor* ("steamed tacos") are typically small corn tortillas filled with tender beef that are prepared in steamer trays or pots to achieve the desired moistness and flavor. Their compact size and pleasant greasiness make them ideal for voracious late morning munching, especially after late night imbibing.

Asian-Mex. A wide category that includes Korean, Japanese, and Indian tacos, Asian-Mex tacos feature ingredients and cooking methods native to Asia. The most popular style in Texas are Korean tacos: corn or flour tortillas stuffed with marinated meats, including strips of umami-infused beef bulgogi, and topped with an assortment of cabbage preparations, most notably peppy, aromatic kimchi.

Barbacoa/Barbecue. Before there was Texas barbecue, there was *barbacoa*, which is steamed meat, typically cow's head or beef cheeks. Barbecue tacos are smoked meats wrapped in a tortilla. Both styles combine Texas's two most beloved cuisines, so what's not to love?

Birria. Birria is a comforting, homey stew that can be made with any number of proteins. Especially popular in Texas are *tacos de birria de res* (beef), whose tortillas are slathered in rich, chile-infused consommé (and accompanied by the same broth in cups for dipping) before being fried. When made with cheese, birria tacos can also be called *quesitacos* or *quesibirria*.

Breakfast. Although this category refers to breakfast fillings wrapped in a tortilla, these tacos can be served any time of day. Austin and San Antonio love to argue about which city is the birthplace of this often eggy mainstay, but neither has a legitimate claim. Breakfast tacos actually hail from both sides of the borderlands, where they are commonly known as *tortillas de harina*, referring to the large flour (*harina*) tortillas on which they're served in the region.

Burritos. Yes, burritos are tacos! They are a staple of the U.S.-Mexico borderlands, including a sliver of far West Texas in the El Paso area, where folks keep things traditional. There, large flour tortillas are stuffed with a main ingredient and an optional slathering of refried beans, rolled, and tucked. The beans help the filling—be it picadillo, *barbacoa*, or an egg mixture—stay in there.

Cajun-Mex. Houston, Texas's most diverse city, is home to many burgeoning taco styles, including this hybrid of the indigenous cuisine of Acadian Louisiana and Tex-Mex. Think large flour tortillas packed with gumbo or rice-speckled boudin.

Carnitas. Carnitas ("little meats") are cuts of pork including *cueritos* (skin), shoulder, and butt that are slowly braised in their own fat. Traditional preparation calls for a *cazo*, a large pot with a wide rim and narrow bottom, but carnitas are now more commonly prepared in large pans.

Chef-Driven. These are creative tacos that defy traditional boundaries and incorporate unusual ingredients and flavor combinations (carmelized cauliflower drizzled with a lemon-epazote crema; duck-fat refried beans topped by plops of chorizo-potato puree). They're often sold at a higher price but are worth it when done with integrity.

Costra. Taking its name from the Spanish word for "scab" or "crust," the *costra* taco is a popular after-bar snack in Mexico City that's become popular in Texas. Why? Because the tortilla is replaced by, encased in, or filled with griddled cheese. Perfection.

Guisados. *Guisados* are homestyle, slow-cooked casseroles, stews, and braises, especially those typically eaten from morning to midday. *Guisado* tacos can include fillings as simple as an eggs and chorizo mixture or as complicated as mole, chile relleno, or birria.

Mini. Popularly known as "street tacos"—a misnomer if the tacos aren't ordered from a street stand or side-walk cart—mini tacos are served on three- to five-inch tortillas and usually topped with a single, traditional meat and a simple garnish, such as onions and cilantro.

Pork-Beef-Chicken (PBC). PBC tacos are built around one or more of these three basic, widely available proteins: pork is usually *al pastor* or comes in the form of red chorizo; beef is typically carne asada or *bistec*; and chicken is often nothing more than grilled poultry or, at best, chipotle-stewed *tinga*.

Puffy. This regional deep-fried taco, in which corn tortillas are crimped into a U-shape as they inflate in the oil, is surprisingly hard to find beyond South Texas—particularly its home-town of San Antonio—maybe because it's delicate and has to be made just right. The shell should feel light; a perfect puffy taco, typically filled with ground beef or juicy, shredded chicken, gives the impression that it might float away.

Seafood. Probably the best known in this category is the iconic Baja style of grilled or battered-and-fried fish topped with a flurry of cabbage and squiggles of chipotle mayo. Another classic option is the *taco de camarón estilo San Juan de los Lagos*, ground shrimp folded into a tortilla that is then fried and topped with a loose, tomato-based salsa.

Taco Dorados. The earliest taco recipes printed in the United States required frying the tortillas. More than a century later, *tacos dorados* (literally "golden tacos") continue to be intensely popular, with myriad examples, including rolled *taquitos*, flautas, and the aforementioned San Antonio–style puffy taco (distinctive enough to warrant its own category).

Tacos Estilo Matamoros. A nod to the Rio Grande Valley's cattle ranching heritage, *tacos estilo Matamoros* are made up of small, oily corn tortillas, a beef filling such as *bistec* or *mollejas*

(beef sweetbreads), and crumbled or shredded queso fresco, and they usually come three to five in an order. Although they are wildly popular in Brownsville, they get their name from the Mexican sister city of Matamoros, where the style was invented.

Trompo. There are several kinds of *trompo* tacos, named after the vertical spit on which the meat is prepared (*trompo* is Spanish for "spinning top"). The two most common in Texas are *tacos al pastor*, which feature pork cooked on a *trompo* that's often topped with cilantro, onions, and pineapple on a corn tortilla, and the *taco de trompo*, which is pork seasoned usually with a paprika-heavy marinade and finished off on a griddle.

Vegetarian/Vegan. Historically, Mexican food was heavy on vegetables—meat is expensive—so meat-free preparations aren't trendy; they are an important part of the taco narrative. Beyond the basic bean and cheese, you'll find creative plant-based options including fried cauliflower, jackfruit, and maple-soaked tofu.

West Indian. This emerging style of taco includes corn tortillas filled with West Indian or Caribbean-style stews and preparations, particularly chicken or pork cooked in jerk seasoning. Like Asian tacos, this is definitely a category that will expand in exciting ways over the next decade.

The Coronation of Brisket

By Daniel Vaughn

TEXAS BARBECUE WITHOUT BRISKET would be like Superman without a cape, or Christmas without a tree. Sure, beef ribs are popular, and some folks still smoke massive beef shoulder clods. But our barbecue arguments are over lean versus fatty brisket, and chopped versus sliced brisket, not brisket or no brisket. It hasn't always been this way. The story of how the state's pitmasters turned one of the least desirable cuts of meat—a tough, fatty slab from the chest of a cow—into a cultural phenomenon is a true Texas underdog story, one worth telling around the campfire (or a Big Green Egg).

In the early twentieth century, brisket as a beef cut was often relegated to the pickling barrel. Along with other lesser cuts, it became corned beef. The high fat content of brisket hindered its shelf life in the days before refrigeration, so it would have been one of the first cuts to be ground into sausages. But even then, there was a glimmer of brisket's future when it came to Texas barbecue. A report from the *Austin Daily Statesman* in September 1911 noted that beef production powerhouse Swift & Co. reported "an advance of $1/2$-cent per pound on beef briskets on account of the heavy demand for barbecue meats."

For much of Texas barbecue's history, the brisket has been an afterthought. It was destined for the barbecue pit along with other tough cuts from the forequarter. For years, there was no real distinction made between beef shoulder clod, chuck roll, or brisket on barbecue joint menus. The more generic "barbecued beef" covered them all. Brisket wasn't heavily advertised by name until the late fifties, after significant changes to beef processing changed the model for ordering raw beef. Restaurants and meat markets could request individual cuts by the box rather than having to receive and process a whole side of beef.

After that, brisket quickly became a preferred cut in barbecue joints—for economic reasons. It was too tough to cook quickly like a steak, making it an inexpensive option. Brisket also contained a generous amount of internal fat, so it didn't dry out after hours next to the low fire of a smoker. Even so, its ubiquity didn't raise its reputation to anything more than functionally appropriate for a barbecue pit. Just twenty years ago at the legendary Kreuz Market, in Lockhart, shoulder clod outsold brisket by a wide margin. However, across town, the nearly ninety-year-old Black's BBQ had opted to focus on its brisket. Eventually the rest of Texas started following in Black's footsteps, including an Austin pitmaster named Aaron Franklin, who, in 2009, opened Franklin Barbecue and proceeded to transform brisket from a Texas signature to an exalted cut of beef.

The trajectory of brisket's popularity in Texas over the past decade is like that of toilet paper during a pandemic. Once taken for granted, its value is now difficult to comprehend. A new crop of barbecue restaurants across the world advertise their smoked brisket to seem more Texan and gain some legitimacy as smoked-meat destinations by association. Fast-food companies including Subway and Arby's source commercially smoked briskets for their sandwiches and market them specifically as brisket sandwiches rather than simply using the word "barbecue." The word "brisket" has marketing power that sells burgers made from ground brisket and Chipotle burritos stuffed with brisket. There's even a line of brisket dog food.

Let's not forget that brisket is also delicious. Really, it's a work of art when done well. Michelangelo described each piece of marble he carved as already containing a sculpture. His only job was to reveal it. The statement seems ridiculous to a layman, but sculptors and Texas pitmasters alike can understand it. To a novice, this raw hunk of tough beef disguises its own potential with a blanket of thick fat. The task of transforming a raw brisket into something people pay money to eat seems like alchemy until you've spent the time to carefully carve and patiently coax a brisket to the proper doneness. Once you've successfully smoked a spectacular brisket yourself, you'll know why Texas pitmasters seem more like artists than cooks.

Brisket, of course, is no longer the cheap option it once was. As its popularity has soared, so has the demand for more expensive Prime grade cuts. A few years ago, it seemed the ceiling for the cost of smoked brisket in Texas was headed toward $20 per pound, but a barbecue joint in Houston recently topped the $30 mark. As the higher-grade prime briskets have increased in value, some pitmasters have gone one step further by using Wagyu briskets from steers with highly prized Japanese genetics.

I guess it's possible that brisket's own popularity could make it too expensive for mass consumption, but today it seems no cost is too high for either Texas pitmasters or their customers. Brisket's reputation has come a long way, and its elevated status is now synonymous with the best of Texas culture.

'CUE TIPS

By Daniel Vaughn

THERE'S NEVER BEEN a better time for barbecue amateurs to learn the finer points of smoking meats. Online videos and detailed cookbooks provide more information than the previous generation could have ever hoped for, but that'll just get you started. A bit of experience, and these tips from some of Texas's most respected pitmasters, can help you reach the finish line.

Start earlier than you think you should. "Meat needs to rest, especially large pieces of barbecue. It takes hours for a brisket to cool down, and you don't want to serve it hot off the smoker. The meat can also stay hot in a cooler for a very long time. You'll save yourself a lot of stress if the brisket is already done when the party starts."—*Don Nguyen, Khói Barbecue, Houston*

Build a big fire. "In the firebox, start with a bigger fire than you think you need and let it burn down to a good coal bed. Don't spend the whole cook nursing along a small fire. And whatever you do, get the fire started and the pit temperature where you want it before putting the meat in the smoker."—*Aaron Franklin, Franklin Barbecue, Austin*

Start the fire with olive oil. "We use butcher paper soaked in beef fat to start the fires at the restaurant. Not everyone has beef fat lying around at home, but take some butcher paper and soak it in olive oil to get a similar result. Olive oil is a little more expensive than vegetable oil, but I swear it makes a better fire."—*Emma Mendoza, Evie Mae's Barbeque, Wolfforth*

Keep the meat moist. "Add some sort of liquid to the meat—use a mop sauce or a spritz—every thirty to forty minutes. I use a mixture of half apple juice and half apple cider vinegar and spritz it on everything. Don't worry about losing heat from checking on the meat that often. It won't extend your cook that long. Raise the lid, spray the meat, and close the lid."—*Derrick Walker, Smoke-a-holics BBQ, Fort Worth*

That Texas Terroir

By Paula Forbes

AT HIS WARM, UPSCALE Austin restaurant and butcher shop, Dai Due, which started as a supper club before moving into a permanent space on the city's east side, chef Jesse Griffiths works exclusively with Texas ingredients: if onions are done for the season, you're not getting them on your wild boar burger or with your venison tartare. For Griffiths, an author who also leads hunting, fishing, and cooking classes, the "keep it local" philosophy even applies to the restaurant's centerpiece live-fire grill, which only uses wood from the region.

"It's hard to discuss any food in Texas without talking about the way that you cook it," he says. "Whether you're down in the [Rio Grande] Valley cooking over direct heat with mesquite, or Central Texas using indirect heat over post oak, Texan food is that interplay between the traditional way of cooking and the resources."

Those resources vary greatly. Texas has snowy winters and tropical summers, desert droughts and hurricanes. The ten ecological regions, with their varied soils and seasons, offer a bounty of fruits, nuts, grains, and game and fish unlike anywhere else on earth, with scores of species of plants and animals that exist only here. Some of the state's native offerings have evolved in Texas over eras; some have been cultivated through great effort. Some are destructive, some a happy accident. But they all have one thing in common: they taste of Texas—of the soil and water and sun and air, and of the taut cords that pull Gulf shrimp traps out of the water, the thick thud of pecans falling in a shaded grove, the rustling of quails running through dry leaves, the smell of blue post oak smoke unfurling on a chilly February morning.

Long before the Spanish invaded, the indigenous tribes in what would become Texas fished, farmed, and foraged their food. In the north and east, the Wichita and Caddo grew corn, beans, and squash and hunted large game, including bears and deer. In the south, the Karankawa studied the seasons and moved where the food was abundant, be it oysters or snapper or turtles. And in the harsher southwestern climate, the Coahuiltecan foraged prickly pear, mesquite, and pecans.

Many of these traditions—eating crawfish in the spring, storing pecans in the fall—continue today. And some are just starting to be rediscovered by new generations. Revived interest in mesquite flour, a sweet, nutty, and versatile source of protein that lends its unique, cocoa-like flavor to chocolate chip cookies and gluten-free pancakes, has led to it being more widely available. You can now buy gin flavored with yaupon holly, one of the only North American native plants containing caffeine, from Treaty Oak distillery in Dripping Springs. And more and more frequently, you can order a tiny ceramic *copita* of sotol, a tequila-like spirit distilled by the likes of Desert Door in Driftwood, from a succulent particular to the Chihuahuan Desert.

In 2019, Texas became the last Gulf state to allow oyster farming, which should both help rejuvenate reefs and produce tasty oysters, whether they're eaten raw with hot sauce and saltines or grilled with cheese and bread crumbs. The Gulf's harvest offers so much more than the baskets of fried fish served in Galveston or South Padre tourist joints (although those are delightful). Along the coast, sweet, plump Gulf shrimp get pickled, ceviched, and nestled in grits; redfish is blackened or pan-fried. And Gulf blue crabs get the barbecue treatment invented at a long-shuttered roadhouse in Sabine Pass and carried on at crab shacks today. It's a technique vastly different from what Texans typically call barbecue; rather, the crabs are stunned in ice water and mercilessly sliced open alive before they are seasoned, dunked in sauce, and deep-fried or grilled, honing their shells to a rust-colored lacquer.

Texas ingredients aren't all indigenous. Among the tastier invasive species is the milk snail, hailing from the Mediterranean, which tastes as great as anything in France when slathered in butter and garlic. The appropriately named bastard cabbage threatens the habitat of bluebonnets and other beloved wildflowers yet is an easy swap in recipes for cabbage or collards. And there are several varieties of carp that have the potential to choke waterways but are better suited to be stuffed with herbs and citrus and thrown on the grill. But none threaten the land quite so terrifically as feral hogs. Centuries ago, the Spanish brought and subsequently abandoned these hogs, which breed fast and trample or devour much that's in their path. The damage can be devastating, whether they're digging up fields of produce or barreling across freeways, cars be damned. Restaurants like Dai Due cook hogs that have been trapped, glazing and grilling ribs or breading and frying chops for a fine schnitzel. Feral hogs also make great carnitas, cooked down in their own fat until crisped and wrapped in tender tortillas.

Ruby Red grapefruit, the pride of the Rio Grande Valley, are neither native nor invasive. They were simply cultivated here. Likewise the wine grapes that give us the Cinsaults and *tempranillos* and *viogniers* and *mourvèdres* grown in the northwestern High Plains, varietals chosen to thrive despite the region's extreme temperature shifts. Hill Country wineries such as Southold Farm + Cellar use such Texas grapes to make weird and wonderful wines.

Every day, Texan food tastes more and more like Texas. Barton Springs Mill, outside of Austin, is working with farmers to grow heirloom wheat, spelt, buckwheat, and more. That means Texas bakers can bake loaves of 100 percent Texas bread, and taquerias can serve tortillas made from locally grown landrace varieties of corn in all the colors of the rainbow. Butcher shops specializing in locally raised meats make artisanal Tex-Mex sausages flavored with cumin, chile powder, and black pepper. Restaurants hire foragers to seek out delicate, earthy mushrooms. Breweries flavor sour ales with prickly pear; pitmasters throw stuffed quail on the smoker. And chefs like Jesse Griffiths shepherd the state's food traditions into the twenty-first century.

TASTE OF THE GULF

By June Naylor

TEXANS TAKE SPECIAL pride in their fat and juicy Gulf Coast oysters: we love 'em raw, we love 'em fried. But, honestly, there is no better way to eat them than the way Hugo Ortega prepares them. Inspired by a long-ago beach cook-out in Acapulco, the Houston chef and James Beard Award winner cooks the oysters on their shells over a live fire, adding a rich chipotle butter and toasty bread crumbs. To serve his oysters, Ortega arranges them on a big metal serving dish atop rock salt scattered with black and pink peppercorns and sprigs of rosemary, thyme, and oregano. Whether you cook on a Weber grill or in a Big Green Egg or even in the kitchen oven, you'll find these oysters are easy to master—and good for impressing friends.

Hugo Ortega's Wood-Roasted Oysters

Serves 3 to 4

1 tablespoon minced fennel bulb

1 tablespoon minced shallot

1 tablespoon minced roasted red
  bell pepper

1 tablespoon minced fresh thyme

1 tablespoon minced fresh oregano

1 tablespoon toasted and ground
  guajillo chiles

1 tablespoon toasted and ground
  chipotle chiles (not canned)

1 tablespoon coarse sea salt

1 pound unsalted butter, room

  temperature

1 dozen shucked oysters on half shells

  with their liquor

¾ cup coarse seasoned bread crumbs

Preheat grill to high heat. (If using a gas grill, set to medium-high indirect heat. For a broiler, set to high.) In a large bowl, mix first 9 ingredients with a whisk to create chipotle butter, mashing until thoroughly incorporated. Generously spoon butter mixture over each oyster and sprinkle with bread crumbs. Grill until butter is bubbling and the bread crumbs are golden brown, 3 to 5 minutes. (You can cook the oysters either directly on the grate of your grill or on a bed of rock salt in a shallow metal or heavy pottery dish.) Consume immediately.

A Steakhouse to Drive For

By Patricia Sharpe

THE TOWN OF BUFFALO Gap sits 215 miles, or four and a half hours by car, from where I live in Austin. But this drive—which I have made at least ten times—is more than something you log on an odometer or a clock. To me, this trip from Central to West Texas marks the distance between urban and rural, between frenetic and easygoing. When I finish the trek along the two-lane blacktop and finally get on the little road leading to town, I inevitably find that the journey through red earth and cacti has somehow put my mind in a different, calmer place. By the time I've reached tiny Buffalo Gap, I've loosened my normal death grip on the steering wheel and rolled down a window or four. This burg of 464 people (give or take a few) looks much the way it did fifty years ago.

I have a routine that I like to follow when visiting, which is to drive slowly along the little dog-leg road through town. I check to see if anyone is at one of the old-timey youth camps and then stop in at the folksy but stylish gift shop on one corner. Finally I head on down to the road under towering trees to the turn-off for Perini Ranch Steakhouse. This is the region's premier dining destination, serving a clatch of local regulars during the week and a changing cast of characters from nearby Abilene (population 123,000) and points beyond—often way beyond—on the weekends. Some 40 percent of Perini Ranch diners travel more than 150 miles to get here.

The food deserves a lot of the credit. Many folks come because they've read about the restaurant's America's Classic Award from the James Beard Foundation, or because they've seen its burger featured on the *Today* show. They may have previously sampled one of Perini Ranch's peppered tenderloins, available by mail order, or they've heard stories about the staff catering events at the White House and the James Beard House.

For a place with such credentials, Perini Ranch doesn't take itself very seriously. The one-story building, which sits by a large field that serves as overflow parking, looks like a country store, or maybe a ranch outbuilding. Indeed, it used to be a hay barn. Now there's a fire in the redbrick hearth all winter long, and mesquite smoke drifts from the terrace out back. Unlike the faux-Western steakhouses that have sprouted up across America, this place is the real thing: a family enterprise located on a working ranch started by a man who wears a Stetson and owns a chuck wagon.

That man would be Tom Perini. He and his wife and business partner, Lisa, are another big draw. The Perinis are Texas aristocracy, pure and simple. Tom grew up in the area in the fifties as part of a prominent local family and ended up going into ranching for eighteen years before opening his middle-of-nowhere restaurant. Lisa married into the family after she met and fell in love with Tom.

There was a time when Tom was at the steakhouse every night, back in 1983 when it was new and the bet that people would make the drive out was still a long shot. He spent considerable time drilling the kitchen crew on the principles of chuck-wagon classics. Now that the machine can run on its own, Tom and Lisa are able to take a couple evenings off. Or they might take a week or two off and travel to Europe to check out the wines of, say, Italy. Those trips serve as R&D for the annual Buffalo Gap Wine and Food Summit, a small annual conference they hold on the grounds, in a big tent and under the oak trees. But often the Perinis are at their customary table in the steakhouse. They can barely have an uninterrupted bite, they are so busy greeting friends and customers.

The dining room, decked out with long strings of dusty, dried red chiles and at least one pair of mounted longhorn horns, invites visitors to settle in and get comfortable. This is a restaurant where the regulars appreciate tradition, and while they expect things to be nice, they don't want anything gussied up.

One great way to start an evening meal is with Tom's Pomtini (vodka plus red grapefruit and pomegranate juices). You can ask to see "Lisa's List" if you fancy a serious bottle of wine. I like the good, straightforward chopped lettuce and bacon salad with crumbled blue cheese. Chicken-fried quail legs are adorable, and they still leave room for a steak, which is always Certified Angus Beef (choice, not prime, so as to keep prices in line with the surroundings) and grilled over live mesquite coals. An equal if not greater draw is the spread of grandmother-quality southern vegetables and desserts. At any given time, you'll find some of the following: black-eyed peas; chunky, garlicky "cowboy potatoes"; cheese-topped zucchini Perini; flat green beans with

bacon; and mesquite-roasted, chile-butter-drenched corn on the cob with the shucks pulled back to make a handle. Piscivores go for the super-crusty fried catfish, with a side like bacon-and-green-chile hominy. Maker's Mark whiskey sauce perks up the sourdough-pecan bread pudding.

If it all sounds overindulgent, consider that the roughly 600-acre ranch offers overnight guest lodging, including rooms in the original 1885 farmhouse or in the rustic but more modern camp house. In any case, a trip over to see the circa 1890s chuck wagon is a must. The relic isn't in use by the restaurant, but Tom takes it to rodeos for cooking demonstrations. If you ask a leading question when he's making his rounds of the dining room, he will explain how trail-drive cooks made Dutch-oven biscuits and son-of-a-gun stew. Pay attention, because that is not something you'll hear in any big-city meat emporium, no matter how tender their steaks. A trip to Perini Ranch is a trip back in time.

A friend and I once ate lunch out

at the picnic tables, under the lean-to, and we became so engrossed in our food that we jumped when we looked up and found a (very tame) young longhorn standing a few feet away. He seemed to be eying our green beans, or maybe he just wanted someone to scratch his ears. Who knows? We didn't give him anything, but that day remains in my memory all these years later. We laughed about it every fifteen minutes all the way home.

Fried and Stuffed

By Dan Solomon

TO UNDERSTAND THE WEEKS-LONG paean to deep-fried gluttony and powdered-sugar excess that is the State Fair of Texas, you need only look at its official mascot. And that's easy to do, because you can't miss him. At fifty-five feet tall and 25,000 pounds, wearing custom Lucchese boots (size 96), a pair of Dickies jeans, and a ninety-five-gallon cowboy hat, Big Tex welcomes more than 2 million fun seekers to historic Fair Park for twenty-four days every fall. But he's not the only thing that sets this wondrous bazaar apart from every other state fair.

No, what happens once a year in Dallas is an ode to the culinary ingenuity of some of Texas's greatest artists—those who use bacon as a brush and a deep fryer as the canvas, their inspiration a desire to put greasy, sweet, and savory confections into our mouths. Any yokel in Oklahoma can deep-fry a Twinkie. At the State Fair of Texas, the true masterpieces are honored in the Big Tex Choice Awards, an annual contest started in 2005 that recognizes the most decadent fried inventions. Fair Park is where a saturated-fat savant thought to deep-fry *lobster tail* and serve it with champagne-infused gravy (a 2015 Big Tex Choice Award finalist). Only in Texas can you be rewarded for burying an expensive northeastern delicacy under layers of breading so that it tastes just like chicken fingers.

Let the presidential hopefuls rubbing elbows with the rubes at the Iowa State Fair thrill to the base-level novelty of the traditional funnel cake. In Texas, that funnel cake might merely be the bun on which a burger topped with bacon and queso is served (a 2017 winner). The names of State Fair of Texas foodstuffs can be straightforward yet evocative (the Tamale Donut, 2017), or they can indicate that a handheld concoction is in fact an entire meal (Fried Thanksgiving Dinner, winner, 2013; Picnic on a Stick, 2012). Sometimes they're even in Italian (Deep Fried Chicken Tetrazzini Parmesana, 2018).

There are always, of course, traditional fair foods. But even those are part of the story of innovation that has emerged from the State Fair of Texas. The corny dog—or "corn dog," in a less enlightened place—which is a staple of every state fair in every part of the Union, was first popularized by Neil and Carl Fletcher at Fair Park back in 1942. The spirit that inspired the Fletchers to batter a hot dog, fry it, and shove it on a stick is the same one that led to the invention of something called the Southern Fried Chicken Fettuccine Alfredo Ball (finalist, 2019).

Yes, you can get standard French fries or cotton candy. Nostalgia, after all, is a powerful force, and it must be sated. But that simple fact ultimately reveals the true genius at work in the Big Tex Choice Awards. These confectionary masterpieces tap into the sentimentality that accompanies being with your family as you consume something that, when it's deep-fried, on a stick, or served with a half-pound of candied bacon, is still something radically, ridiculously, unnecessarily *new*. Why does a man choose to eat a Lone Star Pork Handle (a bone-in pork chop, battered in Lone Star beer, deep-fried, and smothered in BBQ sauce, consumed by gnawing it while holding the bone)? Because he's never had one before, but it will taste familiar nonetheless.

And from there, you can't stop. Cotton candy tacos (winner, 2018)? Yes, please. Fried Coke (winner, 2006)? Why not! Yes, we know, everything in moderation—but the state fair is, after all, held only once a year.

STRAIGHT OUTTA THE MELTING POT

By Paula Forbes

ALL HAIL QUESO, one of the world's perfect foods and arguably the premier example of the Texan knack for brilliant but lowbrow culinary ingenuity. Queso can be a sauce, a dip, or even dinner. It has the power to turn around the most mediocre of days. And it is especially suited to the slow cooker, which is often where you'll find it: on the kitchen counter at a football-watching party, bubbling away on a folding table at a church function, or anywhere else Texans are gathering. This recipe is queso at its finest, with fresh chiles, garlic, onion, tomato, a good amount of kick from cayenne and hot sauce, and two kinds of cheese. Don't skip the processed cheese! As any Texan will tell you, it's the key to proper queso.

Slow Cooker Queso

2 tablespoons vegetable oil

2 poblanos, stemmed, seeded, and finely diced (about 2 cups)

1 jalapeño, stemmed, seeded, and finely diced (about 2 tablespoons)

4 cloves garlic, chopped (about 2 tablespoons)

½ small white onion, finely diced (about ½ cup)

1 teaspoon salt

1 large tomato, seeded and finely diced (about 1 cup)

1 teaspoon cumin

1 teaspoon cayenne (optional, for spicier queso)

1 cup whole milk

2 pounds processed cheese, such as Velveeta, cut into cubes

½ pound shredded cheddar or
  Colby cheese

Chopped cilantro and your favorite
  hot sauce, for garnish

Chips for serving

Heat a skillet over medium heat and add the vegetable oil. Sauté the peppers, garlic, and onion until softened, 3 to 4 minutes. Add the salt, tomato, cumin, and cayenne (if using) and sauté for one more minute. Use a rubber spatula to scrape the mixture into your slow cooker. (If your slow cooker has a sauté or brown function, you may do this step directly in the slow cooker.)

Add the milk and both cheeses and stir to combine. Set the slow cooker to low and cook until melted and bubbly, about 2 hours.

Taste for spice level and adjust with hot sauce as desired. Before serving, top with chopped cilantro and dashes of hot sauce. Serve directly from the slow cooker set to the lowest possible setting. If the mixture becomes too thick at any point, add a splash of milk and stir until smooth.

Longnecks and Longhairs

By John Spong

IT WAS ONE OF the finest marketing slogans ever hatched, a simple, unmistakable declaration of pride and resolve: "Long live long necks." Fittingly, it was conceived over cold Lone Star beers in the parking lot of Austin's Armadillo World Headquarters sometime in early 1974.

Jim Franklin, the concert hall's wild-eyed resident artist and occasional master of ceremonies, was unwinding not far from the backstage apartment he shared with a boa constrictor and a chicken. His conferee was Jerry Retzloff,

Lone Star's local district manager, and talk had turned to the beer business. Retzloff was a reluctant newcomer to Austin, having been abruptly transferred from the brewery's San Antonio headquarters the previous summer. Budweiser had started taking huge bites out of Lone Star's Austin sales, in large part by targeting college kids. Retzloff knew that Lone Star president Harry Jersig, a first-generation German Texan and beer man of the old school, was unwilling to court the youth market. Their long hair sat ill with Jersig's buttoned-up sensibility, and he didn't want to appear to encourage underage drinking. And even if Jersig eased up, Retzloff would still have Lone Star's long-standing image to contend with. Its slogan at the time, as voiced in commercials by Ricardo Montalbán, was "The Beer from the Big Country." It was a rural, outdoorsman's beverage, a beer for cattle pens, deer blinds, and bass boats.

But when Retzloff arrived in Austin, he saw a surefire new angle emerging. He spent his days cultivating rela-tionships with the distributors who brought Lone Star to town and the bartenders who sold it. His nights, however, were spent listening to music in the city's budding progressive country scene, and he noticed an ungodly amount of Lone Star being drunk at its epicenter, the Armadillo. A check of the books at the brewery confirmed his impression: more Lone Star draft beer was sold at the 'Dillo, capacity 1,500, than any venue in the state except the 44,500-seat Astrodome. Whether it was a Texas nativism that even a hippie couldn't shake or some precursor to modern-day hipster irony, the longhairs were threatening to make the cowboy beer their own.

Retzloff persuaded his superiors to let him pursue them. He brought the vice president of marketing, a thick-necked Canadian named Barry Sullivan, to the 'Dillo to hear the scene's golden boy, Michael Murphey. When Murphey opened the second verse of his anthem, "Cosmic Cowboy, Pt. 1," by singing, "Lone Star sipping and skinny-dipping," every hippie in the room raised a Lone Star toward the rafters and screamed. Sullivan was sold.

Then Retzloff went to work on Jersig, who'd instructed him to grow Austin sales by 15 percent in the coming year. "How about I give you thirty percent?" Retzloff proposed to his boss. "But you've got to let me do it my way. I've got to get rid of this coat and tie and get me some cut-off shorts and grow a beard"—all of which were forbidden by strict Jersig policy—"Because I can't sell beer to these kids that way. I'm in there moving kegs around in a tie? They think I'm a narc! I've got to become part of the in-crowd." Jersig acquiesced—but also let Retzloff know his job was on the line.

So Retzloff started thinking about a strategy, and that's what he was doing, out loud, with Franklin in the 'Dillo parking lot. In his ten years with Lone Star, he'd worked in the plant, the front office, and the field, and he knew that to prod a meaningful uptick in sales, he'd need some-

thing to promote other than the beer itself, something that made it seem new. He remembered the Handy Keg, a twelve-ounce can painted to look like a keg that had helped Lone Star to its first year of more than a million barrels sold, in 1965. He looked at the bottle in his hand. It was skinny, with an elongated neck, which in the industry was known as a returnable, as opposed to the stubbier bottles that drinkers could throw away. Budweiser didn't push those longer bottles in Austin because it was too costly to ship them back and forth for refilling.

Studying the bottle, Retzloff recalled a recent sales visit to a bar in Dallas, where he'd bought returnables for some SMU sorority girls. "Oh, look," one had gushed. "Longnecks! Just like we get when we go down to Luckenbach." Her excitement surprised him, and so did her description. "Longneck" was a term he'd heard only in a few small South Texas towns. He kept thinking. He remembered that when he'd worked in the plant, employees would always opt to drink returnables on their beer breaks. From his time in the accounting office, he knew that most of the beer employees took home was in returnables.

"These are beer people," he said to Franklin. "They don't give a darn if you come out with cans that fit in your back pocket, socks, purse, or whatever. They will forever be drinking returnables." That was all Franklin needed. His wonderfully warped mind had already made the lowly armadillo the mascot of the Austin counterculture, and he went to work on a poster design that would similarly elevate Lone Star. It depicted a landscape leveled by an atomic bomb. The only two things still standing were an armadillo and a bottle of Lone Star. And then he came up with that slogan: "Long Live Long Necks."

The beermaker paid Franklin $1,000 for his first poster and asked him to design three more. A "consulting firm" made up of 'Dillo employees and patrons designed "Long Live Long Necks" bumper stickers,

modeling them after the über-patriotic "America: Love It or Leave It!" stickers that rednecks and reactionaries affixed to their pickups. And Retzloff became Jersig's unofficial liaison to the music world, the guarantor that Lone Star would be the on- and offstage beer of every act passing through Austin.

One night, before Retzloff's confab with Franklin, Willie Nelson approached Retzloff with a plan of his own. Just like Lone Star, Willie was chasing the youth market. Why not team up? Not with a formal endorsement deal or ad campaign, but something more organic. So Retzloff made sure that Willie always had plenty of Lone Star, and so too the famous friends who played with him, performers like Waylon Jennings, Kris Kristofferson, and Leon Russell. As Willie grew from local hero to national icon, Retzloff either rode with him or, at a minimum, made sure his bus was loaded with Lone Star. Fans around the country started clamoring just to get their hands on Willie's empties.

The efforts paid off beautifully. In 1975, Lone Star turned around five years of declining sales. The increase was only 2 percent statewide, but it owed entirely to a 46 percent jump in Austin. And as the Austin music scene started to gain wider attention—as the 'Dillo became a nationally known venue and its cosmic cowboys morphed into Nashville's country outlaws— Lone Star's profile rose with it. Now a beer drinker could order a "longneck" anywhere in the state, and a bartender would know he wanted only one thing.

The tone for the next seven years was set by the Franklin posters, the best of which were paintings of landscapes dominated by giant longnecks. One bottle was enclosed in a Spindletop oil derrick and spraying literal liquid gold. Another had a covered wagon inside—think ship in a bottle—and was being dragged across the desert by a team of harnessed armadillos. For Retzloff, life became nearly that surreal; he went with Willie to the White House. Charlie Daniels showed up unannounced in a limo at the brewery one day; he was performing in Austin that night but wanted to see the place where longnecks were made. Another time Kinky Friedman called and asked Retzloff to smuggle some Lone Star to a taco party he was hosting in Hollywood. Retzloff took two cases on the next flight out and arrived at the stately Sunset Tower to find a hotel suite packed with one hundred of Kinky's nearest and dearest. People like Bob Dylan, Joni Mitchell, Jack Nicholson, Dennis Hopper, Tom Waits, members of the Band, and one Rolling Stone. The cool guy, however, was the one who brought the long-necks.

That was in 1976. With sales at their peak, Jersig had cashed out his Lone Star stock and retired, and the new owners, Washington State's Olympia, had parted ways with Sulli-van. But Retzloff plowed on. Perform-ers now begged to record a Lone Star radio spot, acts with national hits, like Freddy Fender, Sammi Smith, David Allan Coe, and Asleep at the Wheel. Friedman recorded one with the Band backing him. Retzloff produced all of those. And then things got really weird. In the summer of 1980, the film *Urban Cowboy* did for cowboy boots and country music what *Saturday Night Fever* had done for wide white lapels and disco, kicking off a nationwide craze for Texas chic. The film's signature image, the one used in movie posters and on the cover of its million-selling soundtrack, was star John Travolta leaning against a bar in a big black Stetson with a longneck in hand, the label facing out.

Lone Star became a bona fide pop-culture phenomenon, not just hip with the college kids but sought out by the jet set as well. When the Kennedy family foundation threw a high-society, Texas-themed fundraiser in Manhattan—it was a chili cook-off at Bloomingdale's—Retzloff booked the band and, of course, supplied the beer.

Lone Star's golden age ended sometime in the mid-eighties. In 1983 Olympia sold out to G. Heileman,

of Wisconsin, and the new owners brought a different strategy. They'd made Old Style beer the top seller in Chicago by pricing it on the cheap, and that was their plan for Lone Star. Retzloff pitched the idea of working with an up-and-coming country singer, George Strait, but Heileman balked. They shut down the endorsements and scaled back the advertising, investing instead in a price drop. Lone Star's image descended with it.

His duties curtailed, Retzloff went back to work at the brewery, eventually running the gift shop and museum. In 1997, shortly after another new owner, Michigan's Stroh, closed the San Antonio plant and moved production to Longview, Retzloff retired, ending his beer man's career after thirty-four years. He received a little bit of glory in 2003, when Merriam-Webster included "longneck" in the eleventh edition of its *Collegiate Dictionary*. But by then he was making his living building boats.

BRAND IDOLATRY

By Dan Solomon

TEXANS HAVE A way of elevating certain homegrown consumer brands, especially food and drink ones, to near religious-icon status.

DR PEPPER. The bubbly confection, born of the Central Texas city of Waco, occupies its own museum there, and a place in the heart of just about every Texan who's ever ordered a drink at a fast-food joint.

WHATABURGER. The fast-food boom of the 1950s led every get-rich-quick dreamer in every small town to open their own burger stand, but it was Corpus Christi's Whataburger, with its iconic orange-and-white stripes, that emerged as the burger brand fetish of Texans from Beto O'Rourke to Selena Gomez.

H-E-B. The H-E-B mythology is well worn at this point: from humble origins in a single-room store in 1905 Kerrville, the grocer grew into one of the nation's largest, despite operating almost solely in Central and South Texas. Humanitarian aid during hurricanes and other crises only cements Texans' fierce loyalty to the brand.

BUC-EE'S. What is it about that beaver? Gas stations rarely inspire so much loyalty, but the legendarily clean bathrooms and vast array of proprietary snack foods at Buc-ee's, combined with the friendly, mischievous mascot, send a sign to road-faring Texans that it's time to pull over—just for the fun of it.

Ode to the Raspa

By Joe Galván

THERE'S NOTHING LIKE A South Texas summer. The air, laden with moisture from the Gulf of Mexico, mingles with the salty brushland for a sultriness and ardency unparalleled in any other part of the state. The days go on forever. Mornings are hot, sticky, and mostly still, with just the faintest breeze to stir the palm fronds. Afternoons might see a refreshing rain shower, followed by breezes that cause the mesquites to sigh into the long blue evenings. When I was a child, life seemed to move very slowly here in the summer, which is why my little brother and I loved going to Tía Nena's house.

My *tía* Nena was not actually my aunt. She was a second cousin, once removed, of my grandfather, who lived two doors down in Harlingen. She lived modestly in a beige and brown frame house. Her dining room was more like a dry-goods store or a concession stand. Among the prints of Our Lady of Fatima and the Sacred Heart and stacks of yellowing phone books stood jars of dill pickles and boxes full of Canel's candies and the beer salt known as SaLimón. She sometimes sold *obleas*, rounds of delicious Mexican caramel sandwiched by edible rice paper, cut into rounds and made to look like communion wafers. But what she was known around the neighborhood for were her homemade *raspas*—carefully arranged rows of clear Solo cups filled with sweet, colorful ice. You paid her a quarter and then ate them right out of the cup with a kitchen spoon, until you could lick out the last drops of the liquid with your tongue. Children from up and down Wright Avenue knew where Tía Nena's house was and came with whatever they could save up to buy their afternoon snacks.

Tía Nena doesn't make or sell raspas anymore, but I buy at least one every time I return to South Texas. Now, you may know them (or versions of them) by other names: sno-cones, Hawaiian ice, *raspadas*, *raspados*—perhaps even *granizado* or *cholados*. In northern Mexico they're called *yukis* (ostensibly from the Japanese word for snow) and have a storied history among connoisseurs of junk food in that country. But there can be no true rival to the South Texas raspa. Like all great food on the border, the raspa is an amalgam of traditions from many countries and cultures, but its Texanness is in its simplicity and singularity of taste.

Homemade raspas like Tía Nena's are a rarity. To get a real sense of what raspas are like, you need to go to roadside kiosks like Tropical Sno Wiz, on M Street in Harlingen, or Mr G's Sno Wiz, in San Benito.

Although tiny and unassuming, these red-roofed huts stand out like beacons in a blistering landscape of scorching blacktop. During the hottest and most intemperate days of the *canícula* you can expect a wait of upwards of thirty minutes for a raspa. It's all worth it when you are handed a tall Styrofoam cup of densely packed shaved ice full of sweet sticky syrup, occasionally crowned by fruit, cream, candy, or maybe even something savory. Raspas conjure up memories of blissful tropical days, replete with the sound of flip-flops slapping on the concrete and the gushing water hoses that sparkled in the triple-degree heat. They were welcome on the return to Harlingen after having spent all afternoon frying on the beaches at South Padre Island; I remember the rarified fruity lusciousness as we sucked up the syrup in the back of my uncle's pickup truck in the surreal purple evening, while the June bugs buzzed under the fluorescent lights of the raspa stand.

There is most definitely an art to making a raspa. In its purest form it is simply corn syrup flavored with natural or artificial flavors, served on grated ice. The ice has a characteristic granular form and is nothing like the sno-balls of the East Coast, which have a finer texture. There is technique in the way the raspa artist (the *rasparista*, if you will) dispenses this liquid ambrosia, with a certain flick of the wrist, a certain Border savoir-faire that knows precisely when the ice has been thoroughly saturated. After that, a simple napkin is tied like a cravat around the neck of the raspa and it's served forth. The taste can be astoundingly sharp and acidic (like the margarita flavor at Mr G's, resplendent with its notes of salt and lime) or mellow and warm (like *leche quemada*, whose taste is pleasantly akin to decadent Mexican caramelized milk, with its notes of browned butter and cinnamon). Other flavors bear mysterious names (what was precisely in Tiger's Blood that made it taste so divine when I was young?) or, for many South Texas children, were foretastes of a cheap night at an overcrowded cocktail bar on South Padre in college (piña colada, anyone?).

We have to hand it to kids for making raspas popular—and not simply because they patronized their stands all summer long. Kids (but especially border kids) have such adventurous tastes. How else can you explain the crazy combinations of savory and sweet items sold at raspa stands? My childhood was full of red-mouthed friends who had the temerity to dip dill pickles into a packet of Tropical Punch Kool-Aid and call it a snack (the citric acid and red dye in the Kool-Aid added a fruity kick to the sour pickle). That is why, at raspa stands all over the Valley, the local special is the Picadilly, a hair-raising assortment of shaved ice covered with dill pickle chunks, covered in Kool-Aid powder and served with any number of sweet or savory combinations, including gummy bears, Sour Patch Kids, Rips (strips of gummy candy covered in salt and citric acid), fruit, or simply a dusting of Tajín seasoning. Sometimes *chamoy*, the Mexican

cousin of Japanese *umeboshi* candy, is added as a pièce de résistance to an already Instagrammable calorie-counting nightmare. You can get the same flavors of a raspa in a cup of tropical fruit either covered with sweet table cream, *chamoy,* or dusted with Tajín seasoning. The real test of how in touch you are with your Chicano heritage, I am told, is based on how much Tajín you can withstand on anything, including fruit.

The real raspa aficionado knows how to manipulate or accentuate flavors to fit a desired palate: the *leche quemada raspa,* already a Valley favorite, can be augmented with cream to make something that tastes rich and decadent. I personally have never liked *chamoyadas* with their excessive, ostentatious, and sometimes offensive use of contrasting flavors and ingredients: call me a raspa minimalist—I like just the basics. Some raspa stands sell savory snacks too, like *duros* (bags of fried wagon-wheel dough soaked through and through with vinegary hot sauce and sometimes *chamoy* or Tajín), Frito pies (which are not and have never been called "walking tacos" where I'm from), and single cans of Coke and Dr Pepper. In South Texas, rare is the raspa stand complete enough to have *elotes* ready to serve; many in fact do not sell them, a task that is the responsibility of your local neighborhood *elotero*.

It's easy to dismiss the raspa as a fluke, some strange mutation of Italian ice in a world of processed corn snacks, red dye 40, chili powder, MSG, and refined corn syrup. Detractors might say that it resembles nothing of its Asian forebears in Hawaii. Mexicans say that it is too American, with its elaborate and fantastic constructions of different colors and flavors. And of course there are practical dietary concerns, such as the oft-told rumor heard in Harlingen that *chamoyadas* can give you stomach ulcers, or

that the sugar content in one raspa is enough to put you in a coma (a real concern in a region beset by the diabetes epidemic). But raspas carry a long, storied history—a history that touches on Chinese, Japanese, Macanese, Filipino, French, German, and American tastes.

Raspas have carved a very sizable (ice-cold) niche in South Texas fare. They serve as an important and necessary reminder of the fluctuating, imprecise worlds that American food inhabits. And whether you like them strong and acidic like a salt tide at Padre or sweet and mellow like a South Texas sunset, the raspa embodies all the lovely innocence and adventure of childhood, the rustle of mesquite fronds and the earthy smell of the south wind, the humidity of a July evening that finds itself at the bottom of a Styrofoam cup.

Texas to the Future

By David Courtney

THOUGH MANY HAVE THEORIZED about the roots of Texans' superiority complex, science has yet to pinpoint a precise explanation for it. Just something about the soil? Maybe. But the secret may actually lie in something closer to religion: Texans *believe* they possess something deep within themselves that sets them apart, and therefore they kind of do. Certainly, an unwavering belief in themselves helps explain how so many Texans over the years have, from an often forbidding landscape, coaxed new ideas and inventions that would go on to shape the world. The fields of ranching, oil and gas exploration, weaponry, medicine, science, and high technology have all been forever affected by the touch of a Texan. And so too have the arenas of sports, music, entertainment, and the visual and culinary arts. That track record, in turn, has further justified and indeed reinforced Texans' high self-regard.

During the rough-and-tumble frontier days, Texas demanded such inventiveness from its inhabitants just so they could survive. When the early Texas rancher Charles Goodnight invented the chuck wagon, in 1866, he didn't just presage today's food trucks; he solved an immediate problem: how to keep cowboys on the remote parts of the range well fed. It wasn't all stoic resolve driving Texans forward, of course; Texas also rewarded its inhabitants' resourcefulness. Consider the Houston-based Hughes Tool Company, whose 1933 tricone rotary rock drill bit was responsible for just about every drop of oil discovered during the Texas wildcatting heyday and helped turn Howard Hughes Jr. into one of the world's richest men.

It's hardly a coincidence that Texas now stands out for its lax land-use rules and low taxes. The state was not only built by wild-eyed dreamers and frontier people but built *for* them— a place where they could spread out and exercise their signature moxie without too much intervention from, well, anyone else. Here was America distilled, a land of endless possibility and true opportunity.

It's worked. Houston, for example, is home to both the world's first artificial heart implantation and the world's first silicone breast implantation. The Screwpull, the world's best corkscrew, is also a Houston invention. So is the Weed Eater. George Ballas, a World War II bombardier and Houston dance studio owner, liked to keep a neat lawn, but his two-acre Bayou City spread was crowded with more than two hundred trees, which posed a lawn-mowing nightmare. Ballas's idea was born as he

observed the spinning brushes of his local automated car wash.

Also consider for a moment San Antonian Frank Liberto, without whose exciting 1970s brainchild of pumpable cheese sauce there would be no stadium nachos. And speaking of nachos, what about Dallas restaurateur Mariano Martinez? The year was 1971, and Mariano's Mexican Cuisine was at the time blessed with hundreds of frozen margarita orders a night. Unfortunately, the fledgling restaurant was equipped with just one blender. Martinez, while visiting an area 7-Eleven (the world's first convenience store, also a Dallas invention), had a eureka moment upon glimpsing the Slurpee dispenser, and it wasn't long before the world had its very first frozen margarita machine.

The hamburger, the corny dog, and chili are, arguably, all Texan. So are Fritos, Cheetos, Doritos, the Ruby Red grapefruit, the Colt Walker pistol, the rotisserie smoker, and Liquid Paper. Having failed with an ahead-of-its-time product known as meat biscuits, Gail Borden Jr. gave the world condensed milk, as well as his namesake town, Borden, Texas. Famous soft drinks Dr Pepper and Big Red were both first formulated in Waco. The Astrodome, the Eighth Wonder of the World, the first domed sports stadium (with air-conditioning), opened in Houston, in 1965.

Speaking of big ideas, it was Texas Instruments electrical engineer Jack Kilby who dramatically changed the course of human events when, on September 12, 1958, in a lab in Dallas, he successfully demonstrated the integrated circuit for the first time. Without the microchip we would never have gotten to the moon, and there would be no International Space Station, no Hubble Space Telescope, no personal computing, no cell phones, no Internet.

Indeed, there's a lot for which the world can thank Texas. But will the next hundred years see as many great advances spring from within these borders as the last? Fossil fuels, long the engine of Texas prosperity,

are slowly going the way of the open range and the chuck wagon. Climate change is pushing beef cattle ranching ever northward, out of the state most known for it. But even as the storied version of the Texas frontier fades into history, a new one emerges. Houston, now as famous for its diversity as for being the energy capital of the world, is a beacon to immigrants from around the globe. Austin, now as famous for its technology industry as for being a shaggy-haired music capital of the world, is a beacon to ambitious thinkers from all over. In 2020, the steady trickle of companies relocating their headquarters to Texas turned into a torrent. Even Elon Musk, the man perhaps most responsible for summoning the end of the internal combustion engine, moved to Texas.

It's not uncommon to hear established multigeneration Texans grumble about the droves of newcomers. It's become a pastime of sorts. Theirs is a noble and worthy cause: to protect and preserve tradition. And yet there's no tradition that runs deeper in Texas than that of the wild-eyed dreamer, the headstrong pioneer possessed of big ideas and the need for a patch of land (perhaps with a favorable tax environment) upon which to throw down stakes and get to work.

True believers tend to find their way to Texas, and then Texas finds its way into them. It has always been this way. And, with a little faith, always will.

Acknowledgments

WE KNEW FROM THE start that creating a book called *Being Texan* would require enlisting a big crew of contributors if we had any hope of reflecting the state's diversity. That crew included, of course, the staff writers and contributing writers who consistently make *Texas Monthly* the magical place that it is and whose work appears throughout these pages. (You can read their bios starting on page 309.) Just as important were the editors who helped shape the book. So much of editing depends on bolts of inspiration, and those rarely occur without healthy collaboration.

Thanks to executive editor Kathy Blackwell for her tireless help building out *Being Texan*'s food and drink coverage, as well as the style pieces; to senior editor Paula Mejía for her insight into Texas arts and culture; to deputy editor Jeff Salamon for his wise counsel at various points; and to the inestimable David Courtney (a.k.a., The Texanist) for his wit and deep well of knowledge about all things Texana. Senior editor Jason Heid deserves special notice for his invaluable contributions when it came to polishing the essays herein to their eventual shine.

That list is woefully inadequate, though. The truth is, almost no one on the staff of *Texas Monthly* did not help shape this book at some level. Others of particular note include Cat Cardenas, Dan Solomon, Forrest Wilder, John Spong, Katy Vine, Mimi Swartz, Patricia Sharpe, Rose Cahalan, and Wes Ferguson—all of whom gamely shared ideas and feedback. Thanks, too, to the magazine's managing editor, Anna Walsh, and Texasmonthly.com's editorial director, Michelle Williams, for allowing members of the team to take their eyes off daily web journalism and monthly print production to heed something

Acknowledgments

as seemingly far-off as a book deadline. Kathy McFarland, meanwhile, kept us faithful to these book deadlines and parsed the details of innumerable contracts.

Of course, no amount of painstaking planning and editing eliminates the need for fact checking, and for that we were beyond lucky to enlist Jaclyn Colletti and Will Bostwick, who pored over every line of the manuscript. (Example: In 1983 the Silverado was not, in fact, a model of Chevy truck but rather a trim level for the C/K models.)

Texas Monthly design director Emily Kimbro and art director Victoria Millner set the kind of visual direction that consistently allows the magazine and its various digital products to so elegantly channel the look and feel of a fast-evolving state. Artist Christopher DeLorenzo, whose work has been a signature part of *Texas Monthly*'s identity since 2018, delivered smart illustrations throughout and a stunning cover concept. At Harper Wave, Joanne O'Neill designed the cover, and Bonni Leon-Berman crafted the interior pages. Thanks, also, to production editor Rebecca Holland and editorial assistant Emma Kupor.

None of the above would matter if we didn't get the word out about the book, and for that effort we owe many thanks to Brian Perrin and Laura Cole on the HarperCollins marketing team, as well as Yelena Nesbit in publicity—all of whom worked closely with *Texas Monthly*'s Caitlyn Perry and Tori Mohn, plus our publicity team at Jackson Spalding.

A huge thanks goes to our agent, Amy Hughes of the Dunow, Carlson & Lerner Literary Agency, for pairing us with such a great publishing house, and to Harper Wave Editorial Director Julie Will for so enthusiastically believing in the idea from the start and for sharpening it along the way.

Which brings us, finally, to *Texas Monthly*'s Editor-in-Chief Dan Goodgame, under whose leadership this national treasure of a publication has become more nimble and more diverse than ever before—both in content and form. No longer just an award-winning magazine, *Texas Monthly* tells the stories of

Acknowledgments

this colorful place in podcasts, videos, live events, and much more—including, of course, books. Owner Randa Duncan Williams; President Scott Brown; and the whole *Texas Monthly* business team make that work possible by believing in the power of uncompromised editorial.

It sounds so simple, but it's actually a miracle when so many people can align around that kind of purpose. It's how a brand like *Texas Monthly* can manage to grow its ambition and its audience in a punishing time for this industry. And it's how an unconventional, often surprising book like this one can make it into your hands. From quite a few of us: Enjoy.

—Tom Foster, Editor-at-Large, *Texas Monthly*

Contributors

KATHY BLACKWELL

Blackwell is an executive editor at *Texas Monthly*. The South Carolina native has worked at newspapers including the *Orlando Sentinel* and the *Austin-American Statesman* and was editor in chief of *Austin Way* magazine. She lives in Austin with her husband, son, and dog.

JOHN BLOOM

Best known as "Joe Bob Briggs," Bloom is a nationally syndicated "drive-in movie critic" whose take on B movies was featured on two long-running late-night television shows. That tradition continues with his series *The Last Drive-In*, on AMC's Shudder streaming platform. Briggs is also a successful journalist, actor, and author.

COURTNEY BOND

Bond is a senior editor who specializes in food and travel. She was born in Austin and went to college in Atlanta. She returned to Austin, then moved to San Francisco, then moved back to Austin, where the enchiladas are better. She has been with *Texas Monthly* for a quarter century.

JORDAN BREAL

Breal was a *Texas Monthly* staff writer from 2005 to 2017.

Contributors

BRYAN BURROUGH

A longtime special correspondent at *Vanity Fair*, Burrough is the author of six books, including the *New York Times* best sellers *The Big Rich, Public Enemies*, and *Barbarians at the Gate*. His latest book, written with Chris Tomlinson and Jason Stanford, is *Forget the Alamo: The Rise and Fall of an American Myth*.

STERRY BUTCHER

A writer at large for the magazine, Butcher has contributed to *Texas Monthly* since 2010, writing chiefly about the land, animals, and residents of the Big Bend. She lives with her family in Marfa.

ROSE CAHALAN

An associate editor at *Texas Monthly*, Cahalan was previously managing editor of the *Texas Observer* and a senior editor at the *Alcalde*, the University of Texas alumni magazine.

CAT CARDENAS

Cardenas is a Mexican American writer and photographer from San Antonio. Since joining *Texas Monthly* as associate editor in 2019, she's interviewed drag queens and politicians, written about immigration, Texas history, film, music, and the state's Latino community.

OSCAR CÁSARES

Cásares is the author of the story collection *Brownsville*, and the novels *Amigoland* and *Where We Come From*. His stories and novels have earned him fellowships from

Contributors

the National Endowment for the Arts, the Copernicus Society of America, the Texas Institute of Letters, and the Guggenheim Foundation.

DAVID COURTNEY

A Temple native, senior editor Courtney joined *Texas Monthly* in October 2005 and debuted his wildly popular advice column The Texanist in July 2007. He will, someday, be the recipient of many accolades, honors, and awards.

DAN Q. DAO

Dao is a Houston-born culture and travel writer whose work has appeared in *Vice*, *Condé Nast Traveler*, *Food & Wine*, *Paper*, and more. He previously held food editor roles at *Time Out New York* and *Saveur*.

ANNE DINGUS

Born and raised in Pampa, Dingus attended Rice University and started working for *Texas Monthly* in 1978. She lives and works in Austin and is the author of four books of Texana.

WES FERGUSON

Ferguson is a senior editor for *Texas Monthly*. An East Texas native, he's the author of two nonfiction books, both about rivers.

PAULA FORBES

Forbes is a writer living in Austin whose work has appeared in *GQ*, *Lucky Peach*, *Eater*, *Epicurious*, the *Houston Chronicle*, and more. Her cookbook, *The Austin Cookbook*, features recipes from restaurants across the tasty Texas capital city. She is also the editor of *Stained Page News*, a cookbook newsletter.

JOE GALVÁN

Galván is a writer, artist, and composer living in Portland, Oregon. He was born and raised in Harlingen, Texas.

MICHAEL HALL

Hall graduated from University of Texas at Austin in 1979 with a government degree. He wrote for *Trouser Press* and *Third Coast* and in 1997 joined *Texas Monthly*, where he writes frequently about criminal justice and has won two Texas Gavel Awards from the State Bar of Texas.

STEPHEN HARRIGAN

A writer at large for *Texas Monthly*, Harrigan is the author of twelve books of fiction and nonfiction, including the novels *The Gates of the Alamo* and *Remember Ben Clayton*, and the forthcoming *The Leopard Is Loose*. His most recent book is *Big Wonderful Thing: A History of Texas*.

JASON HEID

Heid is a senior editor at *Texas Monthly*. He was previously editor in chief of *Austin Monthly*, digital editorial director for *D Magazine*, and an editor at the *Dallas Morning News*. He grew up in Denton, in North Texas, and earned a history degree at Trinity University in San Antonio.

Contributors

SKIP HOLLANDSWORTH

Since 1989, Hollandsworth has been a writer at *Texas Monthly*. He is the author of *The Midnight Assassin*, a *New York Times* best seller about a bizarre series of murders that took place in Austin in the year 1885, and in 2010, he received the National Magazine Award in feature writing. He lives in Dallas and grew up in Wichita Falls.

CHRISTOPHER HOOKS

An Austin native, Hooks writes predominantly about Texas politics but occasionally more reputable subjects. He has written for publications including *The Atlantic*, *Gawker*, *GQ*, *Rolling Stone*, the *Los Angeles Times*, the *New York Times*, and the *Texas Observer*. He joined *Texas Monthly* in 2020.

RAINEY KNUDSON

Knudson is the founder of *Glasstire*, the oldest online-only art magazine in the country. She edited the book *One Thing Well: 22 Years of Installation Art*, about Rice Gallery, and is currently writing for magazines and working on a book about *Glasstire*. She lives in Houston.

PRIYA KRISHNA

Priya Krishna is a food writer who contributes regularly to the *New York Times* and other publications, and is the author of the best-selling cookbook *Indian-ish*. In 2020, she was named to *Forbes*'s annual "30 Under 30" list.

Contributors

ANDY LANGER

Langer is a writer at large for *Texas Monthly* and served as host of the magazine's *National Podcast of Texas*. He can also be heard afternoons on Austin City Limits Radio (97.1 KGSR Austin). From 2002 to 2016 he was a contributing editor and the music columnist at *Esquire*.

JOHN NOVA LOMAX

Former *Texas Monthly* senior editor Lomax now is a contributor to *Texas Highways* and edits his own *Lomax Chronicles & Nova Gazette*. He lives in a cabin on the San Bernard River in the Brazoria County hamlet of Wild Peach Village, Texas, where fishing, stargazing, and birdwatching occupy much of his free time.

MAX MARSHALL

A sixth-generation Texan, Marshall grew up in Dallas and lives in New York City. His journalism has appeared in *Texas Monthly, GQ,* and *Sports Illustrated*. His first book, an investigation into a southern fraternity drug-trafficking ring, will be published by HarperCollins in 2023.

EMILY MCCULLAR

McCullar is an eleventh-generation Texan who was hired as *Texas Monthly*'s receptionist in 2014. She soon charmed her way into the Editorial Department, working as a fact-checker and, eventually, a staff writer. She writes about culture, Texana, politics, and history.

Contributors

PAULA MEJÍA

Mejía is a senior editor at *Texas Monthly*. Her work has appeared in the *New Yorker*, the *New York Times*, NPR Music, *Rolling Stone*, and other publications. She is the author of *Psychocandy*, a meditation on the Jesus and Mary Chain's 1985 album.

MICHAEL J. MOONEY

A *New York Times* best-selling author, Mooney writes for ESPN, *The Atlantic*, *GQ*, *Outside*, *Texas Monthly*, and *Popular Mechanics*. His stories have appeared in multiple editions of *The Best American Sports Writing* and *The Best American Crime Reporting*. He lives in Dallas.

DEBORAH D.E.E.P. MOUTON

Mouton is an internationally known writer, educator, artivist, and poet laureate emeritus of Houston. Her recent poetry collection, *Newsworthy*, examines the conflict between the media, police, and the Black body. She lives and creates in Houston.

JUNE NAYLOR

A Fort Worth–native cookbook author and frequent contributor to *Texas Monthly*, Naylor loves searching Texas for the best things to eat and the intriguing people who make them.

Contributors

KATIE NODJIMBADEM

Nodjimbadem is a journalist from El Paso whose work has appeared in *Texas Monthly*, *Smithsonian*, *Air Mail*, and the *New Yorker*. She has been an editorial staff member at *Smithsonian* and the *New Yorker* and was a 2017–2018 Fulbright grantee in Côte d'Ivoire.

DAN OKO

An avid outdoorsman and award-winning freelance writer, Oko is based in Houston. In addition to *Texas Monthly*, his writing has appeared in *Adventure Journal*, *Outside*, the *Texas Observer*, and the *Houston Chronicle*. His book about climate change and the Texas coast is due out in 2022.

DOYIN OYENIYI

Oyeniyi is a writer with a passion for sharing the stories of marginalized people. She was born in Nigeria and has lived in Texas for most of her life. She has written about race, immigration, abortion access, and gun violence in the United States and has interviewed many Texas artists, writers, and filmmakers.

JOSÉ R. RALAT

Ralat is *Texas Monthly*'s taco editor. He is also the author of *American Tacos: A History & Guide*. He has written for *Eater*, the *Dallas Observer*, *D Magazine*, *Vice*, *Cowboys & Indians*, *Gravy*, and more.

Contributors

JOHN PHILLIP SANTOS

Santos is a documentary producer and writer who teaches in the Honors College of the University of Texas, San Antonio. The creator of over forty documentaries for CBS News and PBS, he is a widely published essayist and the author of a book of poems and two memoirs.

PATRICIA SHARPE

In 1974, Austin-native Sharpe joined the staff of then-two-year-old *Texas Monthly*. She presently coedits the Dining Guide and writes a restaurant column. In 2006 she won a James Beard Award for her essay "Confessions of a Skinny Bitch."

DAN SOLOMON

Since joining *Texas Monthly* in 2013, Solomon has published more than 1,700 stories on topics as diverse as the Baylor University sexual assault scandal and gentrification in Austin barbecue. His reporting has appeared in the *New York Times*, *GQ*, *Vanity Fair*, *Wired*, *Fast Company*, and *Deadspin*.

JOHN SPONG

Senior editor Spong has written about popular culture for *Texas Monthly* since 1999. He lives in Austin with his wife, Julie Blakeslee, and their sons, Willie Mo and Leon.

Contributors

KAYLA STEWART

Stewart's work has been featured in the *New York Times, Texas Monthly, Southern Food-ways Alliance, Travel + Leisure, Heated,* and others. She served as a Fulbright scholar in Semarang, Indonesia, and holds a joint master's degree in international relations and journalism from New York University.

MIMI SWARTZ

Swartz has worked at *Texas Monthly* off and on since 1984. She is the author of two books and is a two-time finalist and two-time winner of the National Magazine Award. Over the years, her work has appeared in *Vanity Fair,* the *New Yorker,* and the *New York Times Magazine.* She is also a contributing opinion editor for the *New York Times'* op-ed page.

DANIEL VAUGHN

Texas Monthly's barbecue editor, Vaughn is also the author of *Prophets of Smoked Meat: A Journey Through Texas Barbecue,* and coauthor of *Whole Hog BBQ: The Gospel of Carolina Barbecue.* He has traveled the world sampling smoked meats at more than 1,800 barbecue joints, most of which are in Texas.

CHRISTIAN WALLACE

Wallace worked as a roughneck, a ditch digger, an electrician, a record store clerk, and a radio DJ before joining *Texas Monthly.* In 2020, the West Texas native wrote and hosted the documentary podcast series *Boomtown.* His 2019 *Texas Monthly* cover story on honky-tonks was a finalist for a National Magazine Award.

Index

Index

beef, 241–42
  birria tacos, 266
  brisket, 270–72
  climate change and, 303
  Perini Ranch Steakhouse in
    Buffalo Gap, 281–84
  pork-beef-chicken (PBC) tacos,
    267
  tacos estilo Matamoros, 268
  see also cattle
beer, Lone Star, 289–94
Beethoven, Ludwig van, 216
"being Texan," meaning of, 1–5
Bell, Archie, & the Drells, 208
Bernie, 168
Beyoncé, 16, 20, 50, 213, 214, 226
Big Bend (region), 5, 81, 88, 89, 129,
  259
Big Bend National Park, 2, 127–28
Big Bend Ranch State Park, 129,
  130, 136, 169
Bigfoot sightings, 126
Big Hill, 136
Big Red, 303
Big Tex Choice Awards, 285–86
Big Tex mascot, 285
Big Thicket National Preserve,
  125–26
Big Wonderful Thing (Harrigan), 183,
  191
Biles, Simone, 20
Bill's Junk, Houston, 193–94
Bird Island Basin, 124–25
birds, migratory, 82
birria tacos, 266
bison, 126
Bissinger, H. G. "Buzz," 168, 184
Black Americans, 75, 192, 196, 221,
  222–23, 244
  Beyoncé's "Formation" and, 213

country music and, 220–22
cowboys, 46, 50, 58, 59, 180, 191,
  221
in El Paso, 103, 104–5
Floyd killing and, 41, 46, 98, 227
Johnson's music and, 206–7,
  216–19
Juneteenth and, 40–42
Sayles's *Lone Star* and, 158, 161–62
segregation and, 17, 186
see also slavery
Blackland Prairie, 85, 100
Black's BBQ, Lockhart, 271
Black Seminoles, 42
black tie, dress code for, 49
Blackwell, Kathy, 48–51
black widow spiders, 112–13
Blaffer Art Museum, University of
  Houston, 196
Blanco River, 131–32, 133
Blood and Money (Thompson), 183
Bloom, John, 231–36
Bluebird, Bluebird (Locke), 184
bluebonnets, 90, 142, 143–44, 250,
  277
Blue Hole, 132
blues, 93, 206, 209, 213–14, 216, 217
Boca Chica Beach, 138
Bogdanovich, Peter, 167, 174, 176
Bogota, Texas, 26
Bond, Courtney, 88–90129–130,
  246, 252–54
Bonnie and Clyde, 166
books, 174–87
  essential Texas, 183–87
  histories of Texas, 159–60,
    190–91
  see also McMurtry, Larry
Boone and Crockett Club, 152, 153
boots, cowboy, 43, 58–60, 61

Index

Borden, Gail, Jr., 303
border and borderlands, 104, 188
   ancient migration patterns and,
     191
   cariño in, 103–5
   cattle ranching and, 66–67
   killing of Mexican Texans in, 190
   mixing of races and cultures at,
     192
   Republic of Texas and, 10
   Sayles's *Lone Star* and, 161–62,
     163–64
   writings about, 183, 184
Bosque County, 25
Box, Amber Venz, 50
Boyhood, 169
Boy Kings of Texas, The (Martinez),
   184
brain-eating amoeba, 113–14
Brammer, Billy Lee, 23
brand idolatry, 295
Brazos River, 184–85
breakfast tacos, 266
Breal, Jordan, 56–57
Breton, André, 233
Brewster McCloud, 167
Bridges, Leon, 213
Brighton, Lew, 233, 234
Briscoe Western Art Museum, San
   Antonio, 199
brisket, 270–72
Brokeback Moutain, 176
Broken Spoke, Austin, 205
Brooks, Jack, 14
Brownsville Ship Channel, 138
Bryan, John Neely, 52–53
Bryanston Distributors, 232, 233
Buc-ee's, 295
Budweiser, 290, 291
Buffalo Gap:

   drive from Austin to, 281
   Perini Ranch Steakhouse in,
     281–84
Bullock, Bob, 23, 24
burritos, 266
Burrough, Bryan, 31–36
Busby, Mark, 182
Bush, George H. W., 2, 3, 14
Bush, George W., 30
Butcher, Sterry, 73–79

cabbage, bastard, 277
Cabeza de Vaca, Álvar Núñez, 188
cactus:
   saguaro, 117
   see also prickly pear
cactus juice cocktail (Prickly
   Pear'ita), 256, 259–60 (recipe)
   harvesting cactus for, 256–59
Caddo Indians, 25, 26, 191, 276
Café J, Lubbock, 262
Cahalan, Rose, 198–99
Cajun flavors:
   Cajun-Mex tacos, 266
   Viet-Cajun crawfish (recipe),
     246–48
Calatrava, Santiago, 55
Camino Real road trip (State
   Highway 21), 139
Camp Tonkawa Springs, 132
Cannes Film Festival (1975), 232
capitol of Texas, 10
Capps, Garrett T., 202
Caprock Canyons State Park, 84,
   126–27
Caprock Escarpment, 84
Cardenas, Cat, 95–96, 228–30
Cardi B, 230
cariño, in borderland, 103–5
carnitas, feral hogs and, 278

Index

carnitas tacos, 266
Caro, Robert, 23
carp, 277
Carson, Johnny, 232
Cásares, Oscar, 63–69, 183
Castro, Rosie, 17, 20
catamounts, 115
cattle, 2, 85, 170
  climate change and, 303
  Dallas and, 170, 172
  indigenous grazelands and, 83, 86
  introduced into Texas by Spanish,
    74–75
  McMurtry's novels and, 176,
    177–78, 180–81
  national appetite for beef and,
    241–42
  tended by students, 45
cattle drives, 59–60, 166, 241
  in *Lonesome Dove*, 176, 180–81
cattle fever, 66–67
cattlemen and cattle empires, 32–33,
  165, 241
cattle ranching, 73–79
  settlement of Texas and, 74–75
  at Seven L, 73–74, 76
  time's passage and, 76–77
  working alone in, 77–78
  yen for more property and, 78
  see also cowboys
cattle rustlers, 33
cedars, 82–83, 135
Centering for Centering, Houston,
  195
Chamizal National Memorial, El
  Paso, 104
Chapman, Harve, 100, 101
cheese:
  enchiladas, 245, 249–54
  Enchiladas with Chili Con Carne

(recipe), 253–54
  sauce, pumpable, 302
  Slow Cooker Queso (recipe),
    287–88
chef-driven tacos, 266–67
Cherokees, 12
chicken, in pork-beef-chicken (PBC)
  tacos, 267
The Chicks, 211–12
Chihuahuan Desert, 81, 103–4, 117,
  130, 135, 136, 277
Child, Julia, 243
Chili Con Carne, Cheese Enchiladas
  with (recipe), 253–54
Chilton (drink), 261–63
Chimy's Cerveceria, Lubbock, 262
Chisholm Trail, 59, 241
Chisos Basin, 127
Chisos Mountains, 81, 122
Chisos Mountains Lodge, 127
Chisum, John, 33
Christmas decorations, 135
Christmas songs, 211
chuck wagons, 241, 282, 283, 301,
  303
Cinsaults, 278
Cisneros, Sandra, 185
Civilian Conservation Corps, 81
Civil War, 13, 32–33, 138, 241
Claiborne, Craig, 243
Clark, Annie, 213
Clark, Gary, Jr., 213–14
Clark, Guy, 209
climate crisis, 185, 303
Clover, Carol, 234–35
Coahuiltecans, 96, 276
Coe, David Allan, 293
Coen, Joel and Ethan, 168
Coleman, Ornette, 207
colonialism, 188, 190

Index

Index

Index

Index

Index

Index

indigenous peoples, *see* Native
  Americans; *specific peoples*
individualism, 36, 47, 189
Inks Lake, 133
integrated circuits, 303
"Int'l Players Anthem (I Choose
  You)," 212
invasive species, 277–78
inventiveness, 301–4
I Say Me for a Parable (Lipscomb),
  218
"I Turn My Camera On," 212
Ivey, Lisa, 259–60
Ivins, Molly, 14–15, 16, 17, 20, 23
"I Want to Be a Cowboy's
  Sweetheart," 164

Jaime, A. C. "Beto" and Dora, 67–69
Japanese culinary influence, 244, 245
Jay-Z, 212
Jazz Church of Houston, 194
Jefferson, Blind Lemon, 217
Jennings, Waylon, 209, 292
Jersey Lilly Saloon, Langtry, 136
Jersig, Harry, 290, 291
Jiménez, Don Santiago, 202, 210
Jiménez, Flaco, 210
Johnson, Blind Willie, 206–7, 216–19
Johnson, Lyndon B., 3, 23, 47
Johnson City, 135
Johnston, Daniel, 209–10
Joiner, Dad, 35
Jones, Jerry, 173
Jones, Tommy Lee, 168, 181
R. R. Jones Stadium, El Paso, 119
Joplin, Janis, 208
Jordan, Barbara, 16, 47
Juenke, Arkey, 202
jukeboxes, 202, 203
"June 27th," 211

Juneteenth, 40–42
Justin, Enid, 59
Justin, H. J. "Big Daddy Joe," 69

Karankawa Indians, 276
Katy football stadium, 120
Keen, Robert Earl, 211
Kempner High, Houston, 45–46
Kemp's ridley sea turtle, 82
Kennedy, John F. (JFK), 172
Keystone field, 35
Khói Barbecue, Houston, 273
Kilby, Jack, 303
Kimbell Art Museum, Fort Worth,
  198
King, Freddie, 93
King, Richard, 33, 59
King Ranch, 66, 241
Kiowa Indians, 165
Knowles, Solange, 50
Knudson, Rainey, 193–97
Koch, Stephen, 233, 234
Korean tacos, 265
Kreuz Market, Lockhart, 271
Krishna, Priya, 249–51
Kristofferson, Kris, 157, 161, 208,
  292
Kroll, Jack, 179
Ku Klux Klan, 222

La Feria, Texas Rose Bar in, 203
"La Grange," 208–9
Lake Amistad, 136
lakes:
  Prairies and Lakes region, 85
  resacas, 86
  as swimming holes, 132, 133
Lama, Tony, Bopopts, 59
Lamar, Mirabeau, 12
land grants, 75

Index

Index

Index

Moody Center for the Arts, Rice
University, 196
Mooney, Michael J., 99–101, 118–21
mop sauce, 274
Morris, Errol, 167–68
Morris, Willie, 23
Morrison, Toni, 104–5
mountain lions, 115
Mouton, Deborah D.E.E.P., 141–43
movies, 157–69
  based on McMurtry's novels, 166,
    174–76, 178, 179
  essential Texas, 165–69
  Lone Star, 157–64
  The Texas Chainsaw Massacre, 167,
    231–36
Muñoz Martinez, Monica, 190
Murchison, Clint, 35
Murphey, Michael, 290
Museum of Fine Arts, Houston
  (MFAH), 193, 195–96
Museum of Modern Art, New York
  (MOMA), 233
Musgraves, Kacey, 50, 212–13, 230
music and musicians, 192, 200–230
  essential Texas songs, 206–14
  honky-tonk venues, 137, 200–205
  in Houston, 194
  phonograph records carried by
    Voyager spaceships, 215–
    19
  see also specific genres and performers
Musk, Elon, 138, 303
Mustang-Panther Stadium,
  Grapevine, 119
Mystic Lyon, Houston, 194–95

nachos, 302
Nacimiento de los Negros, Mexico,
  41–42

Naegleria fowleri (brain-eating
  amoeba), 113–14
Narows (swimming hole), 131–32
Native Americans, 25, 33, 74, 75, 160,
  184, 186, 188, 205, 256, 259
  indigenous ingredients and,
    276–77
  prickly pear and, 256
  see also specific peoples
Naylor, June, 279
Neal, Ed, 235–36
Negros Mascogos (Black Seminoles),
  42
Neiman Marcus, 53–55
Nelson, Willie, 47, 203, 208, 209,
  211, 219, 220–23, 292, 293
Neon Boots Dancehall & Saloon,
  Houston, 203–4
New Line Cinema, 236
Newman, Paul, 166, 178
"New San Antonio Rose," 207
New Southwestern Cuisine, 242–43
New Spain, 59, 188
Newsweek, 179
New York magazine, 173
New York Times, 45, 178, 179, 243
Nguyen, Don, 273
"Night Life," 203
Nocona Boot Company, 59
No Country for Old Men, 168
Nodjimbadem, Katie, 103–5
"No Me Queda Más," 229
nopal, *see* prickly pear
Nordic culinary influence, 245
NorthPark Center, Dallas, 54–55
North Texas Commission, 100
Notsuoh, 194
"Nudie-Suits," 50
Nueces River, 111–12, 133
Nueces Strip, 34

Index

Obama, Barack, 44–45
ocotillo, 89, 117
O'Daniel, "Pappy," 23
oil, 2, 31–36, 82, 98, 172
  consumer spending and, 53
  cycles of boom and bust and,
    106–10
  wildcatters and, 2, 31–36, 209,
    301–2
Oko, Dan, 122–28
Old Fred Road, 137
Old No. 9 Highway, 137
Old San Antonio Road, 139
Old Texas, 165
"Old Town Road," 58
Old Tunnel State Park, 137
Old West Portal road trip (US
  Highway 90), 136
olive oil, starting fire with, 273–74
Olympia Brewing Company, 293, 294
"Only the Lonely (Know the Way I
  Feel)," 207
"On the Road Again," 221
opera, dress code for, 49
Opuntia engelmannii (Texas prickly
  pear), 255–60, 278
  buying syrup of, 259–60
  cocktail made with juice of
    (Prickly Pear'ita), 256, 259–60
    (recipe)
  harvesting, 256–59
  indigenous tribes and, 256, 276
Orange County Weekly, 26
Orange Show Center for Visionary
  Art, 196
Orbison, Roy, 207
Ortega, Hugo, 279–80
Outdoor Life, 116
Outkast, 212
Oyeniyi, Doyin, 220–22

oysters, 276
  Hugo Ortega's Wood-Roasted
    (recipe), 279–80

Pace, Linda, 199
Padre Island, 82
Padre Island National Seashore,
  124–25
Pale Horse, Pale Rider (Porter), 186
Palmito Ranch, 138
Palo Duro Canyon, 84, 126–27, 138,
  165
"Pancho and Lefty," 208
Panhandle, 2, 36, 84, 100, 234
  Caprock Canyons State Park in,
    126–27
  football stadiums in, 119
  history of battle between white
    settlers and indigenous people
    of, 184
  Underworld road trip in (State
    Highway Park Road 5), 138
Pantera, 211
panthers, 115
Paredes, Américo, 47, 187, 190
Parker, Carl, 14
Parker, Quanah, 184
parks:
  swimming holes in, 132–33
  see also wildlands; specific parks
Parton, Dolly, 220, 221
Pastoral Ideal road trip (Old No. 9
  Highway), 137
Paulsen, David, 172
PBS *Great Chefs*, 243
pecans, 90, 276
Pecos River, 81, 136
Pei, I. M., 55
Perini Ranch Steakhouse, Buffalo
  Gap, 281–84

Index

Index

Index

Index

Index

Index

University of Texas Press, 227
University of Texas Tower shooting
    (1966), 185–86
Urban Cowboy, 48, 60, 167
urban sprawl, Metroplex and,
    99–101
US Highway 90, 136

Van Zandt, Townes, 208
vaqueros, 59, 190
Vaughan, Stevie Ray, and Double
    Trouble, 209, 218–19
Vaughn, Daniel, 270–74
vegetable gardening, 142
vegetarian/vegan tacos, 268–69
Viet-Cajun crawfish (recipe), 246–48
Vietnamese American student,
    experiences of, 43–46
Villa, Pancho, 199
violence:
    male, Texas as land of, 233–34
    national debate on, 231
Viva! El Paso, 104
vodka, in Chilton, 261–63
Voyager spaceships, phonograph
    records carried by, 215–19

Wagyu brisket, 272
"Wake Up Dolores," 158
"Walk," 211
Walker, Derrick, 274
Walker, Jerry Jeff, 209
Wallace, Christian, 106–10, 134–39,
    200–205, 255–60
"Waltz Across Texas," 207–8
Washington, Bryan, 185
"Wasted Days and Wasted Nights,"
    192
water moccasins, 111–12
Wayne, John, 158, 160, 166, 188

Webb, Walter Prescott, 187, 190
Weed Eater, 302
Wellington, Arthur Wellesley, First
    Duke of, 59
"Western chic" dress code, 62
Westerns (movies), 60
    Lone Star, 157–64
Western wear, 58–62
    cowboy boots, 43, 58–60
    rules of, 60–62
West Indian tacos, 269
West Texas, 123, 134, 167, 212, 256,
    266
    Balmorhea State Park in, 81, 132,
        135
    Big Bend region of, 5, 81, 88, 89,
        129, 259
    boom and bust cycles of Permian
        Basin oilfield in, 106–10
    mountain lion attacks in, 115
    musicians from cotton belt of,
        217
    Perini Ranch Steakhouse in,
        281–84
    stars at night in, 129–30
    see also Chihuahuan Desert
wetlands, coastal, 82
Whataburger, 295
White, James and Annetta, 205
white supremacists, 192
whooping cranes, 82
Wichita Indians, 276
Wilco, 210, 226
wildcatters, 2, 31–36
    cattlemen as precursors of, 32–33
    Clark's "Desperados Waiting for a
        Train" and, 209
    Hughes Tool Company's tricone
        rotary rock drill bit and, 301–2
    see also oil

— **338** —

Index

wildflowers, 135
   see also bluebonnets
wildlands, 122–28
   Big Bend National Park, 127–28
   Big Thicket National Preserve,
      125–26
   Caprock Canyons State Park,
      126–27
   Devils River State Natural Area,
      122–24
   Padre Island National Seashore,
      124–25
Wild West, historic foodways and,
   241
Williams, Larry, 125–26
Wills, Bob, and His Texas Playboys,
   207

Wimberley, 83, 131, 132
Winckler, Suzanne, 143–44
windsurfing, 125
wineries, 5, 278
With His Pistol in His Hand (Paredes),
   187
Woodruff, Ron, 168–69
Wright, Lawrence, 23
Wyatt, Lynn, 17, 18, 20, 51

yaupon holly, 277
Years of Lyndon Johnson, The (Caro), 23
"You're Gonna Miss Me," 208
"Your Hand in Mine," 212

ZZ Top, 208–9

About the Author

SINCE 1973, *TEXAS MONTHLY* has chronicled life in the Lone Star State, exploring its politics and personalities, barbecue and business, true crime and tacos, honky-tonks and hiking. One of the most respected publications in the nation, the iconic magazine has won fourteen National Magazine Awards (the industry's highest honor) for its editorial excellence and outstanding design. The magazine's cinematic storytelling, deep analysis, and expert advice also come to life well beyond the written word—in videos, podcasts, live events, and beyond.